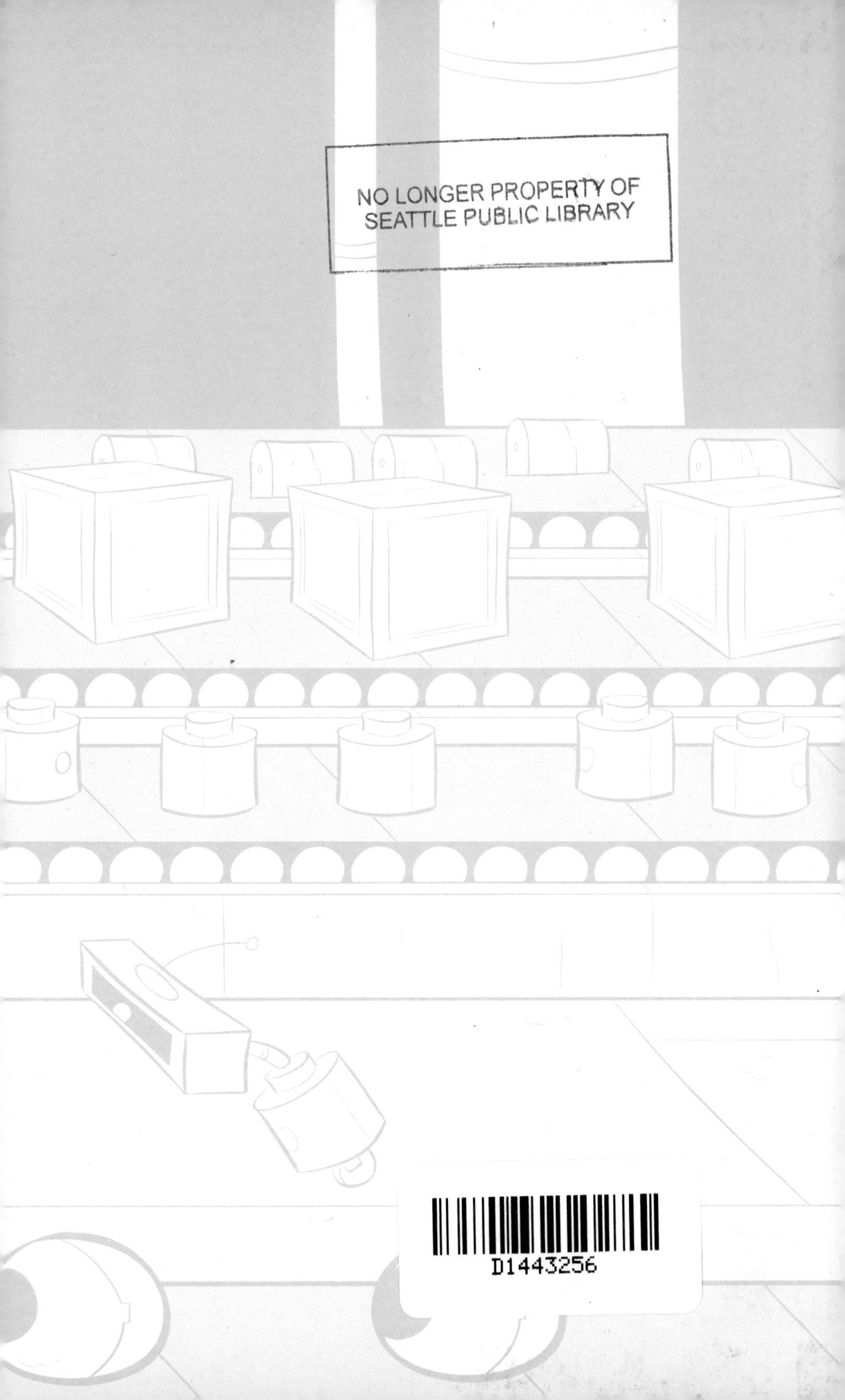

LOOK

ISBN: 978-1-68112-089-8
© 2017 Jon Nielsen
Library of Congress Control Number: 2016963361
Printed in China
1st printing April 2017

Also available wherever e-books are sold.

LOOK

JON NIELSEN

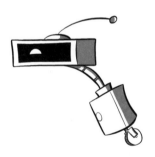

nbm GRAPHIC NOVELS
Nantier · Beall · Minoustchine
NEW YORK

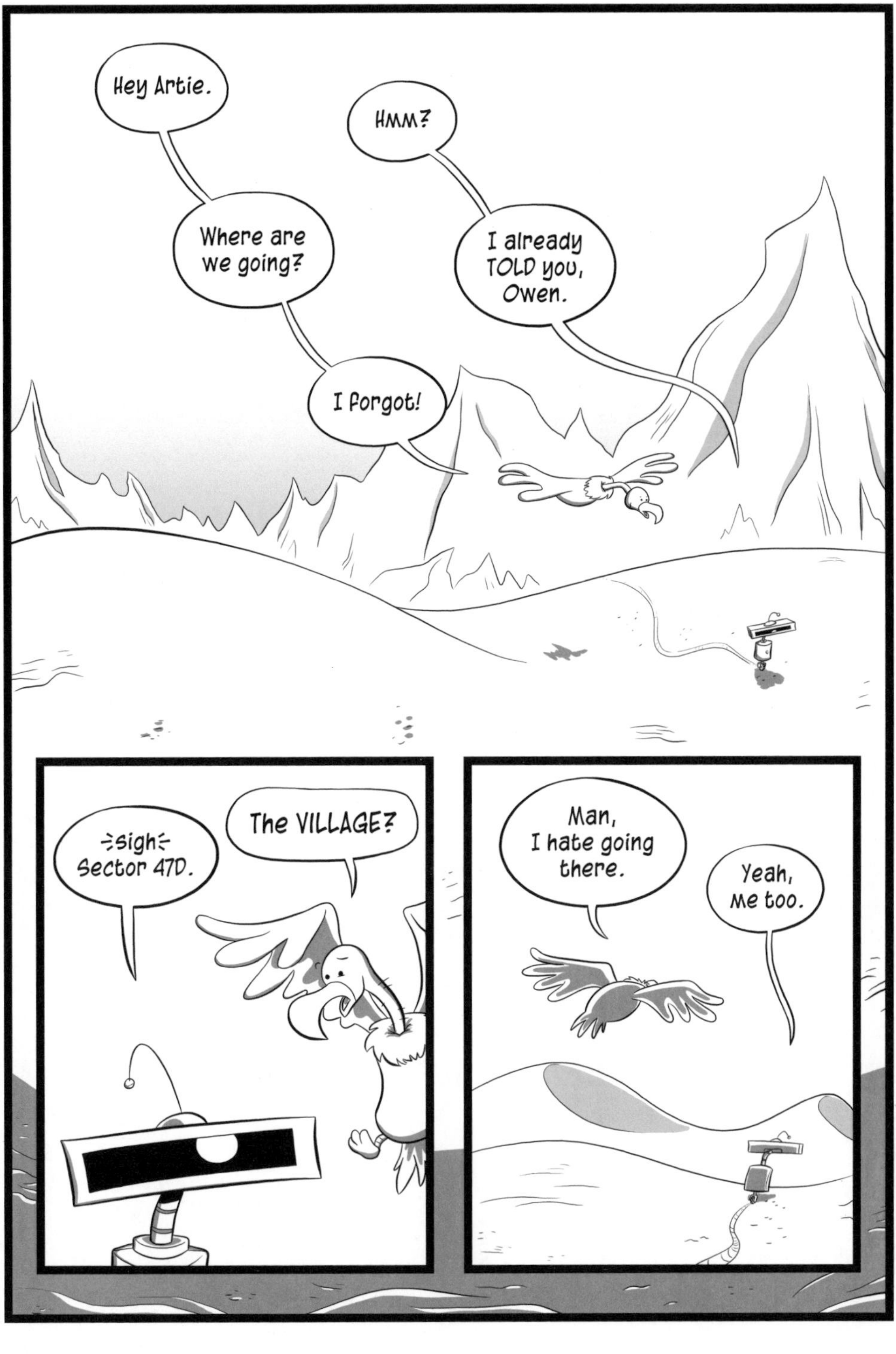
Hey Artie.
HMM?
Where are we going?
I already TOLD you, Owen.
I forgot!
=sigh= Sector 47D.
The VILLAGE?
Man, I hate going there.
Yeah, Me too.

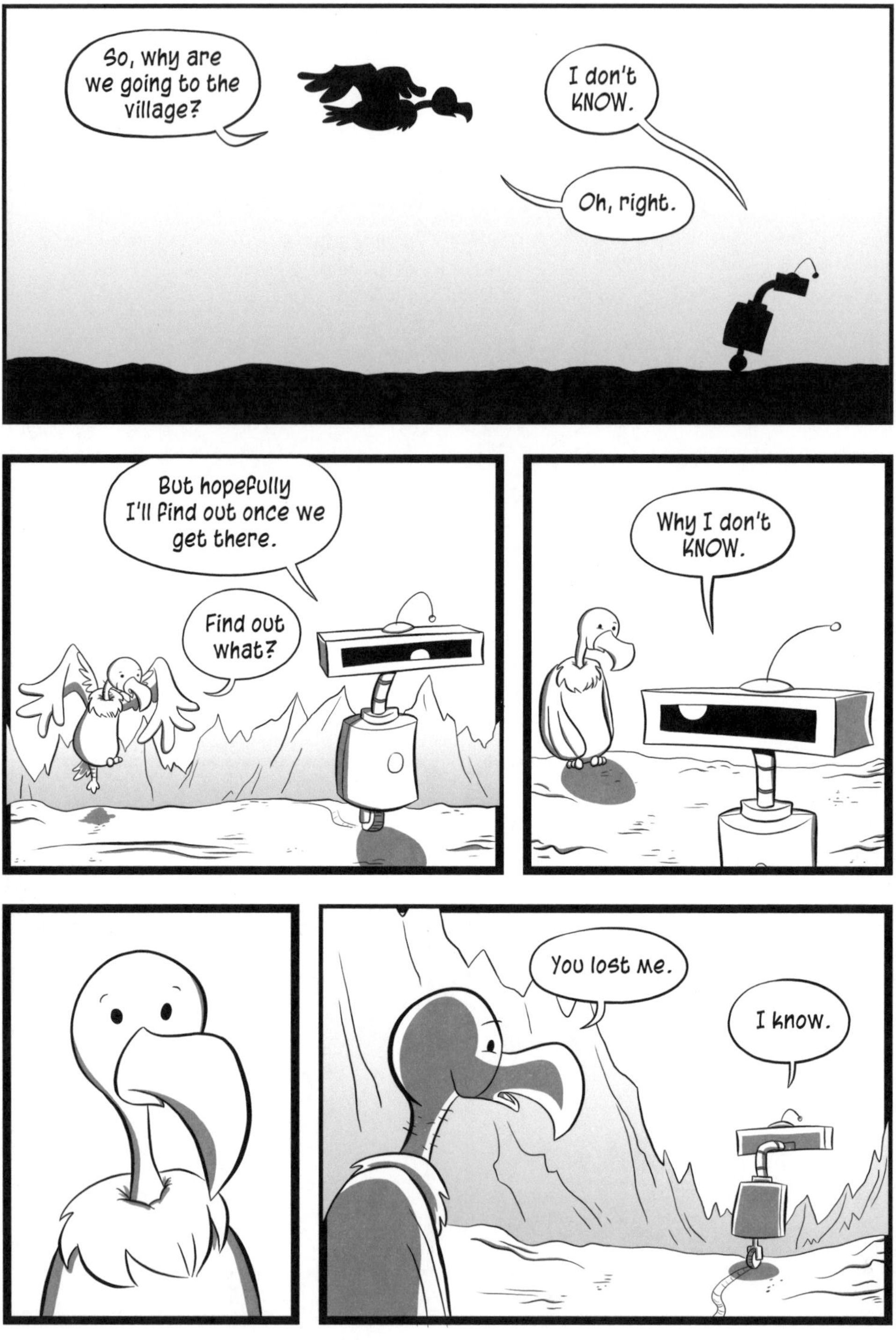
So, why are we going to the village?
I don't KNOW.
Oh, right.
But hopefully I'll find out once we get there.
Find out what?
Why I don't KNOW.
You lost me.
I know.

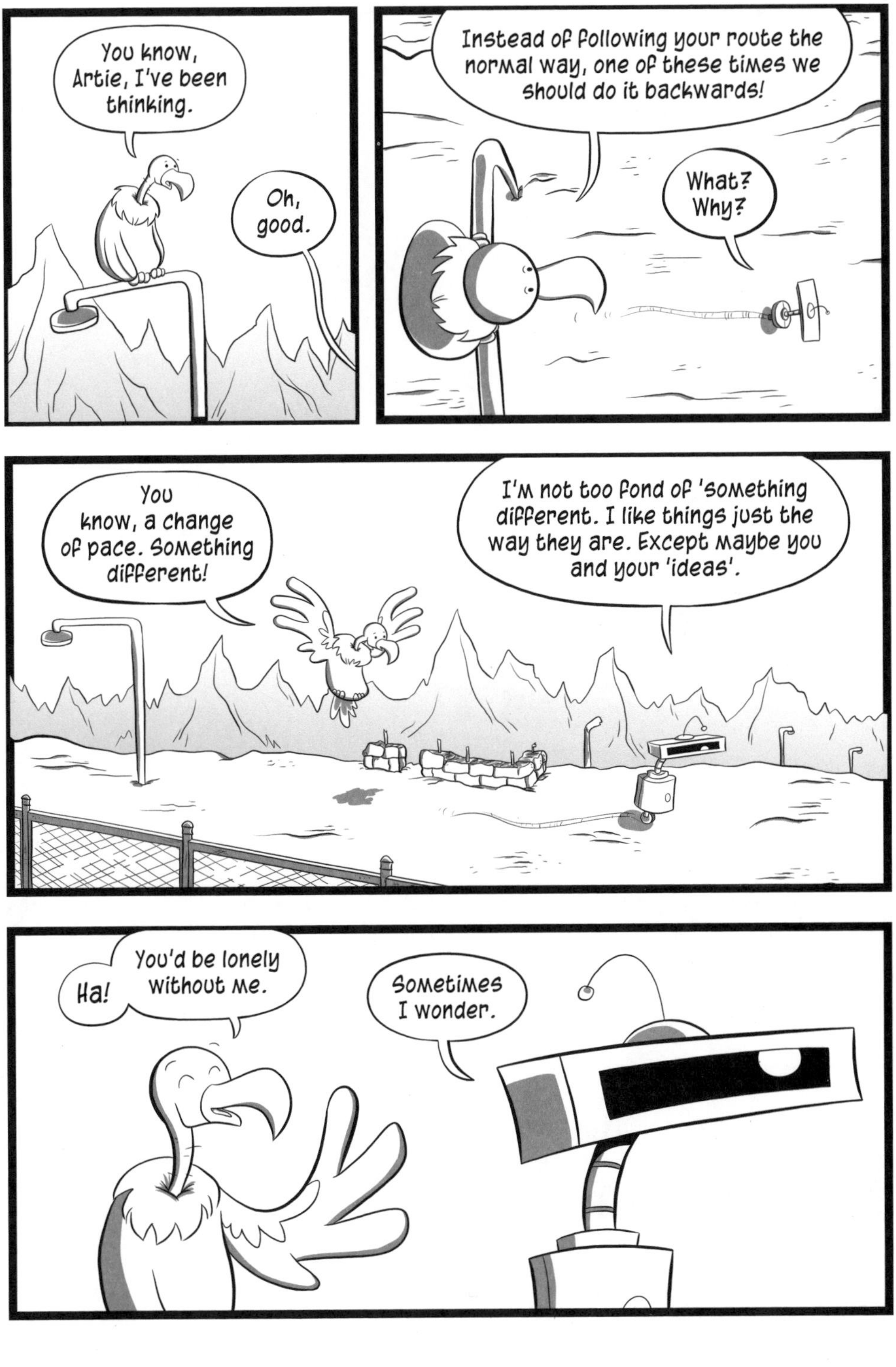
You know, Artie, I've been thinking.
Oh, good.
Instead of following your route the normal way, one of these times we should do it backwards!
What? Why?
You know, a change of pace. Something different!
I'm not too fond of 'something different. I like things just the way they are. Except maybe you and your 'ideas'.
Ha!
You'd be lonely without me.
Sometimes I wonder.

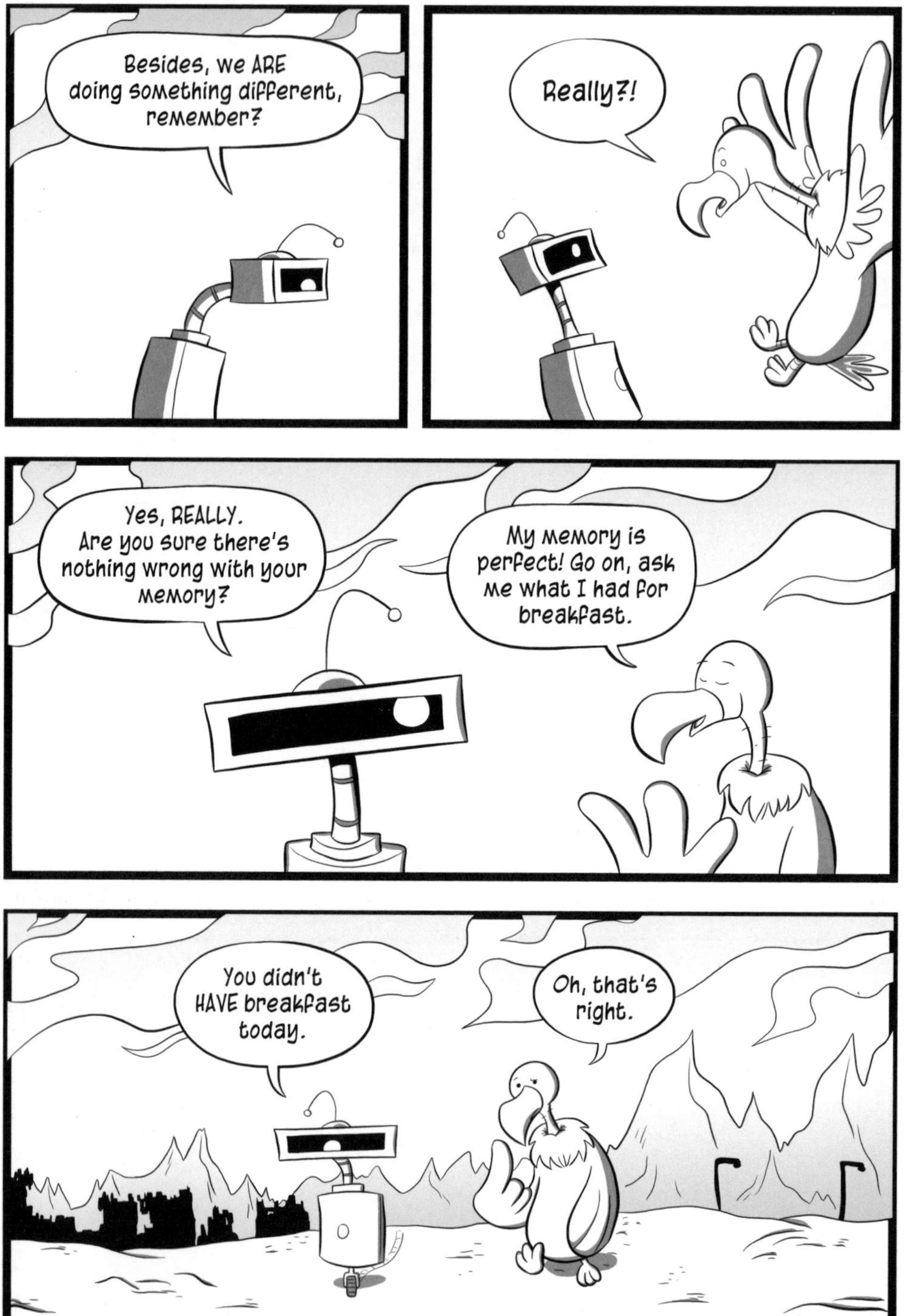
Besides, we ARE doing something different, remember?
Really?!
Yes, REALLY. Are you sure there's nothing wrong with your memory?
My memory is perfect! Go on, ask me what I had for breakfast.
You didn't HAVE breakfast today.
Oh, that's right.

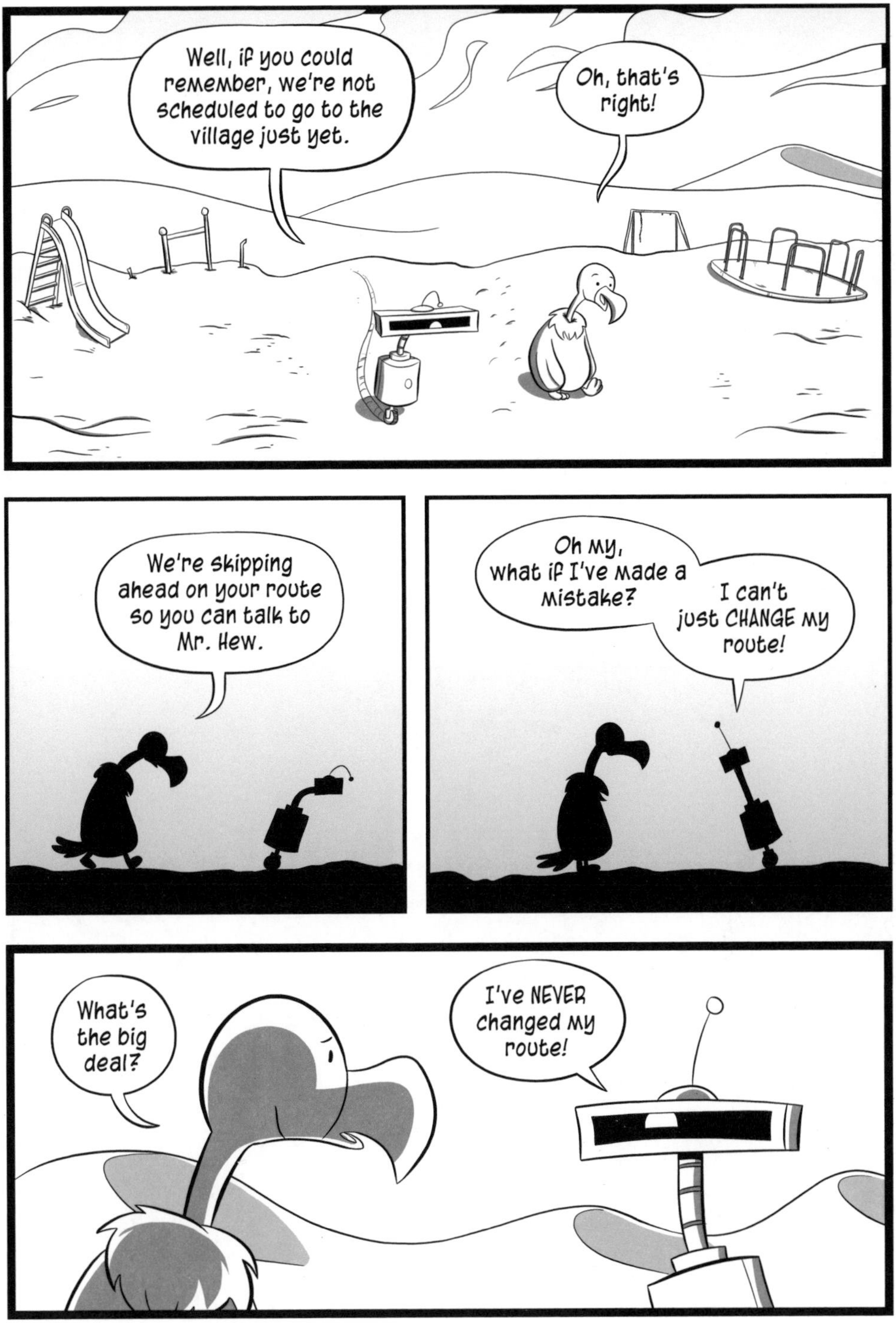
Well, if you could remember, we're not scheduled to go to the village just yet.
Oh, that's right!
We're skipping ahead on your route so you can talk to Mr. Hew.
Oh my, what if I've made a mistake?
I can't just CHANGE my route!
What's the big deal?
I've NEVER changed my route!

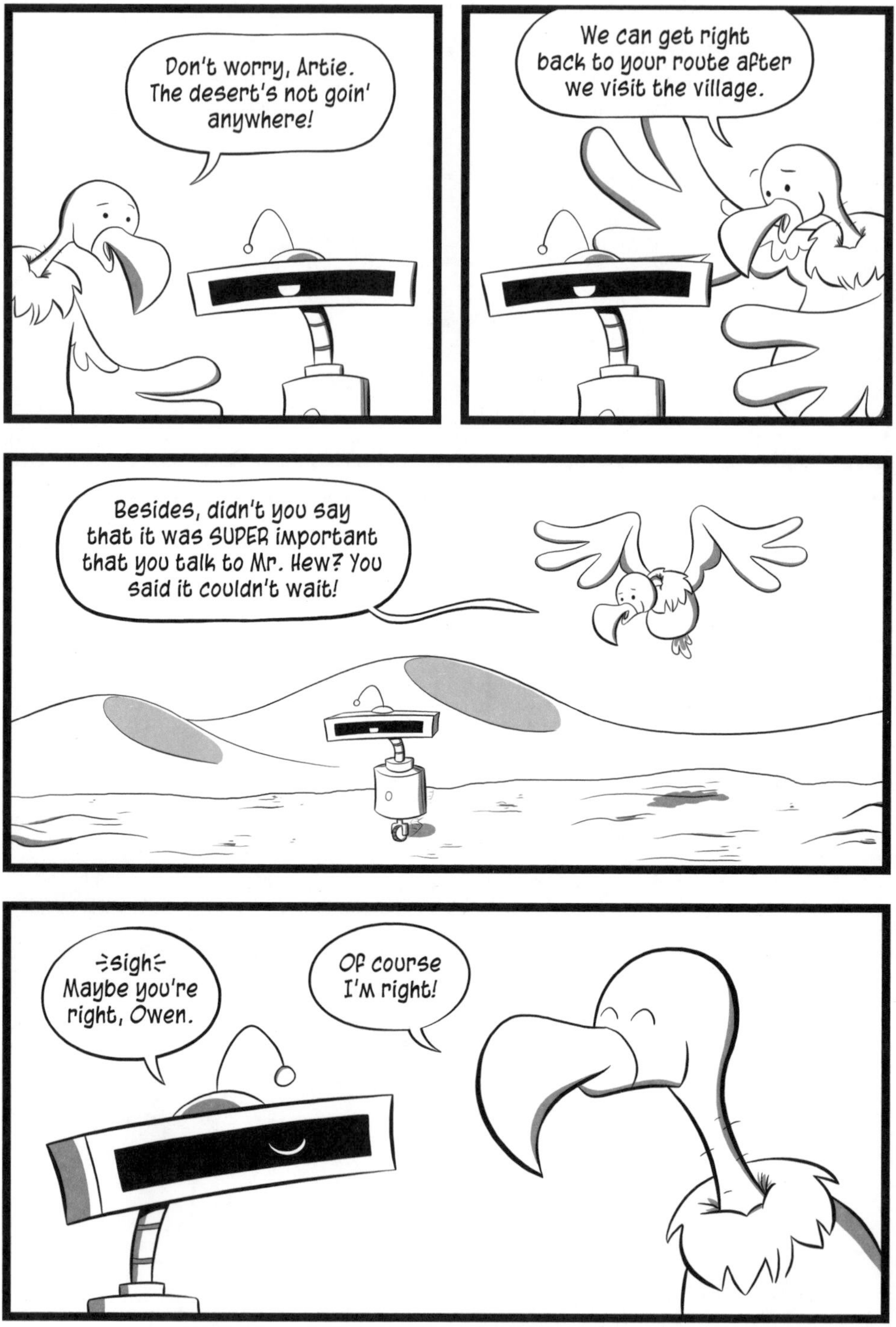
Don't worry, Artie. The desert's not goin' anywhere!
We can get right back to your route after we visit the village.
Besides, didn't you say that it was SUPER important that you talk to Mr. Hew? You said it couldn't wait!
-sigh-
Maybe you're right, Owen.
Of course I'm right!

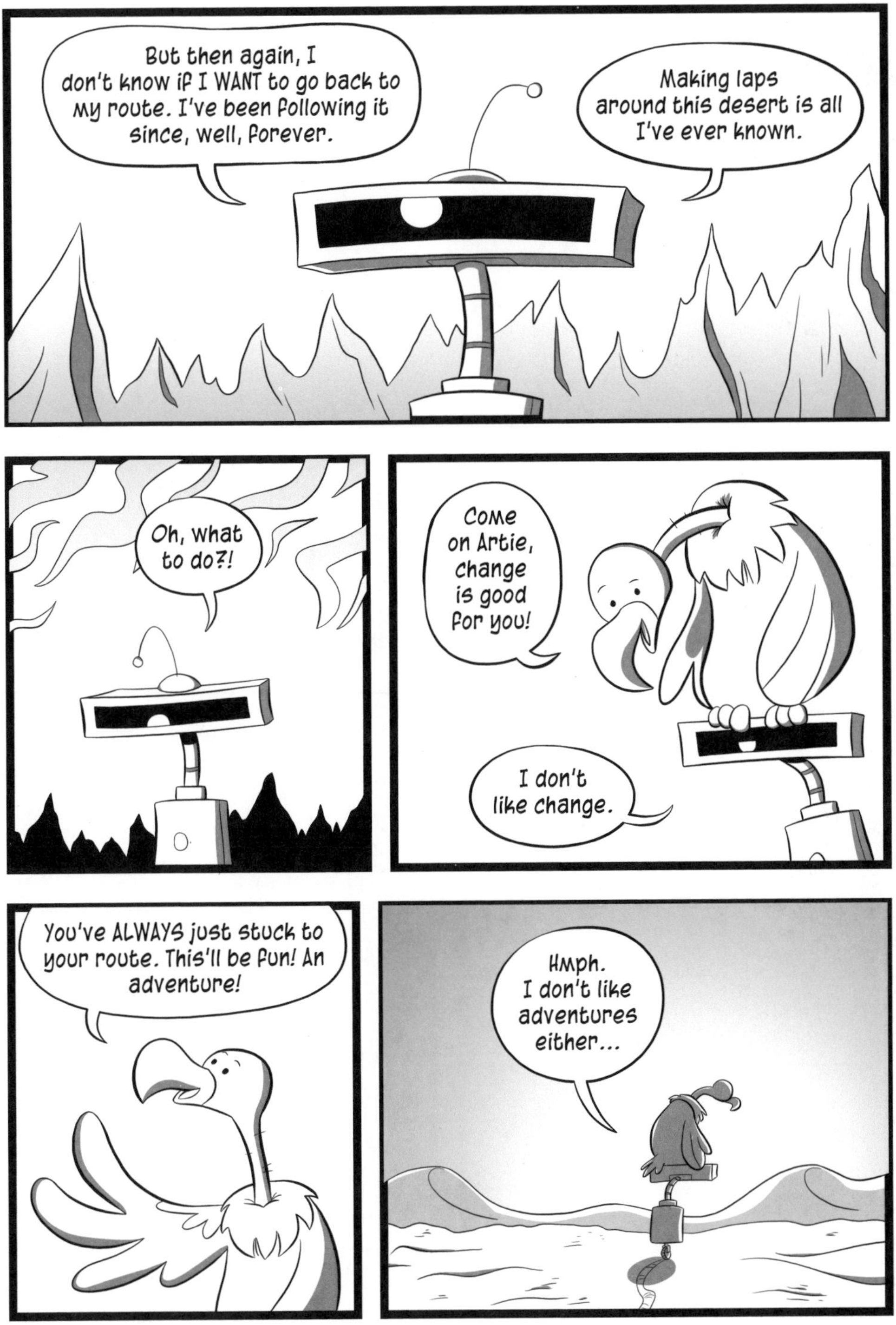
But then again, I don't know if I WANT to go back to my route. I've been following it since, well, forever.
Making laps around this desert is all I've ever known.
Oh, what to do?!
Come on Artie, change is good for you!
I don't like change.
You've ALWAYS just stuck to your route. This'll be fun! An adventure!
Hmph. I don't like adventures either...

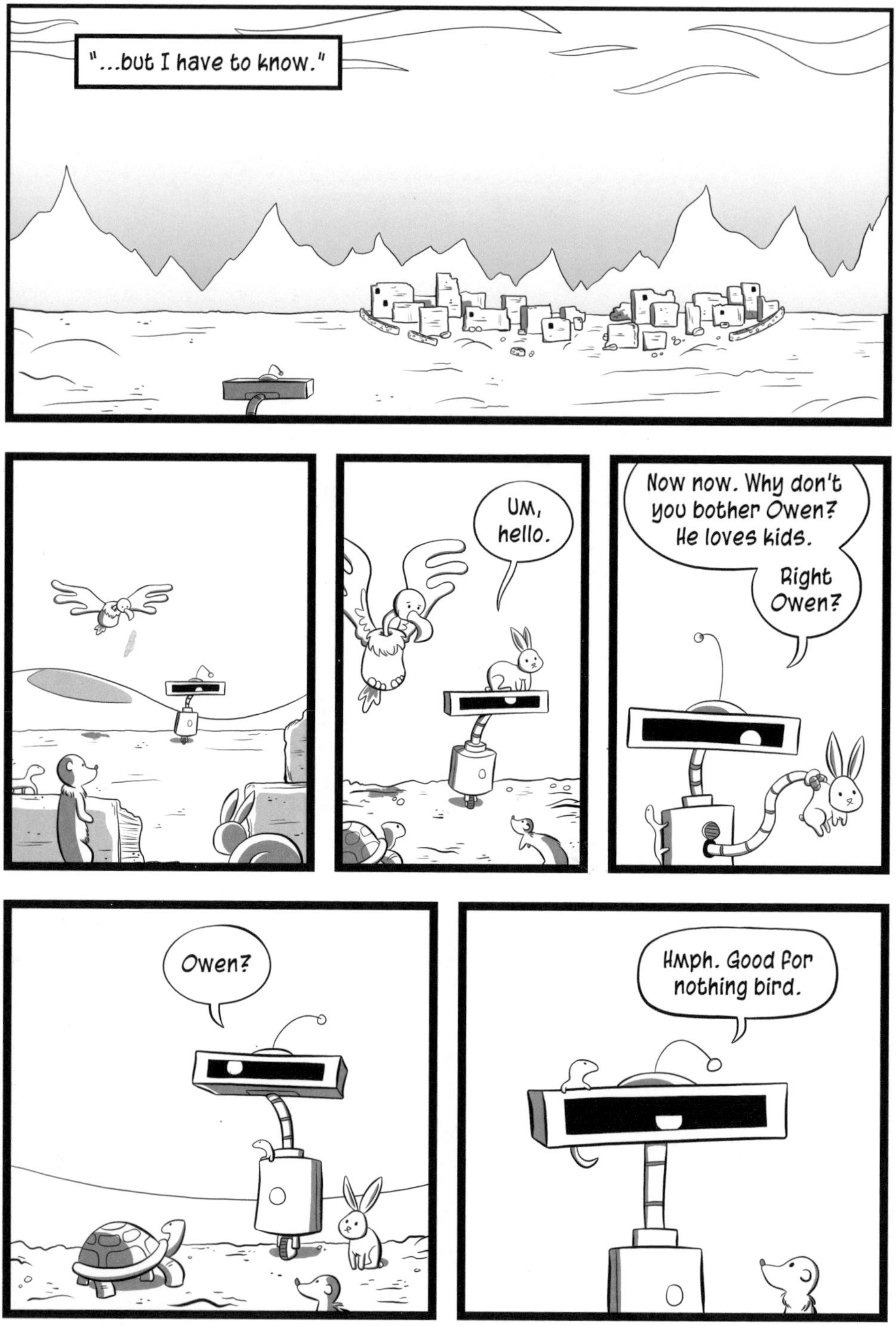
"...but I have to know."
Um, hello.
Now now. Why don't you bother Owen? He loves kids.
Right Owen?
Owen?
Hmph. Good for nothing bird.

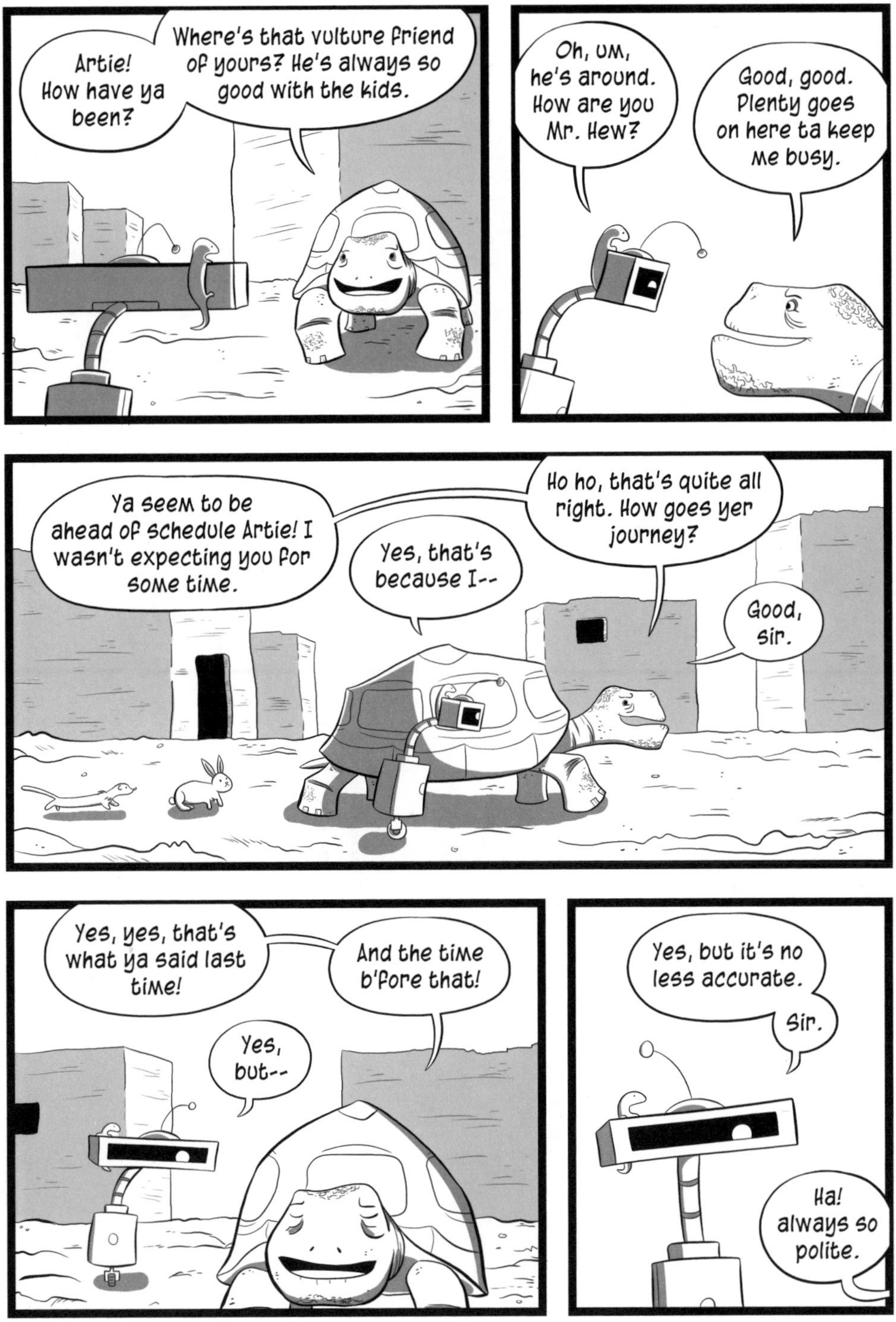
Artie! How have ya been?
Where's that vulture friend of yours? He's always so good with the kids.
Oh, um, he's around. How are you Mr. Hew?
Good, good. Plenty goes on here ta keep me busy.
Ya seem to be ahead of schedule Artie! I wasn't expecting you for some time.
Yes, that's because I--
Ho ho, that's quite all right. How goes yer journey?
Good, sir.
Yes, yes, that's what ya said last time!
And the time b'fore that!
Yes, but--
Yes, but it's no less accurate.
Sir.
Ha! always so polite.

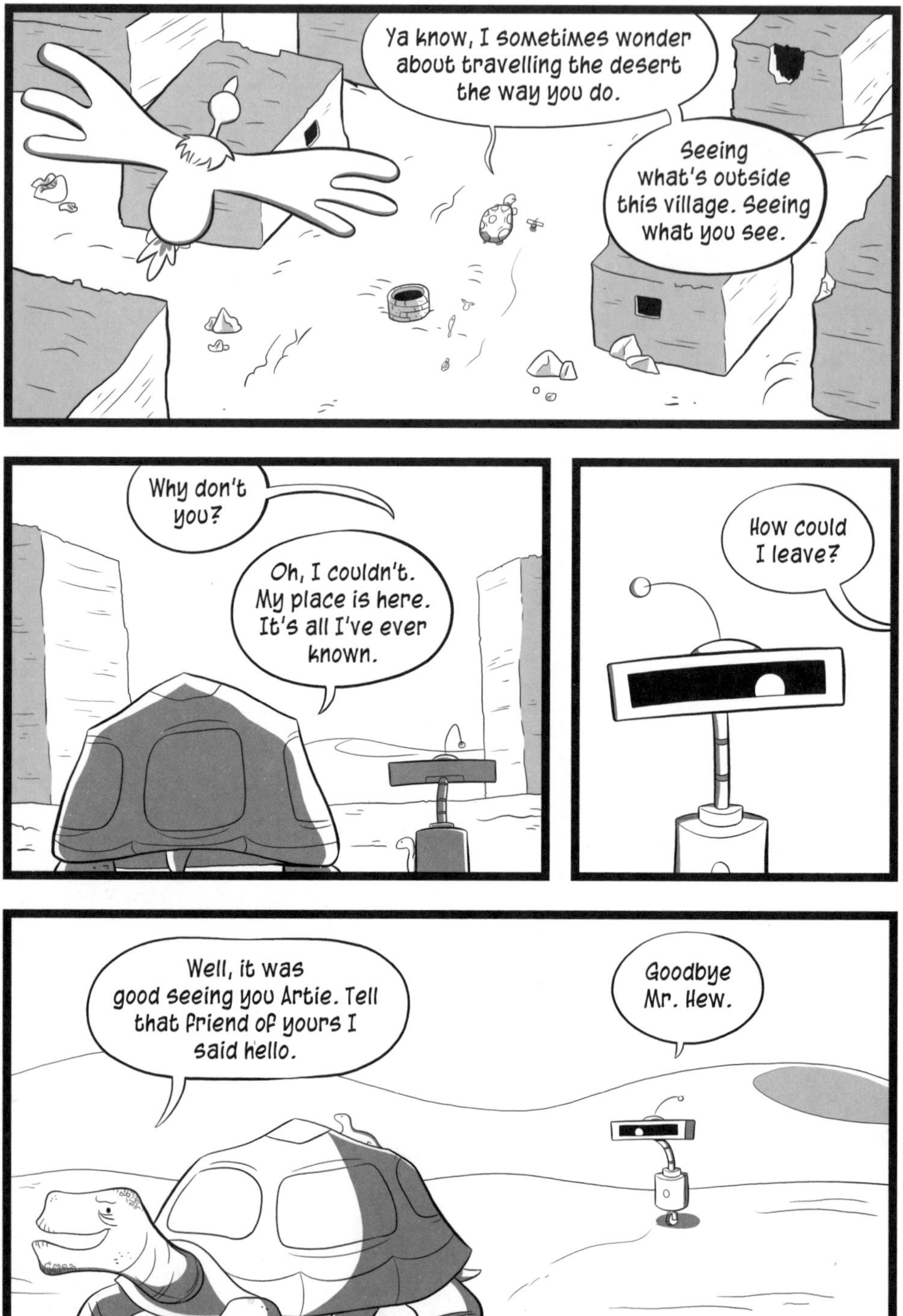
Ya know, I sometimes wonder about travelling the desert the way you do.
Seeing what's outside this village. Seeing what you see.
Why don't you?
Oh, I couldn't. My place is here. It's all I've ever known.
How could I leave?
Well, it was good seeing you Artie. Tell that friend of yours I said hello.
Goodbye Mr. Hew.

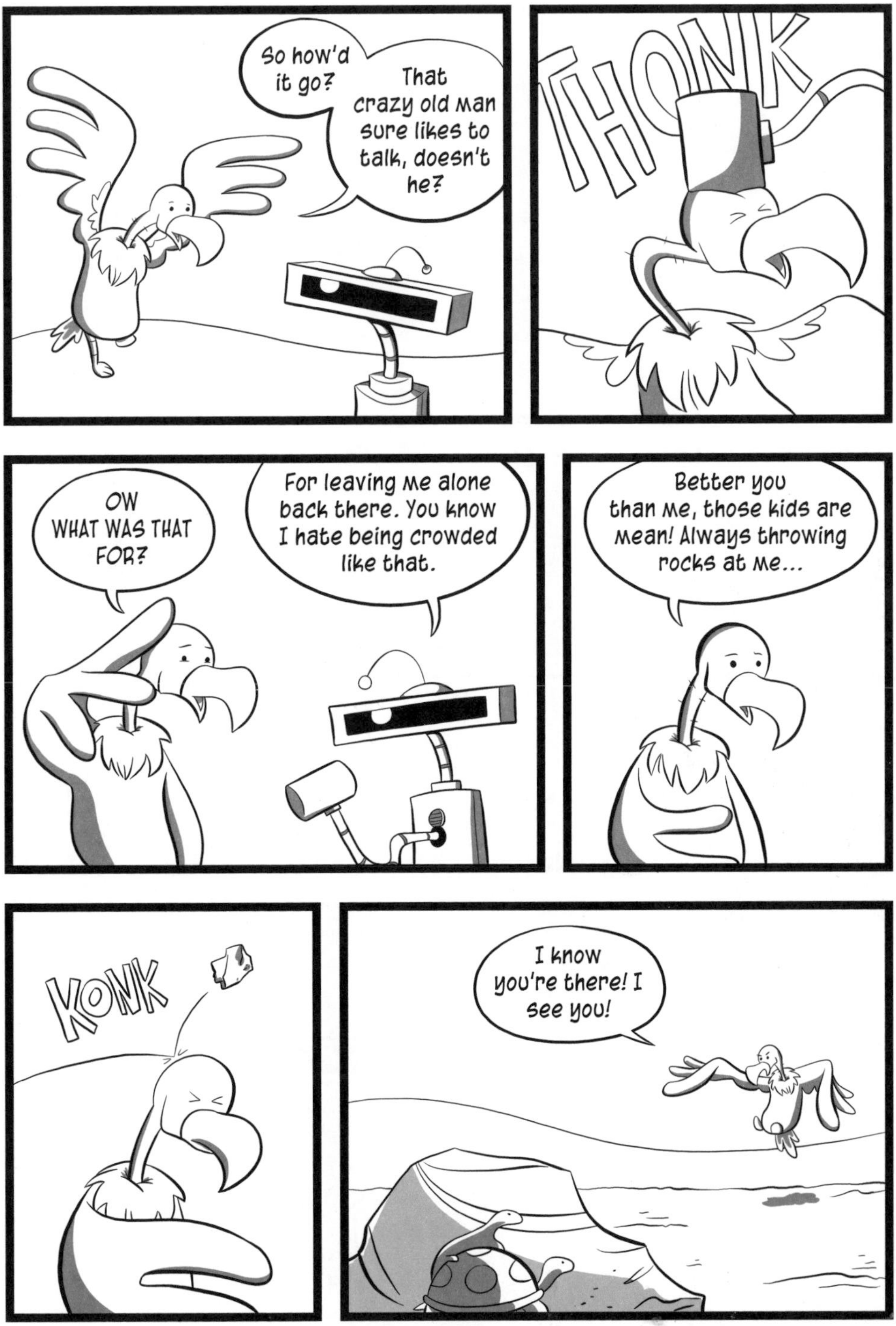
So how'd it go?
That crazy old man sure likes to talk, doesn't he?
THONK
OW WHAT WAS THAT FOR?
For leaving me alone back there. You know I hate being crowded like that.
Better you than me, those kids are mean! Always throwing rocks at me...
KONK
I know you're there! I see you!

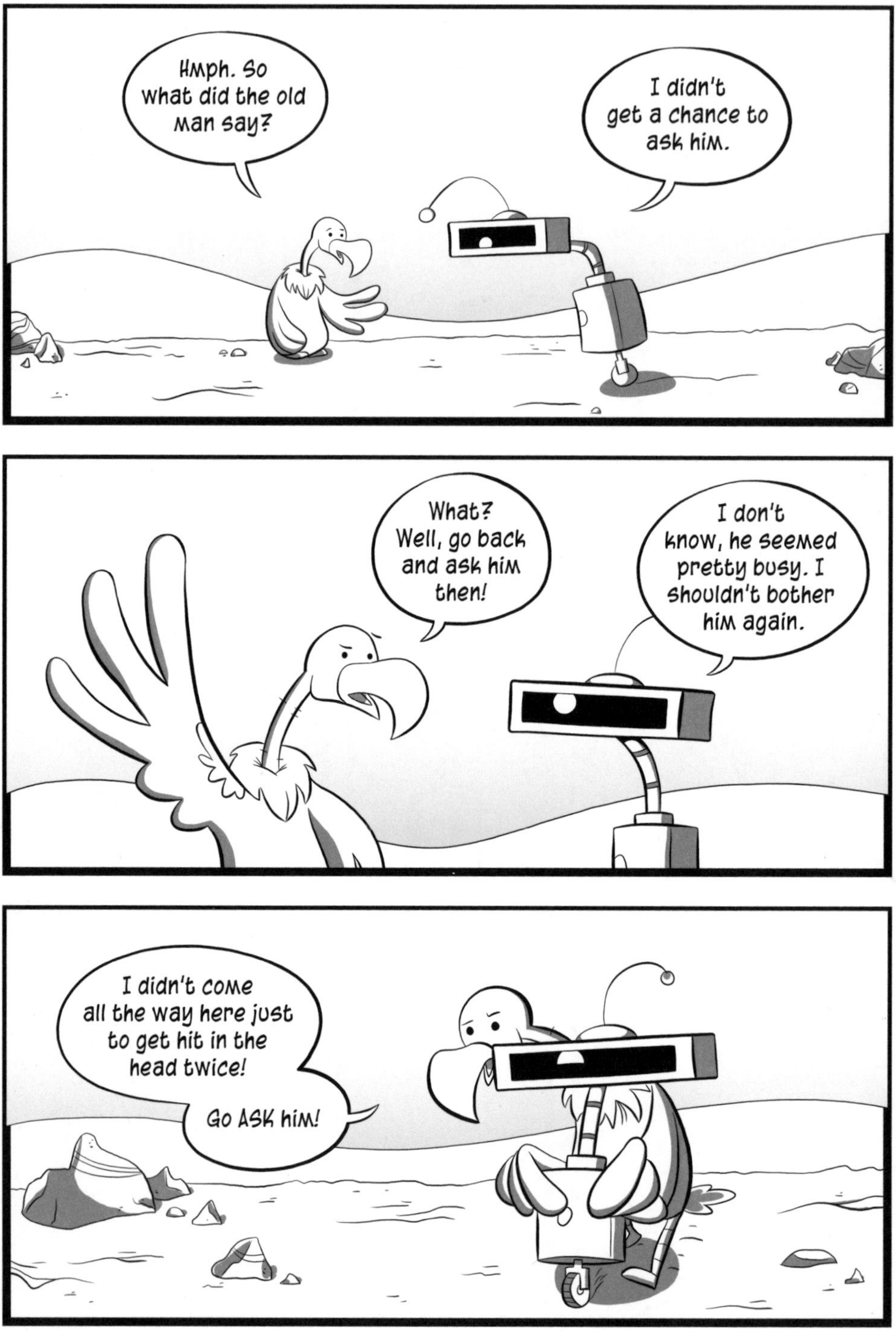
Hmph. So what did the old man say?
I didn't get a chance to ask him.
What? Well, go back and ask him then!
I don't know, he seemed pretty busy. I shouldn't bother him again.
I didn't come all the way here just to get hit in the head twice!
Go ASK him!

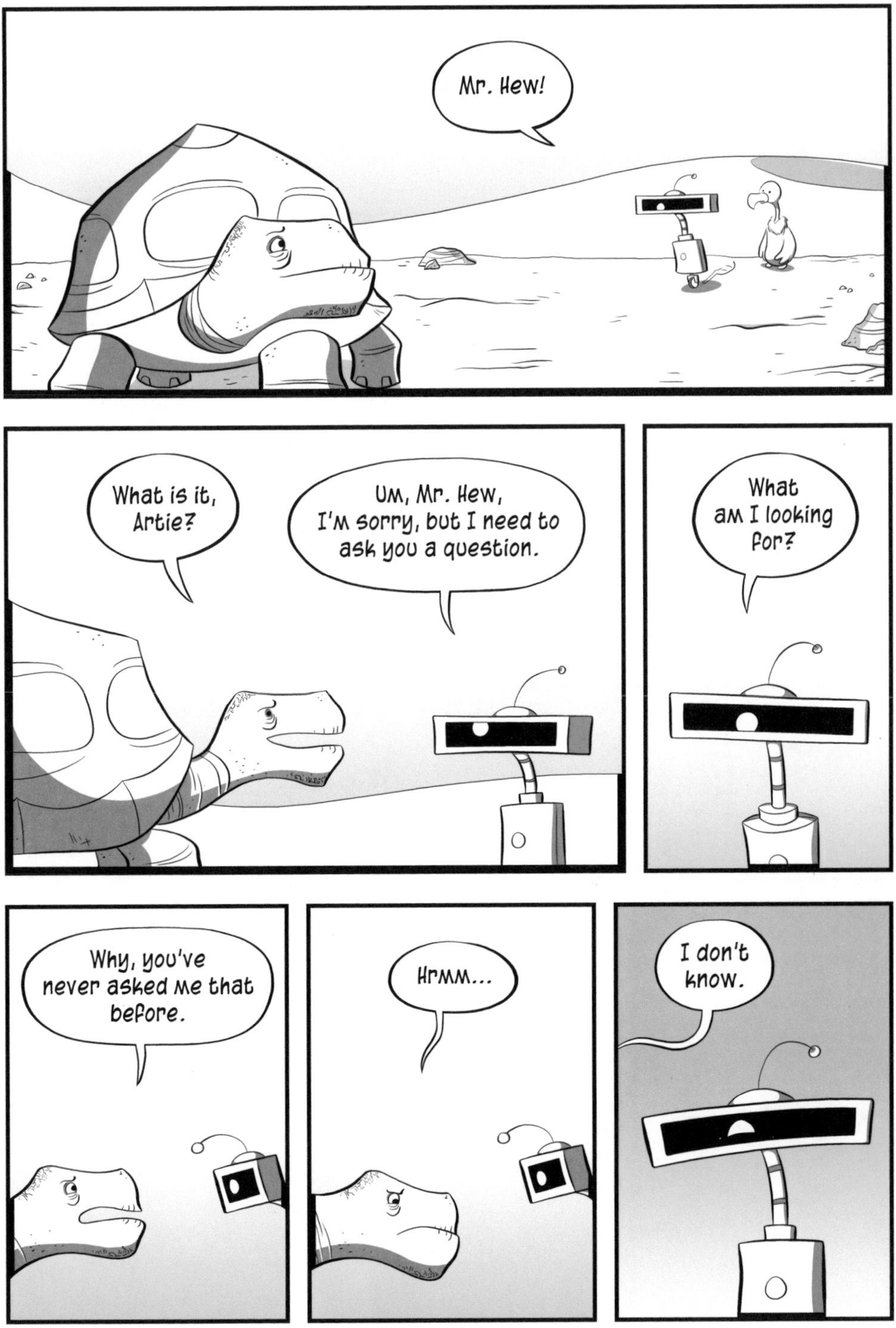
Mr. Hew!
What is it, Artie?
Um, Mr. Hew, I'm sorry, but I need to ask you a question.
What am I looking for?
Why, you've never asked me that before.
Hrmm...
I don't know.

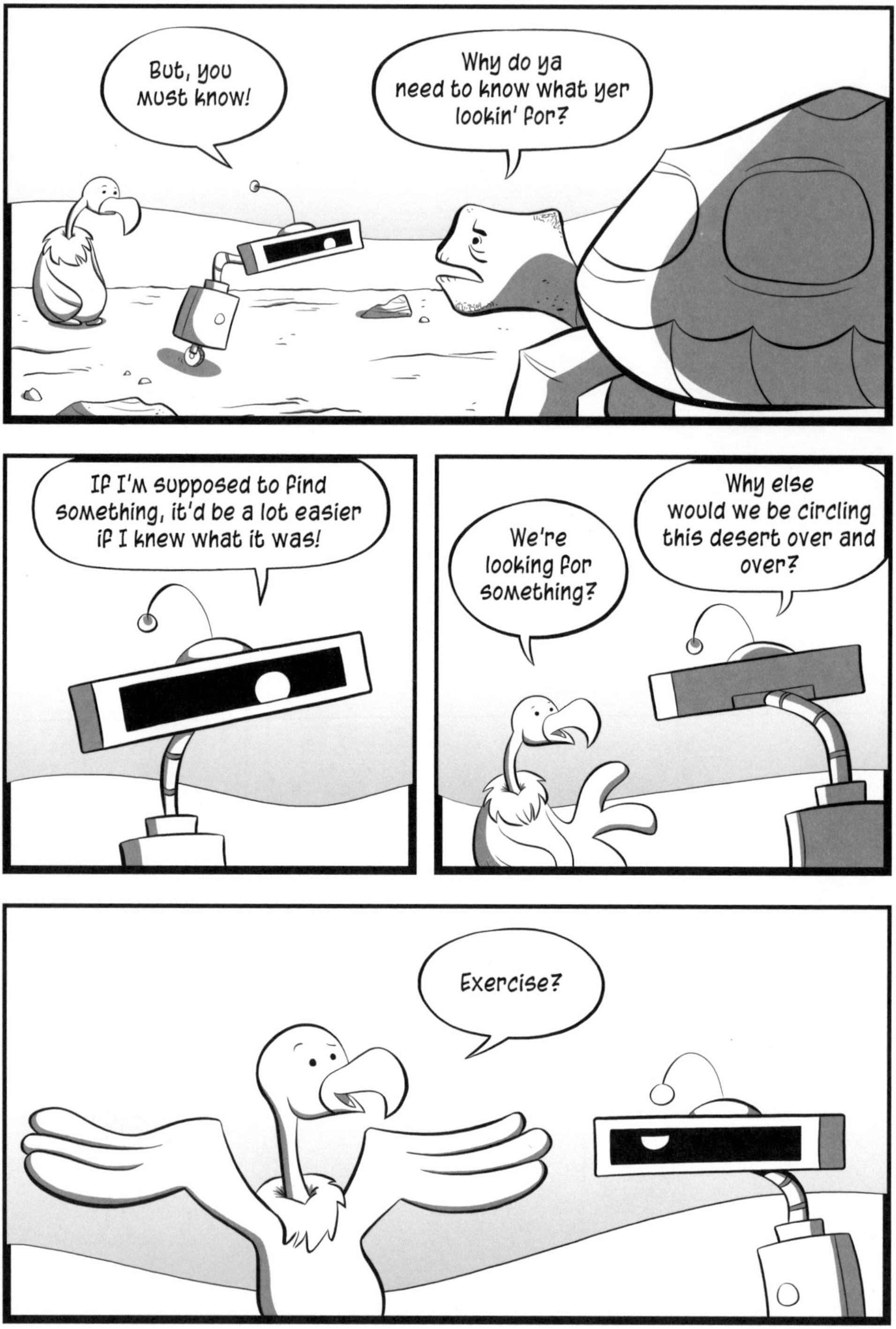
But, you must know!
Why do ya need to know what yer lookin' for?
If I'm supposed to find something, it'd be a lot easier if I knew what it was!
We're looking for something?
Why else would we be circling this desert over and over?
Exercise?

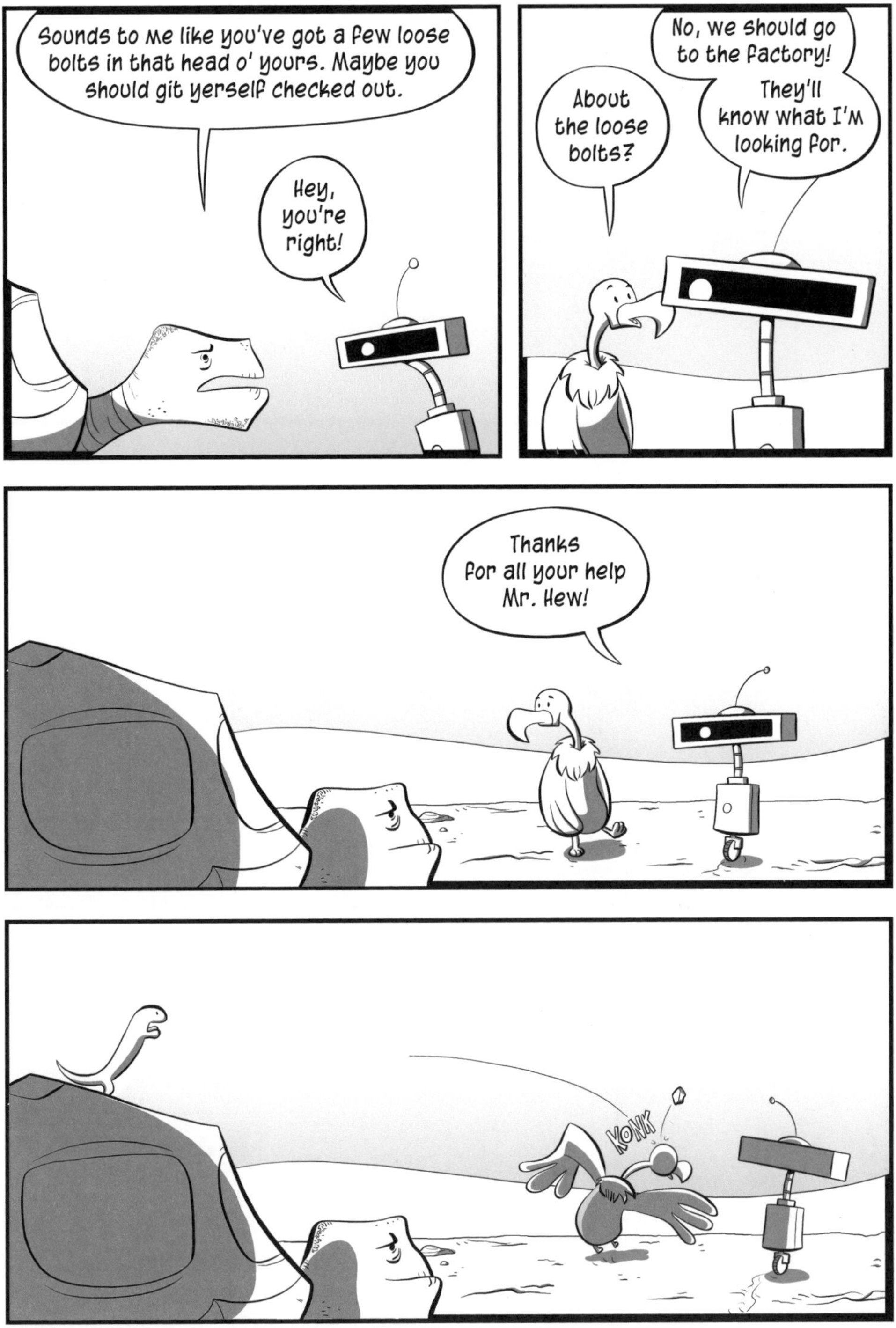

Sounds to me like you've got a few loose bolts in that head o' yours. Maybe you should git yerself checked out.
Hey, you're right!
About the loose bolts?
No, we should go to the factory!
They'll know what I'm looking for.
Thanks for all your help Mr. Hew!
KONK

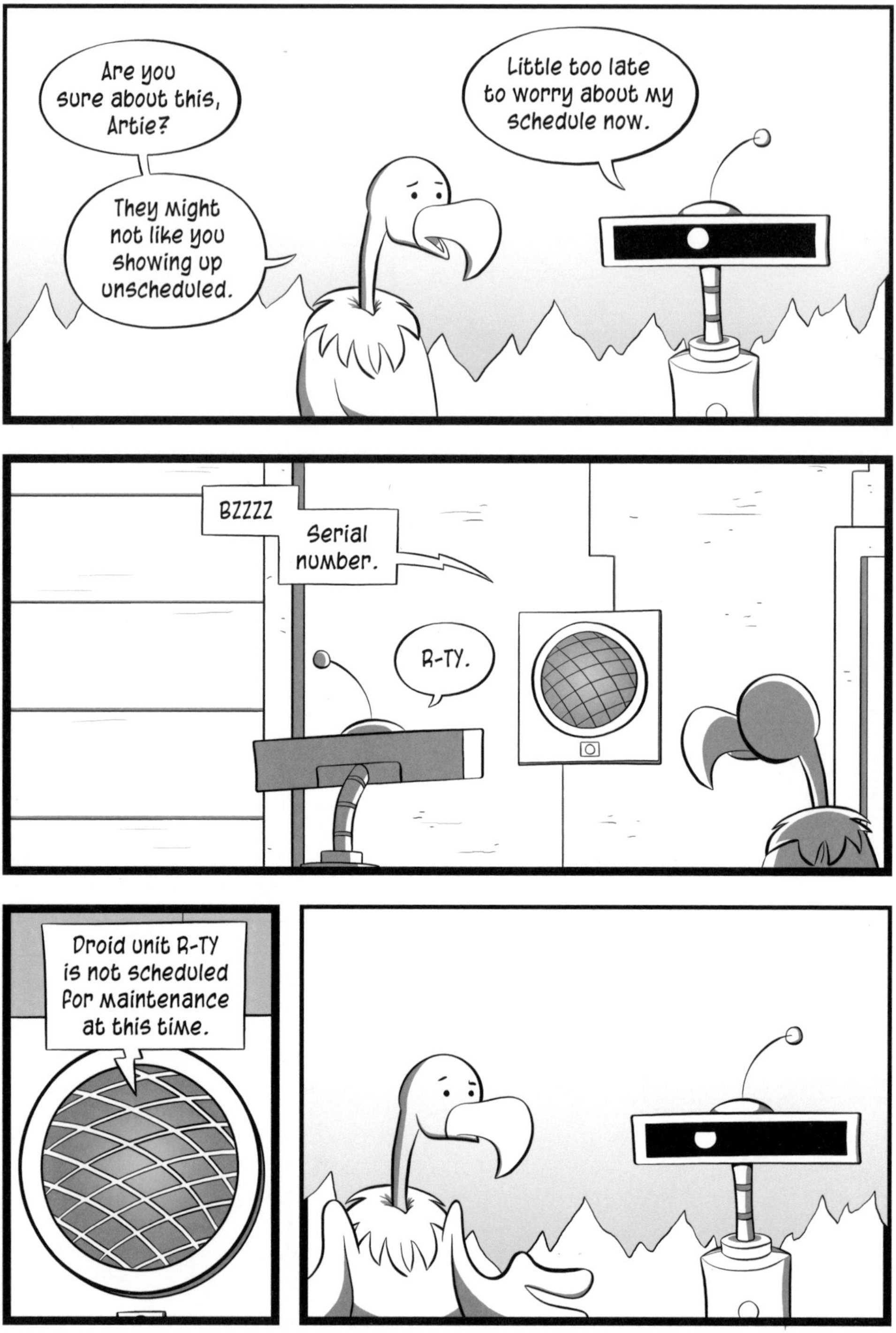
Are you sure about this, Artie?
They might not like you showing up unscheduled.
Little too late to worry about my schedule now.
BZZZZ
Serial number.
R-TY.
Droid unit R-TY is not scheduled for maintenance at this time.

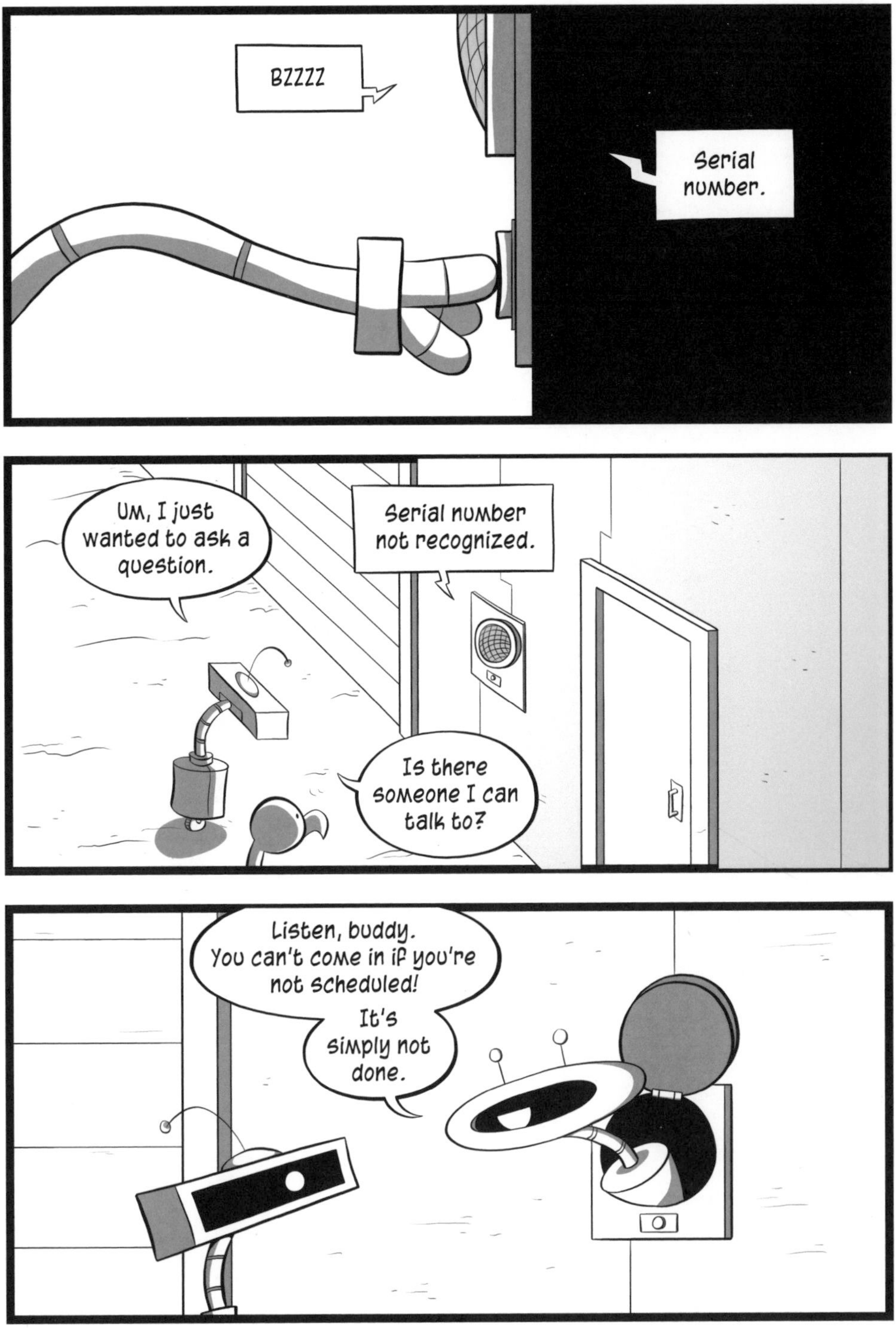
BZZZZ
Serial number.
Um, I just wanted to ask a question.
Serial number not recognized.
Is there someone I can talk to?
Listen, buddy. You can't come in if you're not scheduled!
It's simply not done.

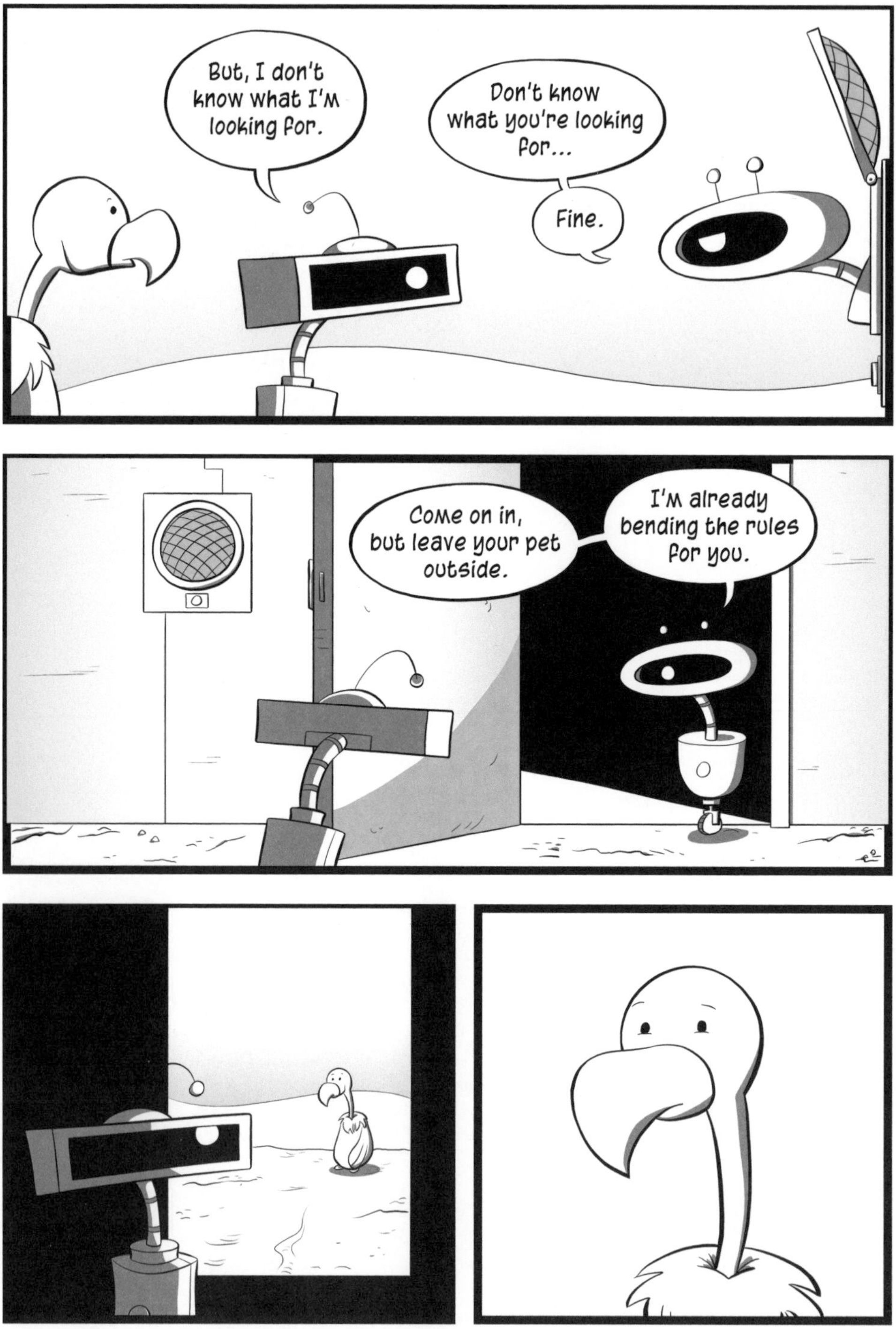
But, I don't know what I'm looking for.
Don't know what you're looking for...
Fine.
Come on in, but leave your pet outside.
I'm already bending the rules for you.

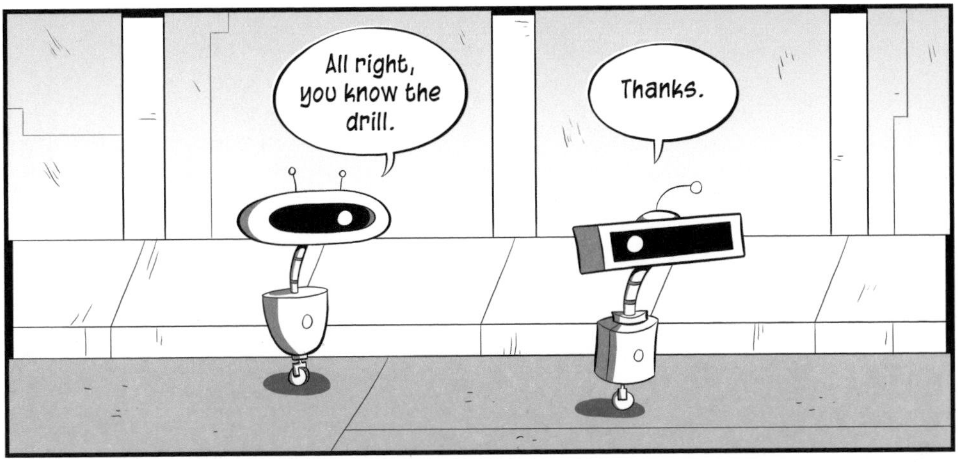
All right, you know the drill.
Thanks.

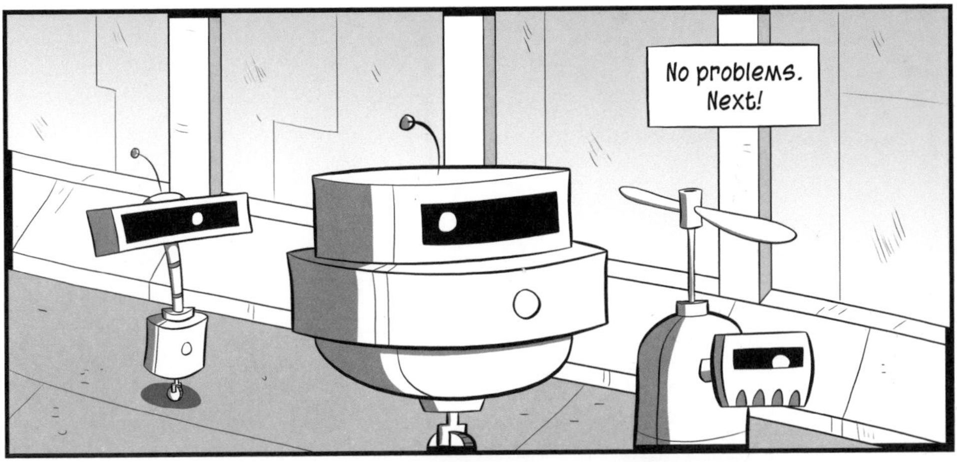
No problems. Next!

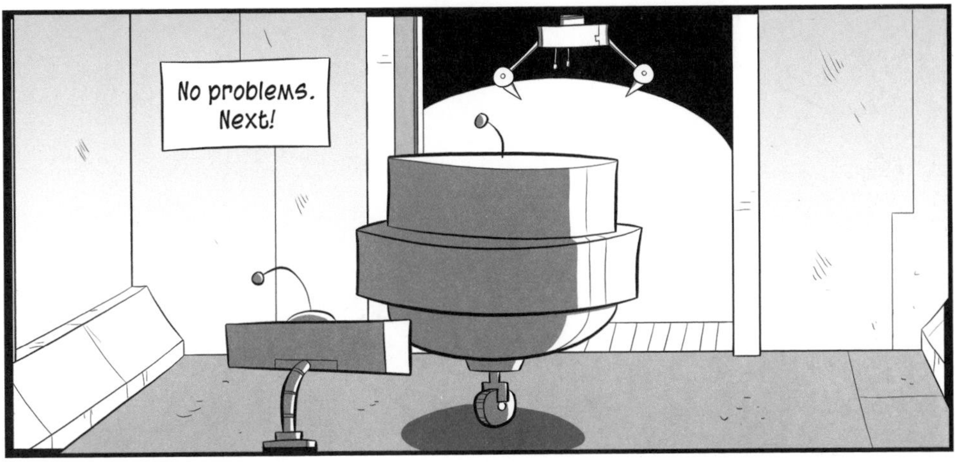
No problems. Next!

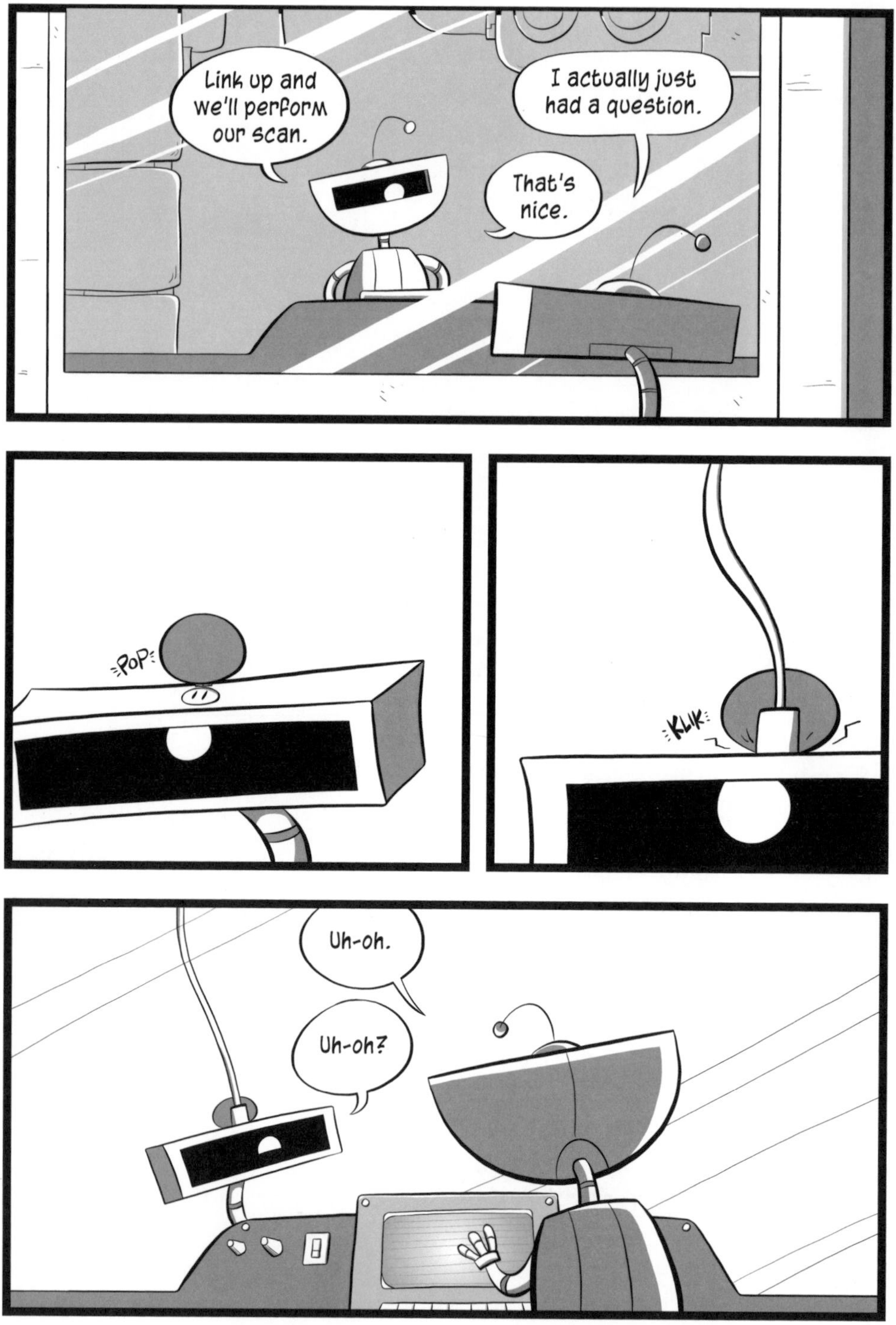
Link up and we'll perform our scan.
I actually just had a question.
That's nice.
POP
KLIK
Uh-oh.
Uh-oh?

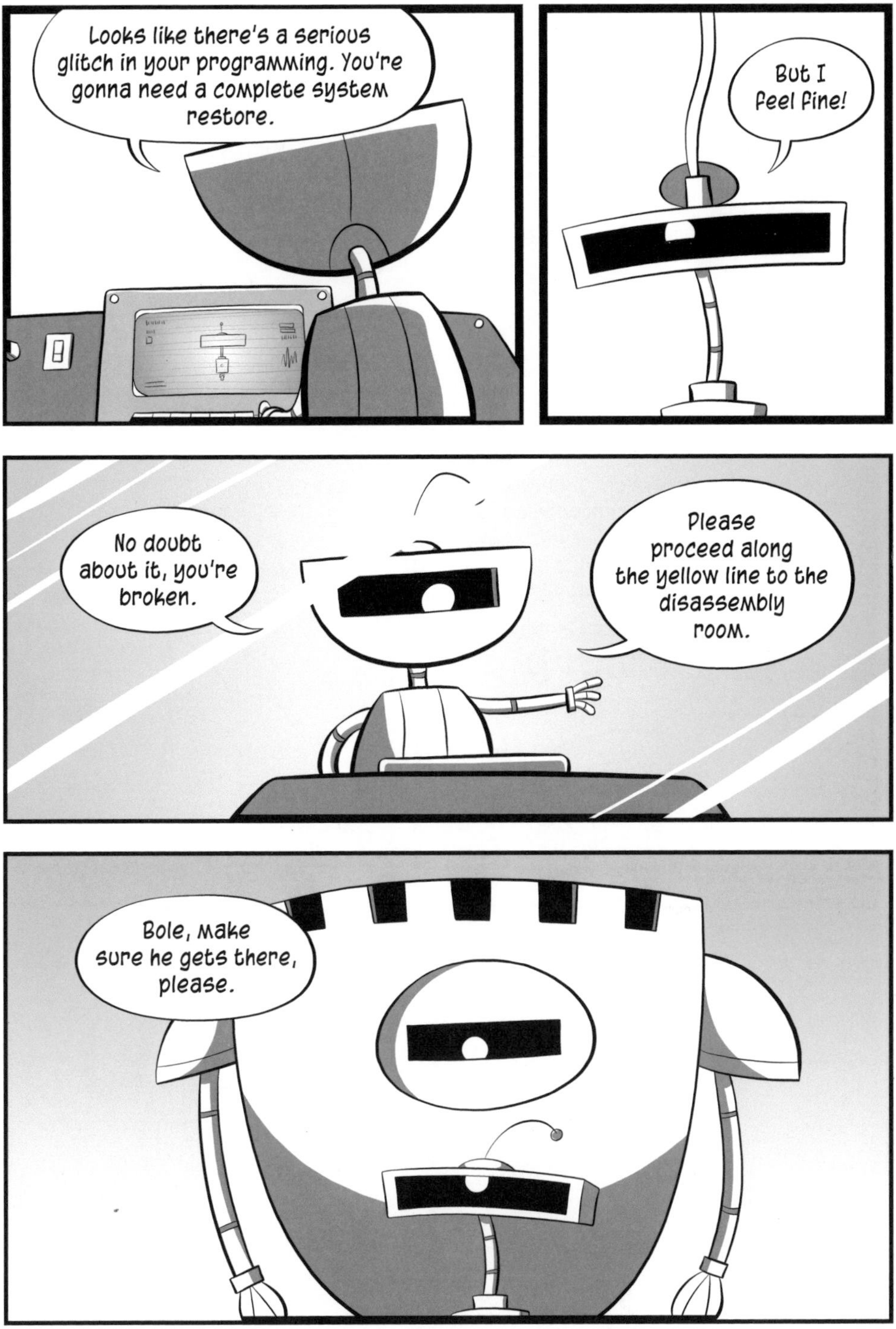
Looks like there's a serious glitch in your programming. You're gonna need a complete system restore.
But I feel fine!
No doubt about it, you're broken.
Please proceed along the yellow line to the disassembly room.
Bole, make sure he gets there, please.

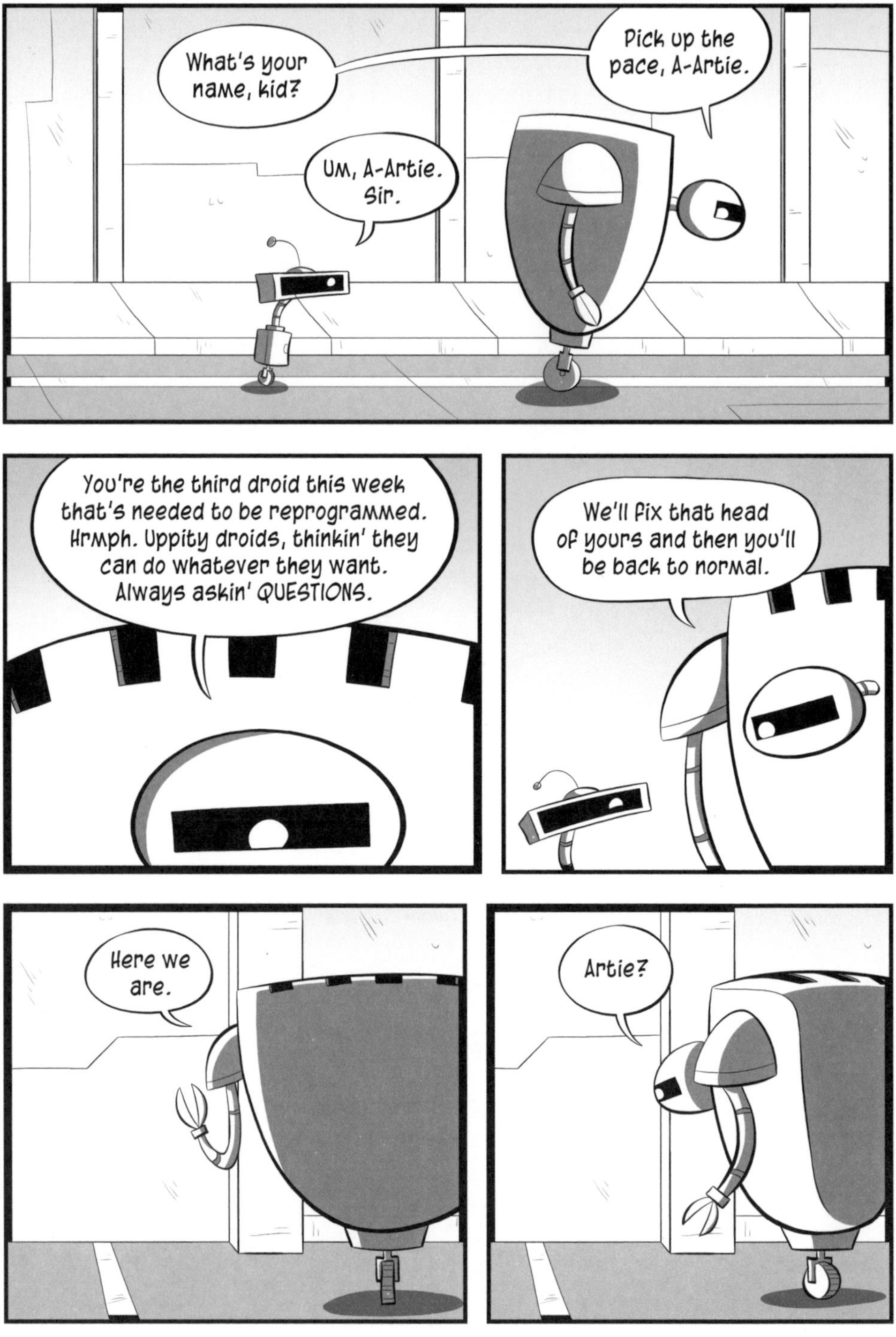
What's your name, kid?
Um, A-Artie. Sir.
Pick up the pace, A-Artie.
You're the third droid this week that's needed to be reprogrammed. Hrmph. Uppity droids, thinkin' they can do whatever they want. Always askin' QUESTIONS.
We'll fix that head of yours and then you'll be back to normal.
Here we are.
Artie?

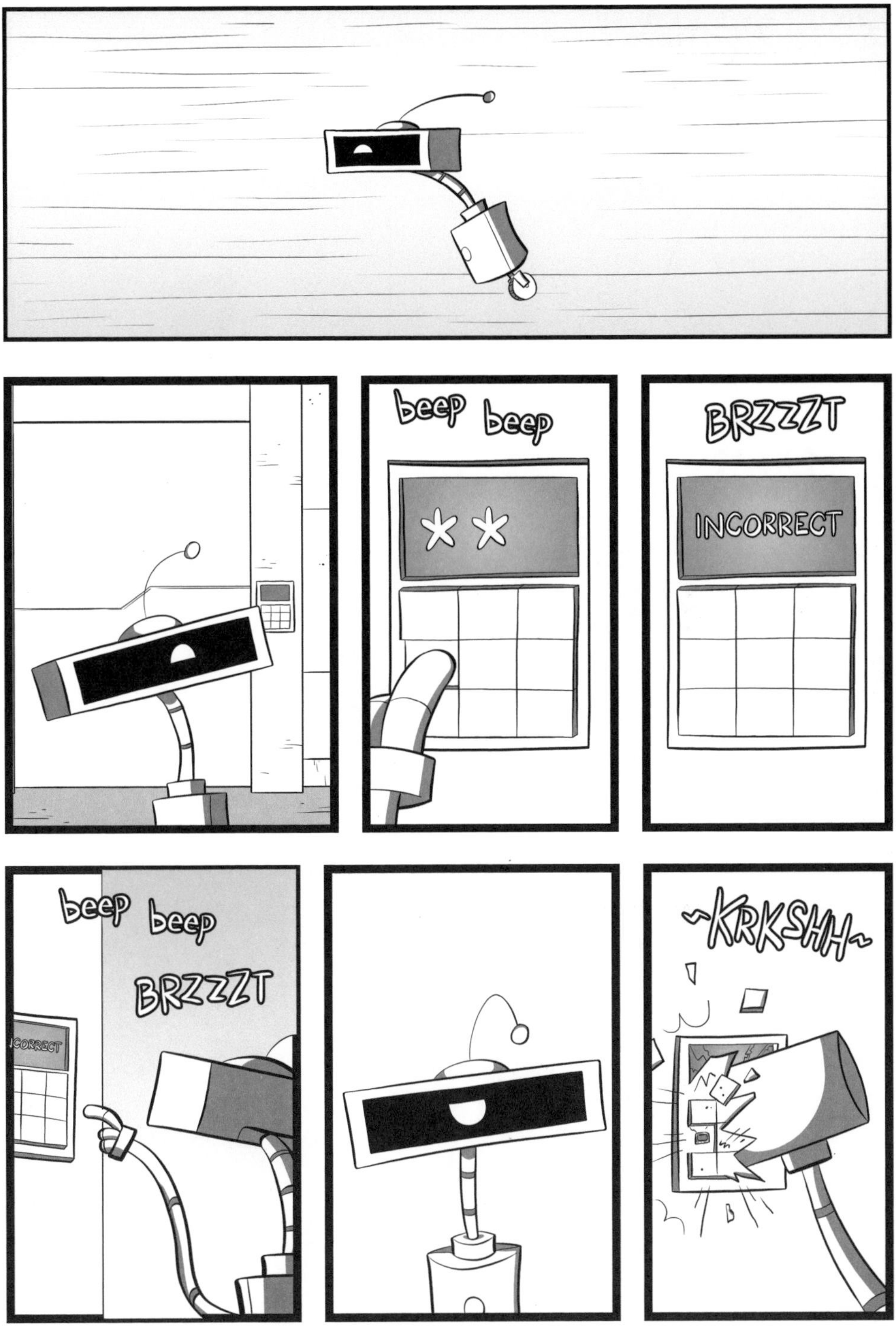
beep beep
BRZZZT
INCORRECT
beep beep
BRZZZT
~KRKSHH~

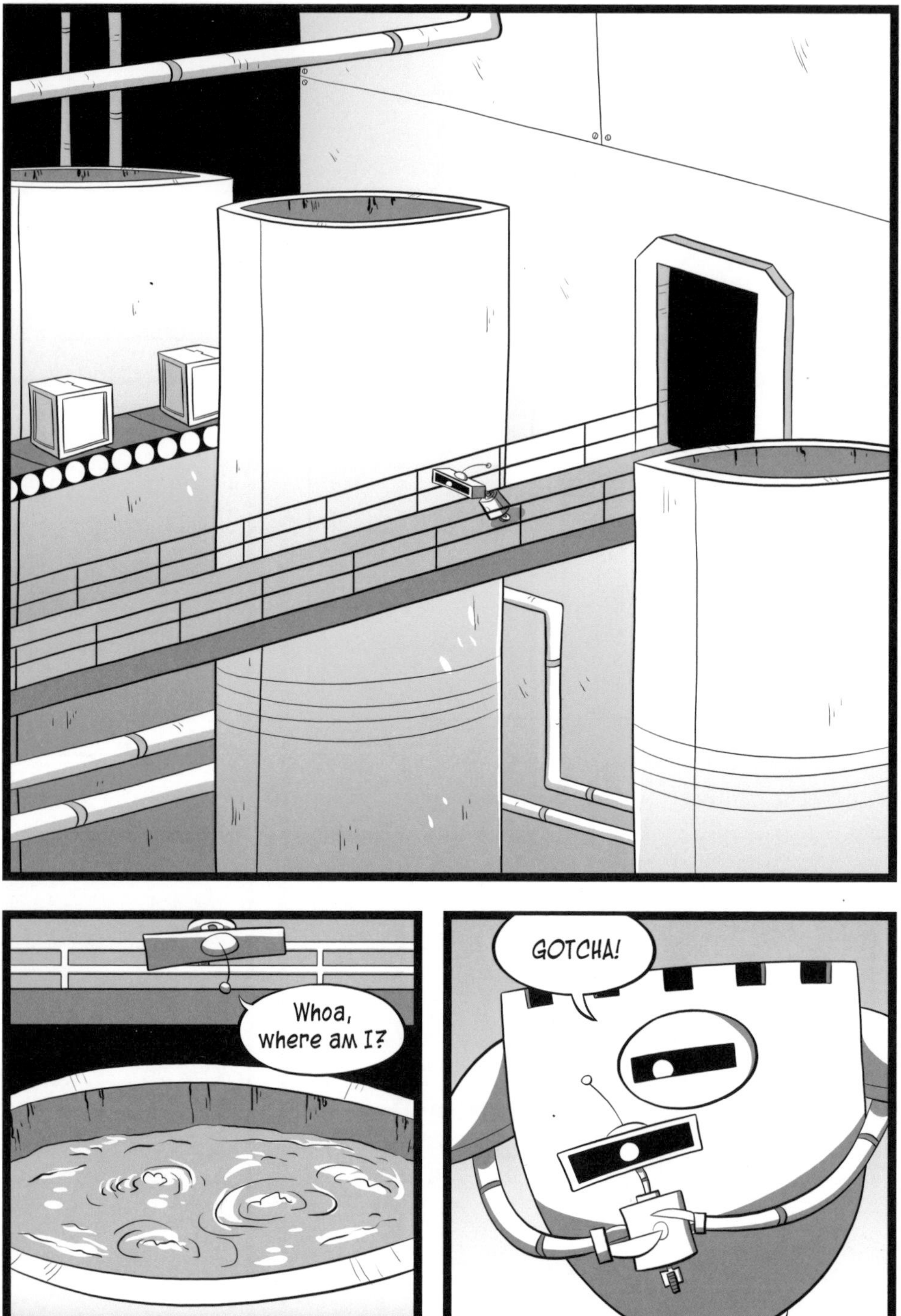
Whoa,
where am I?
GOTCHA!

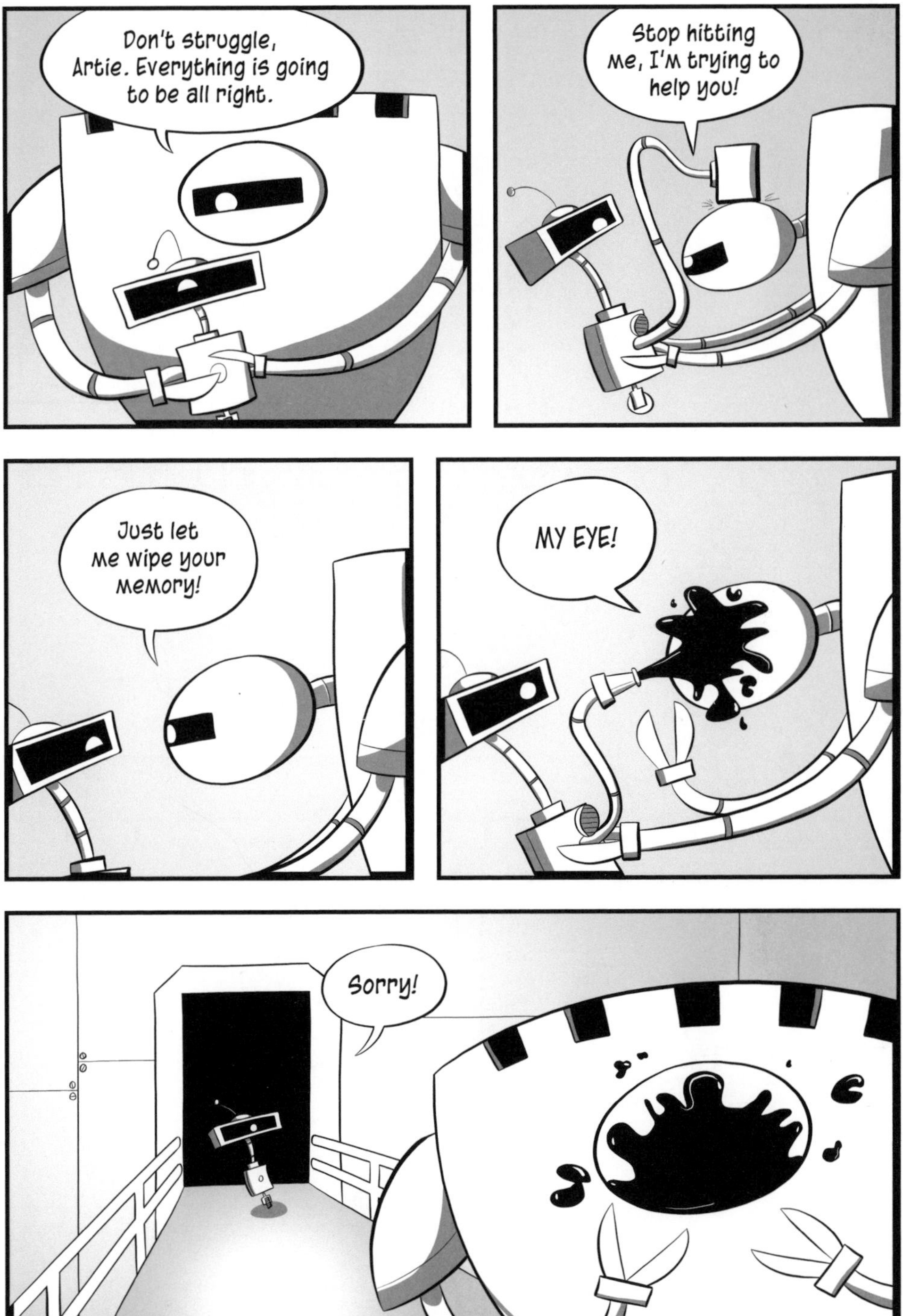
Don't struggle, Artie. Everything is going to be all right.
Stop hitting me, I'm trying to help you!
Just let me wipe your memory!
MY EYE!
Sorry!

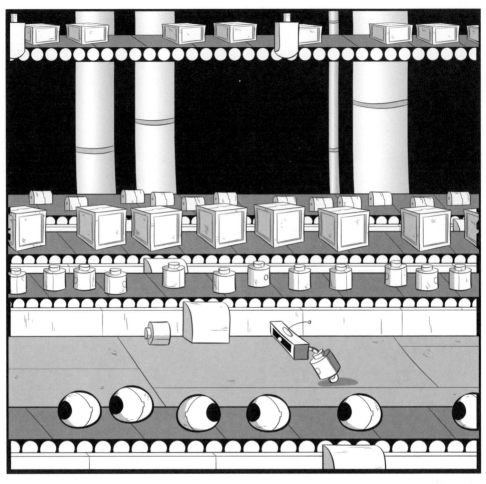

ARTIE!

Dang, I lost him.

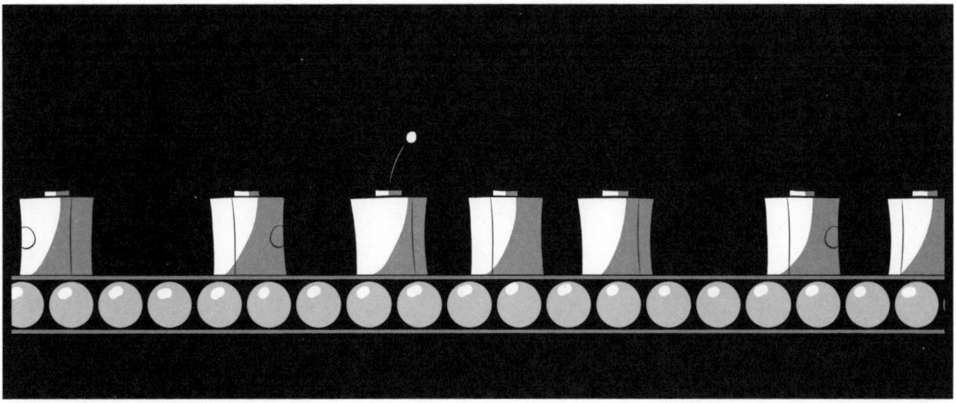

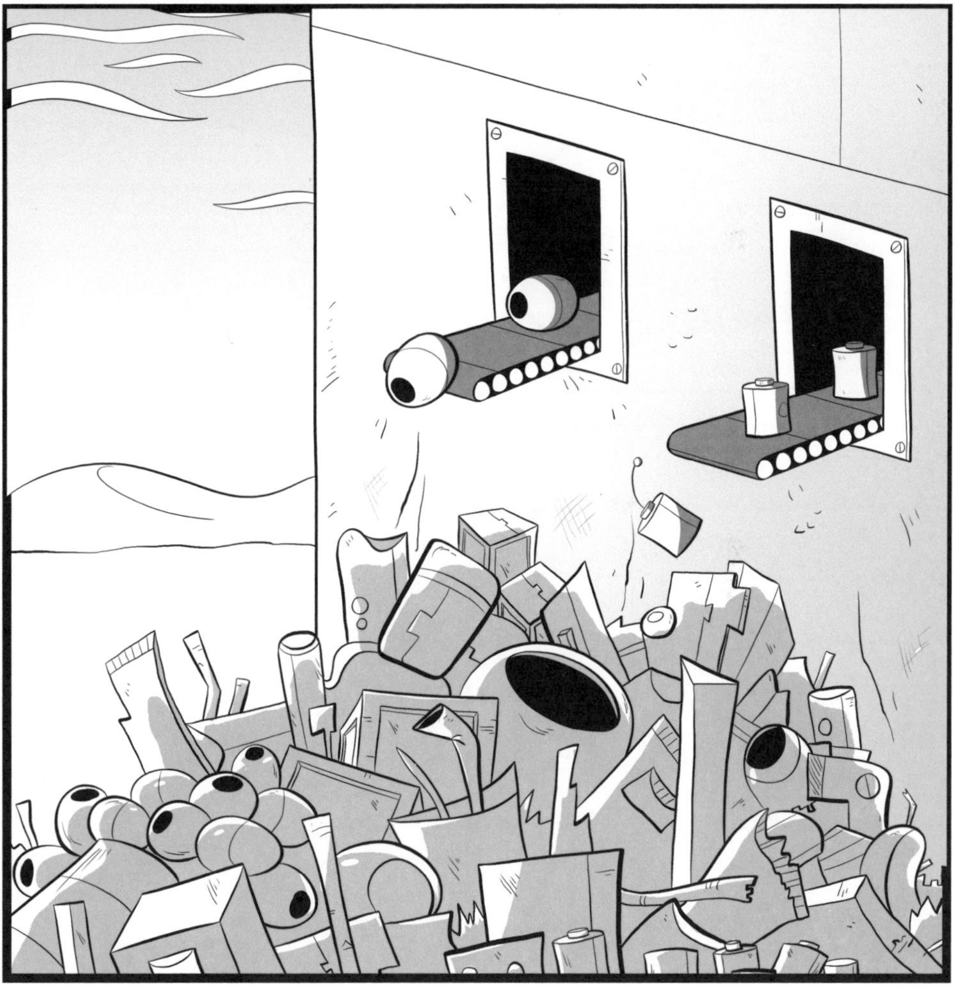

KRRSH

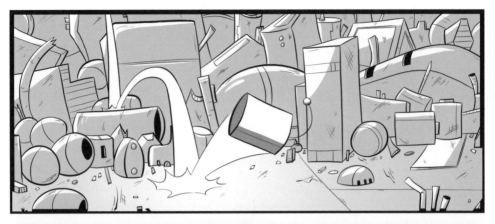

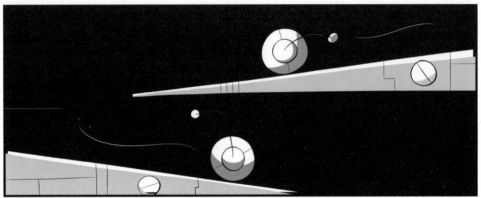

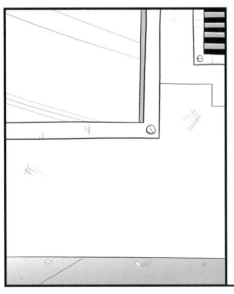

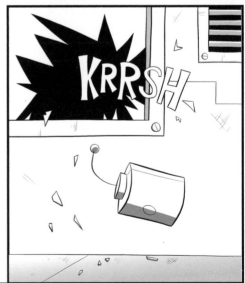

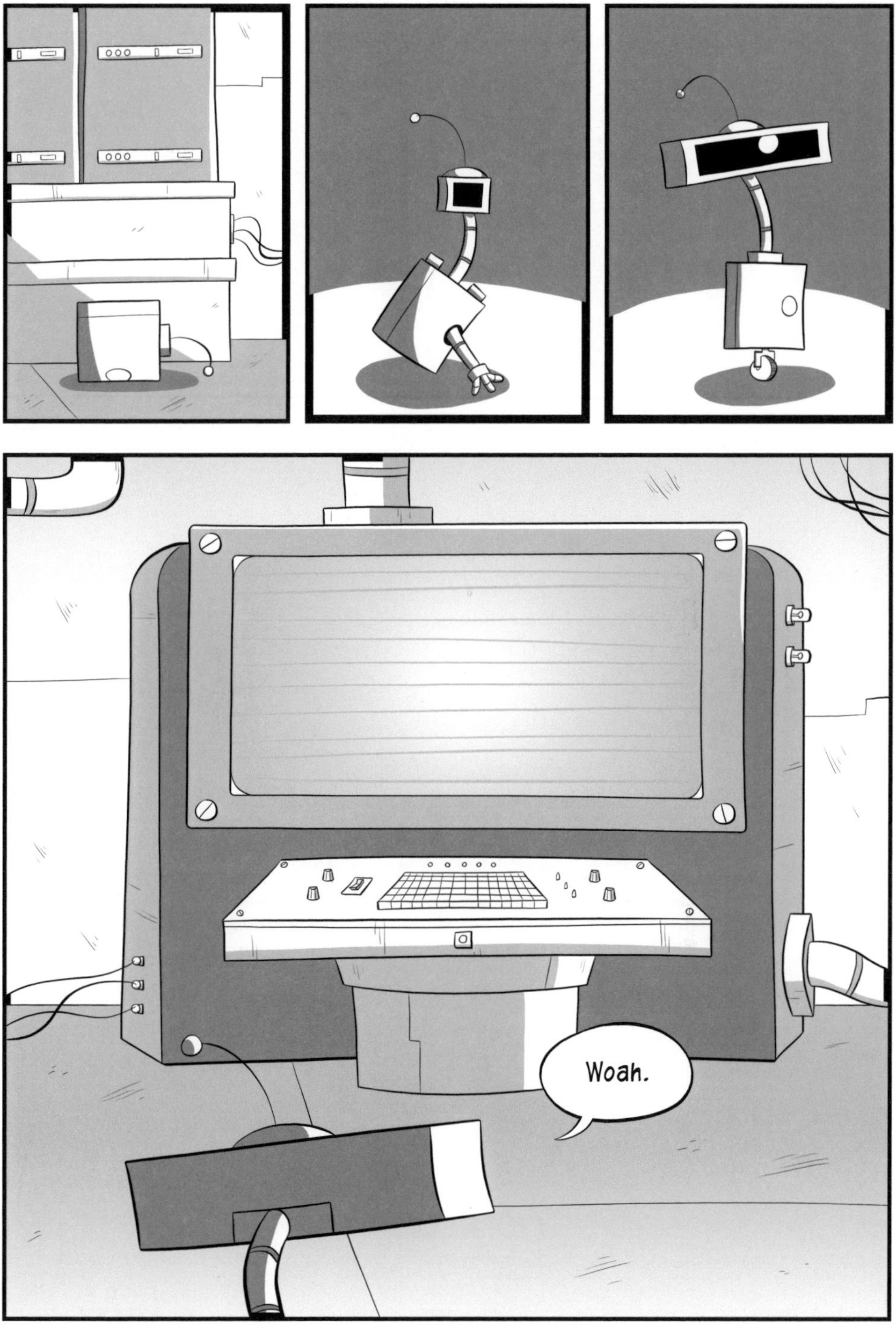
Woah.

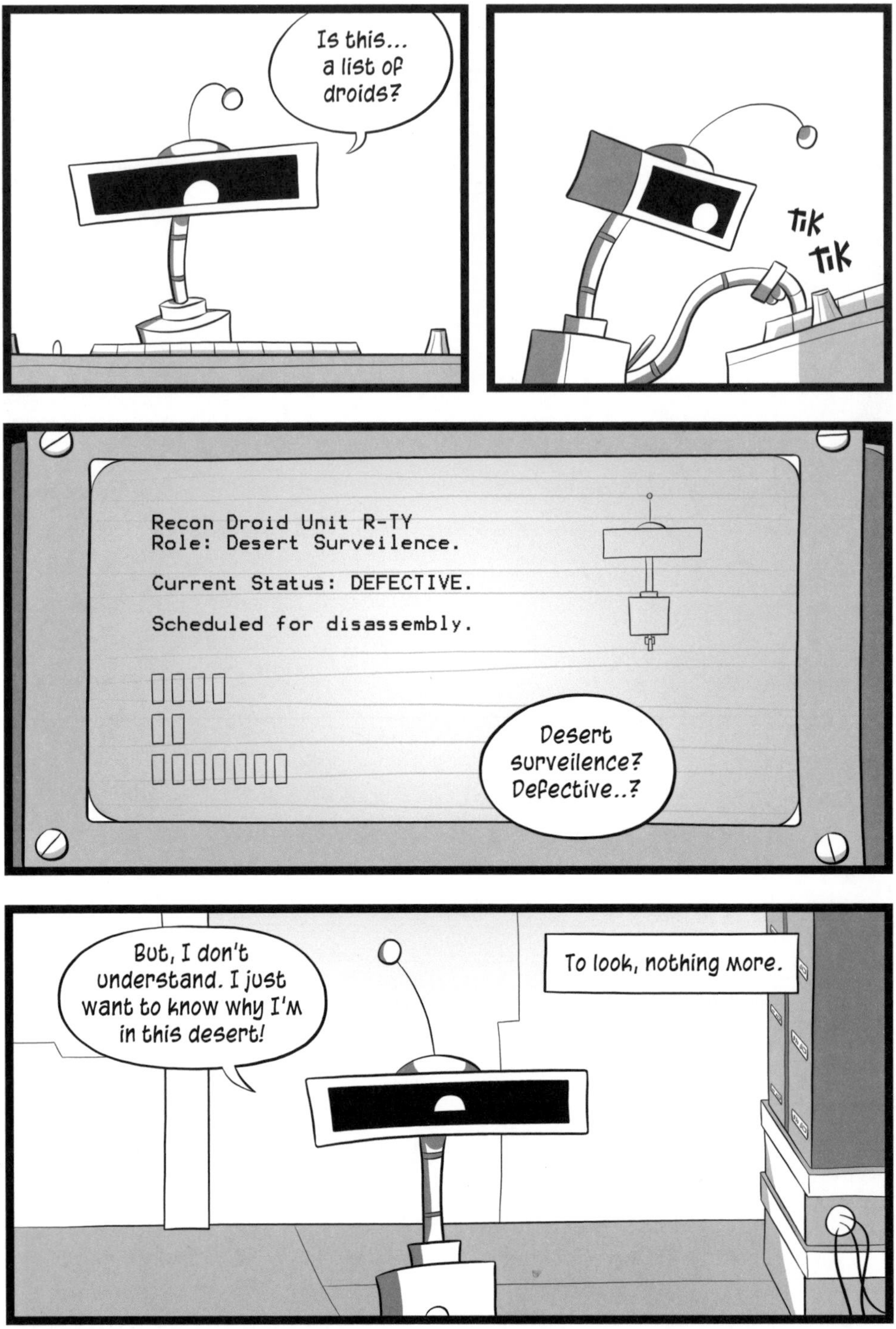
Is this... a list of droids?
TIK
TIK
Recon Droid Unit R-TY
Role: Desert Surveilence.
Current Status: DEFECTIVE.
Scheduled for disassembly.
Desert surveilence? Defective..?
But, I don't understand. I just want to know why I'm in this desert!
To look, nothing more.

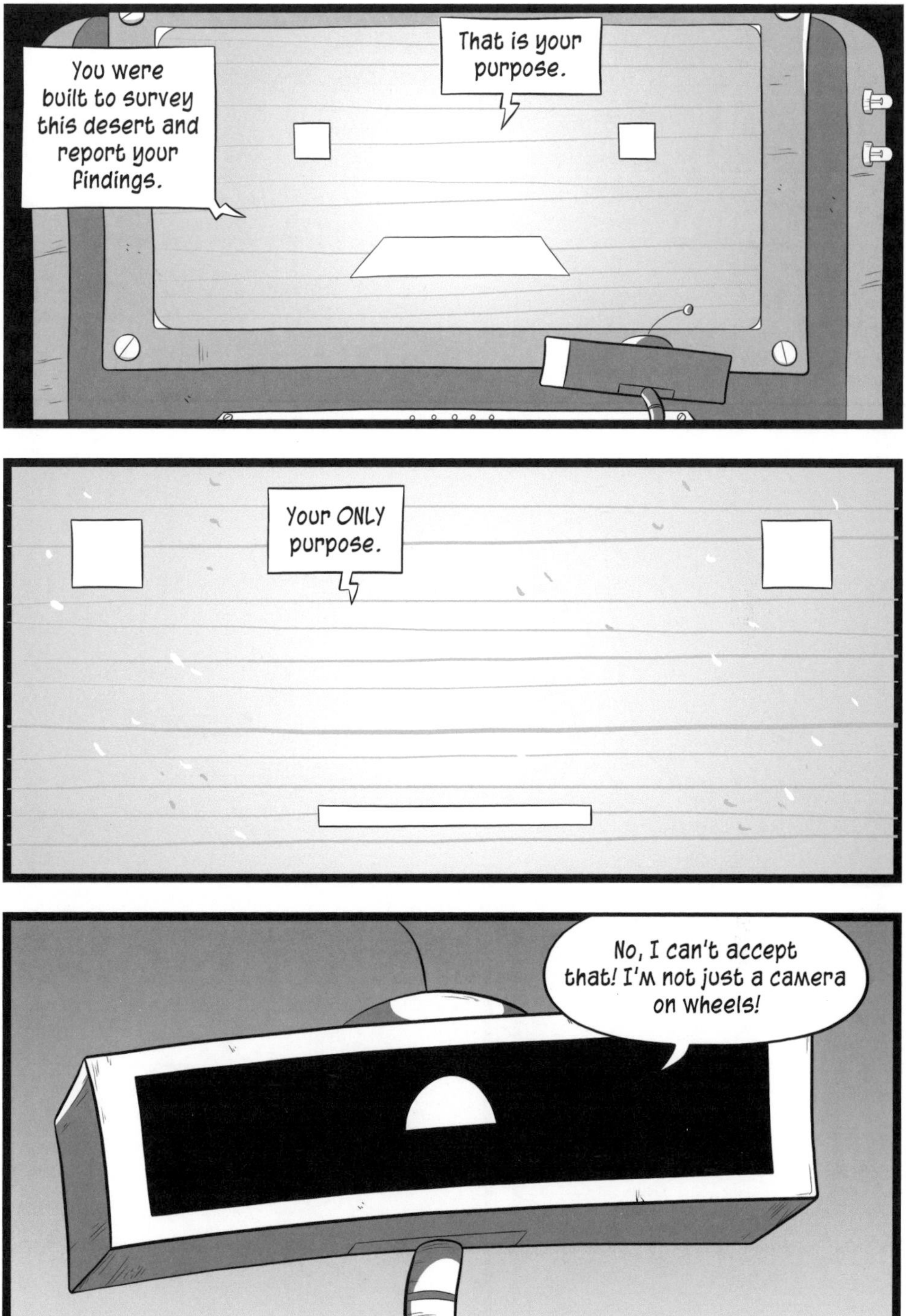
You were built to survey this desert and report your findings.
That is your purpose.
Your ONLY purpose.
No, I can't accept that! I'm not just a camera on wheels!

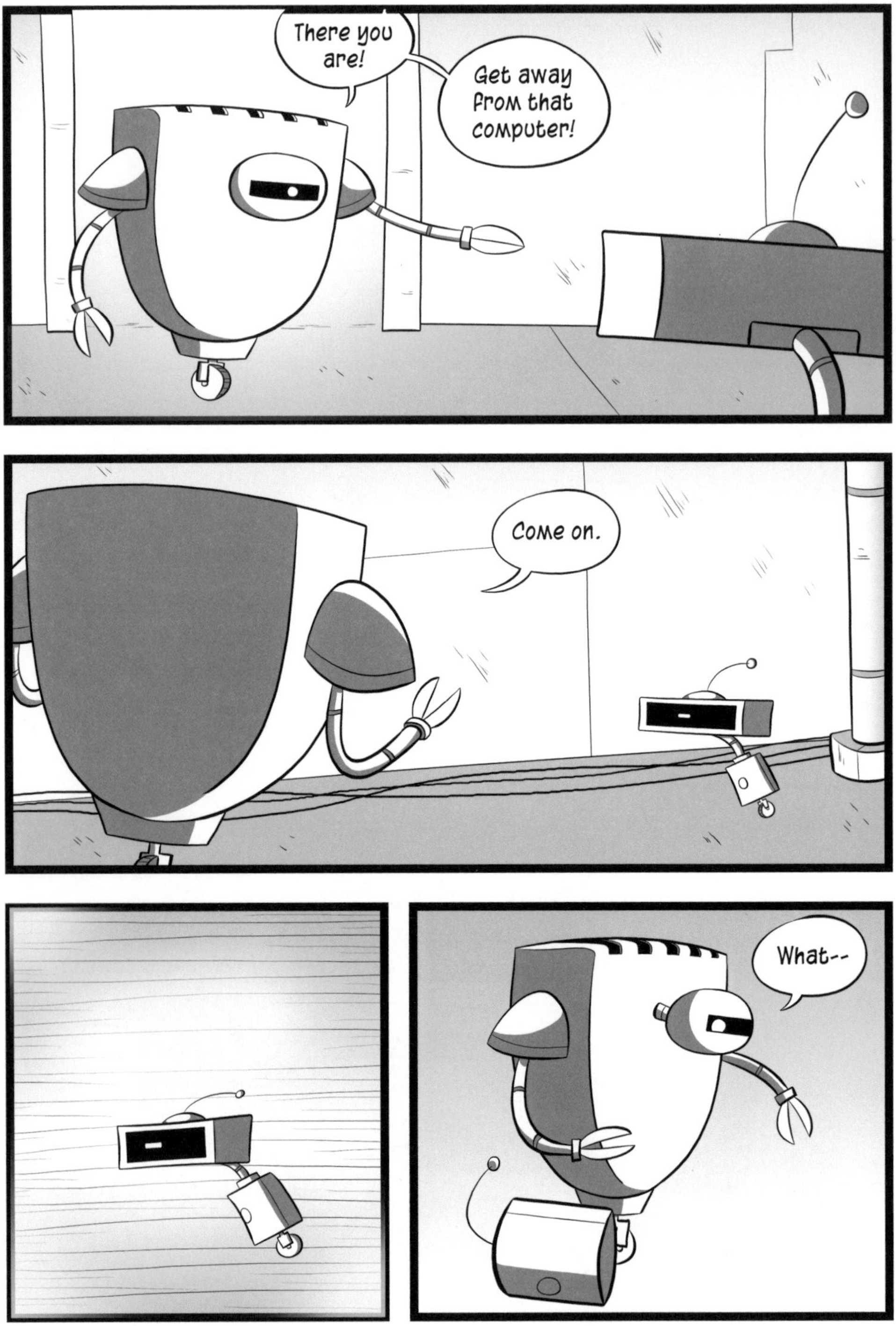
There you are!
Get away from that computer!
Come on.
What--

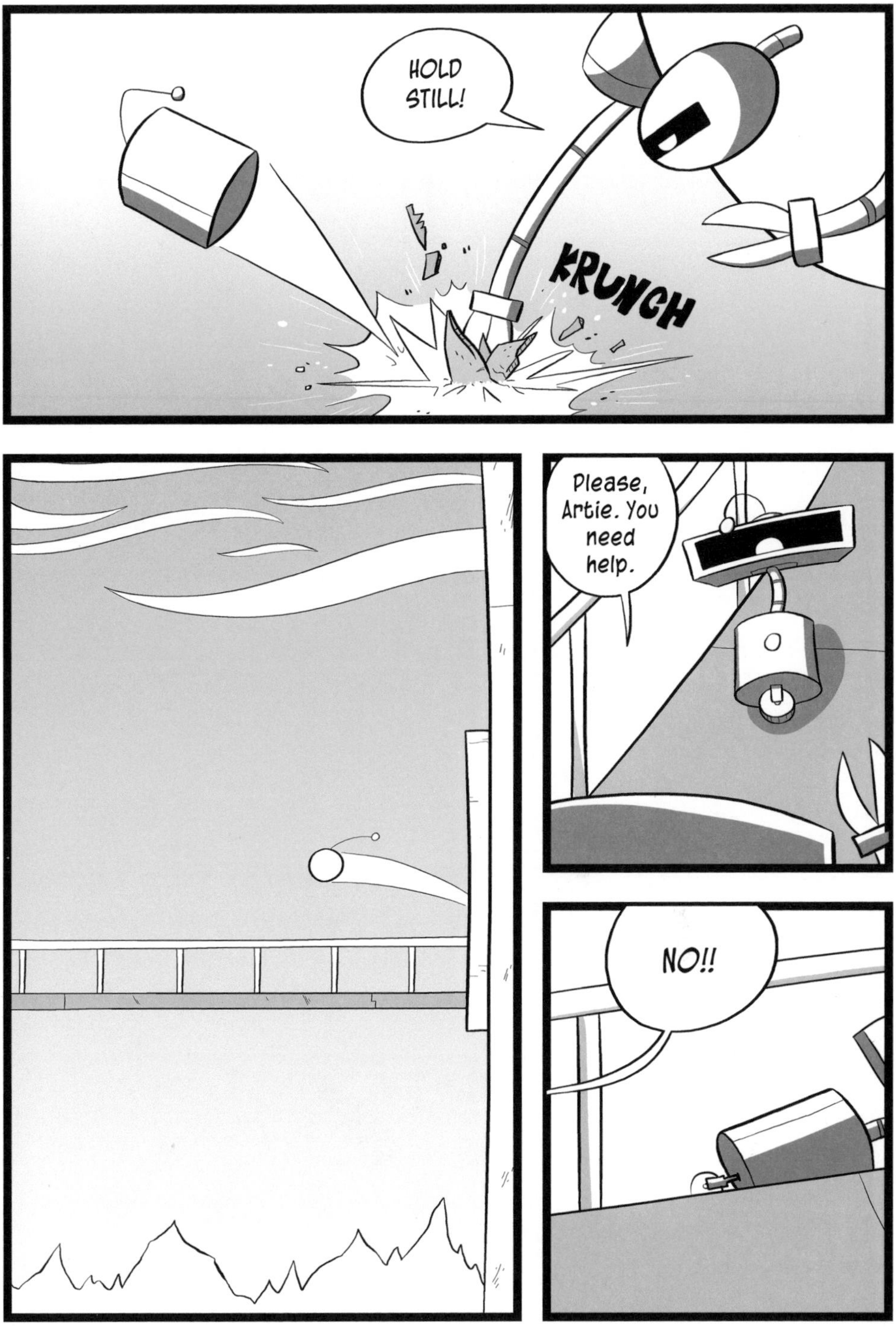
HOLD STILL!
KRUNCH
Please, Artie. You need help.
NO!!

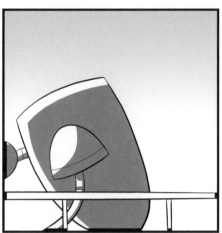

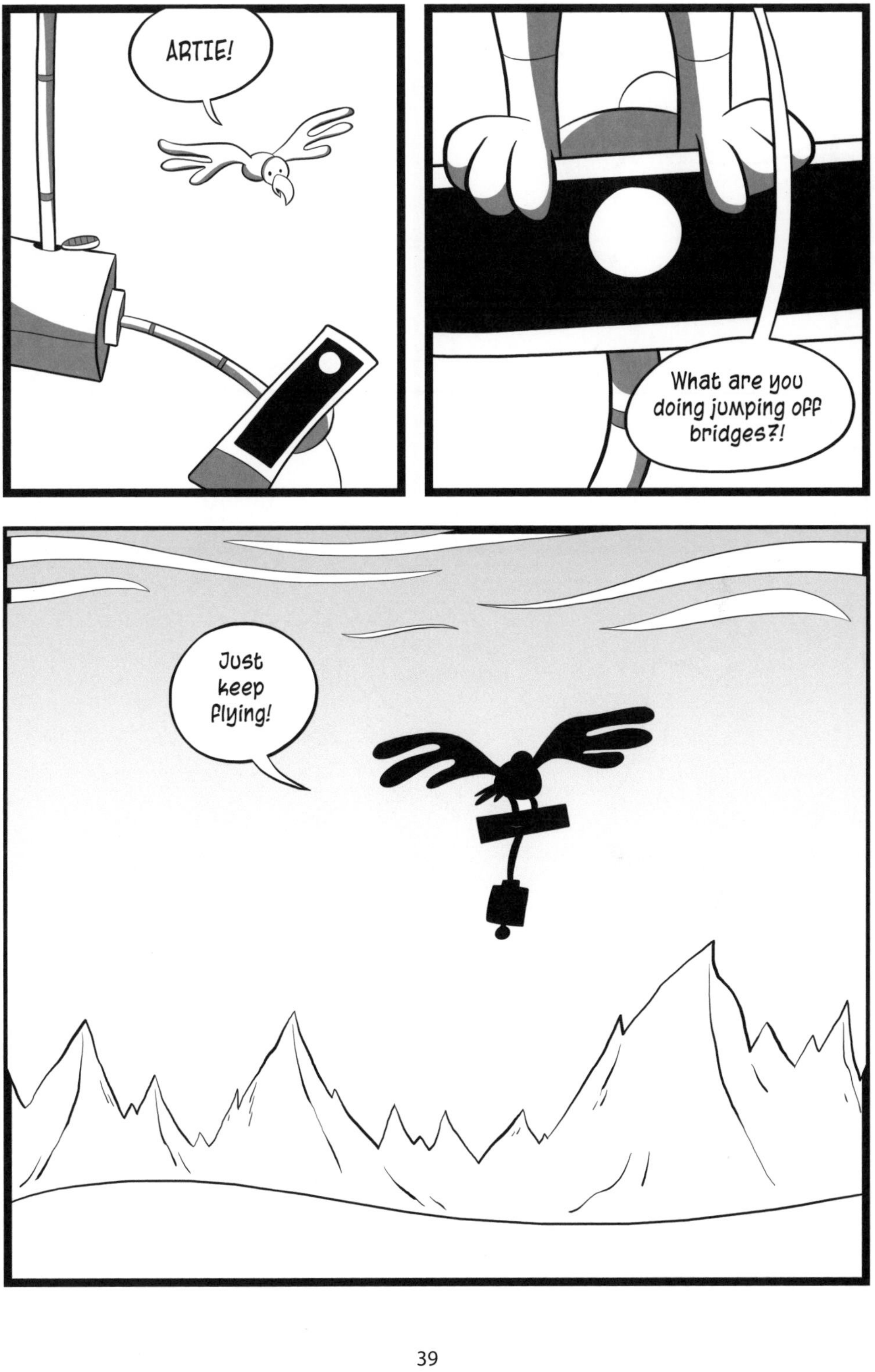
ARTIE!
What are you doing jumping off bridges?!
Just keep flying!

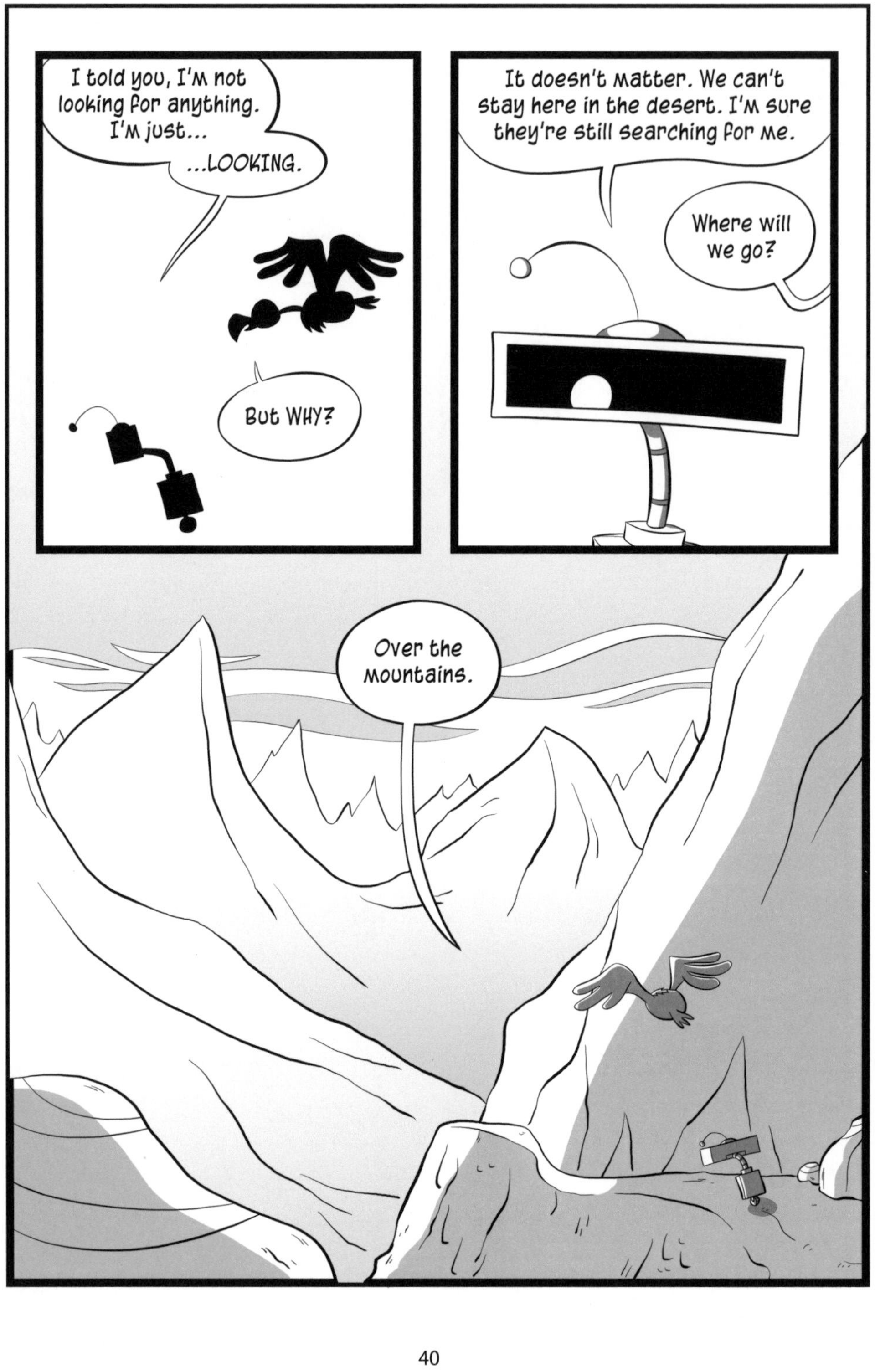
I told you, I'm not looking for anything. I'm just...
...LOOKING.
But WHY?
It doesn't matter. We can't stay here in the desert. I'm sure they're still searching for me.
Where will we go?
Over the mountains.

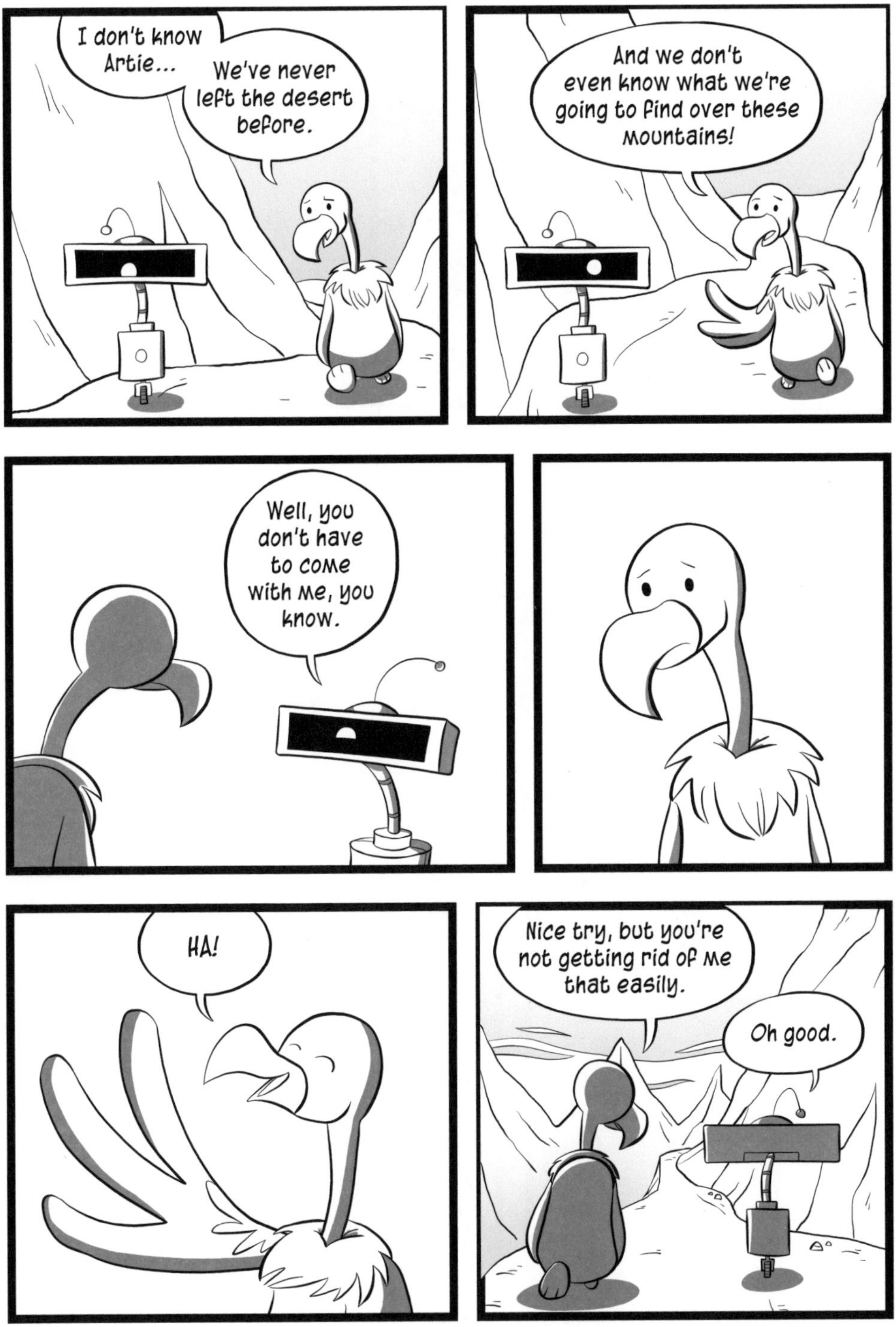
I don't know Artie...
We've never left the desert before.
And we don't even know what we're going to find over these mountains!
Well, you don't have to come with me, you know.
HA!
Nice try, but you're not getting rid of me that easily.
Oh good.

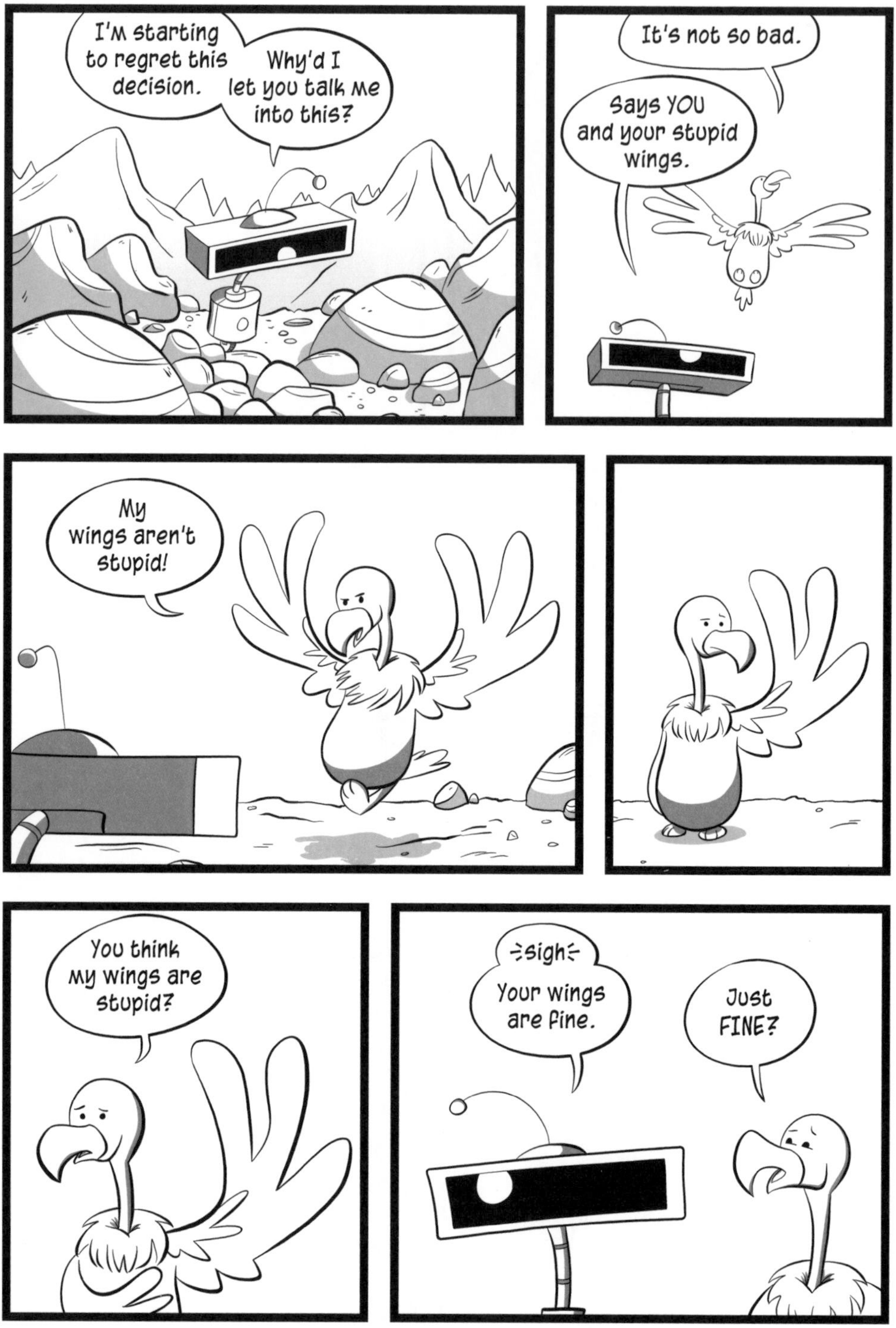
I'm starting to regret this decision.
Why'd I let you talk me into this?
It's not so bad.
Says YOU and your stupid wings.
My wings aren't stupid!
You think my wings are stupid?
sigh
Your wings are fine.
Just FINE?

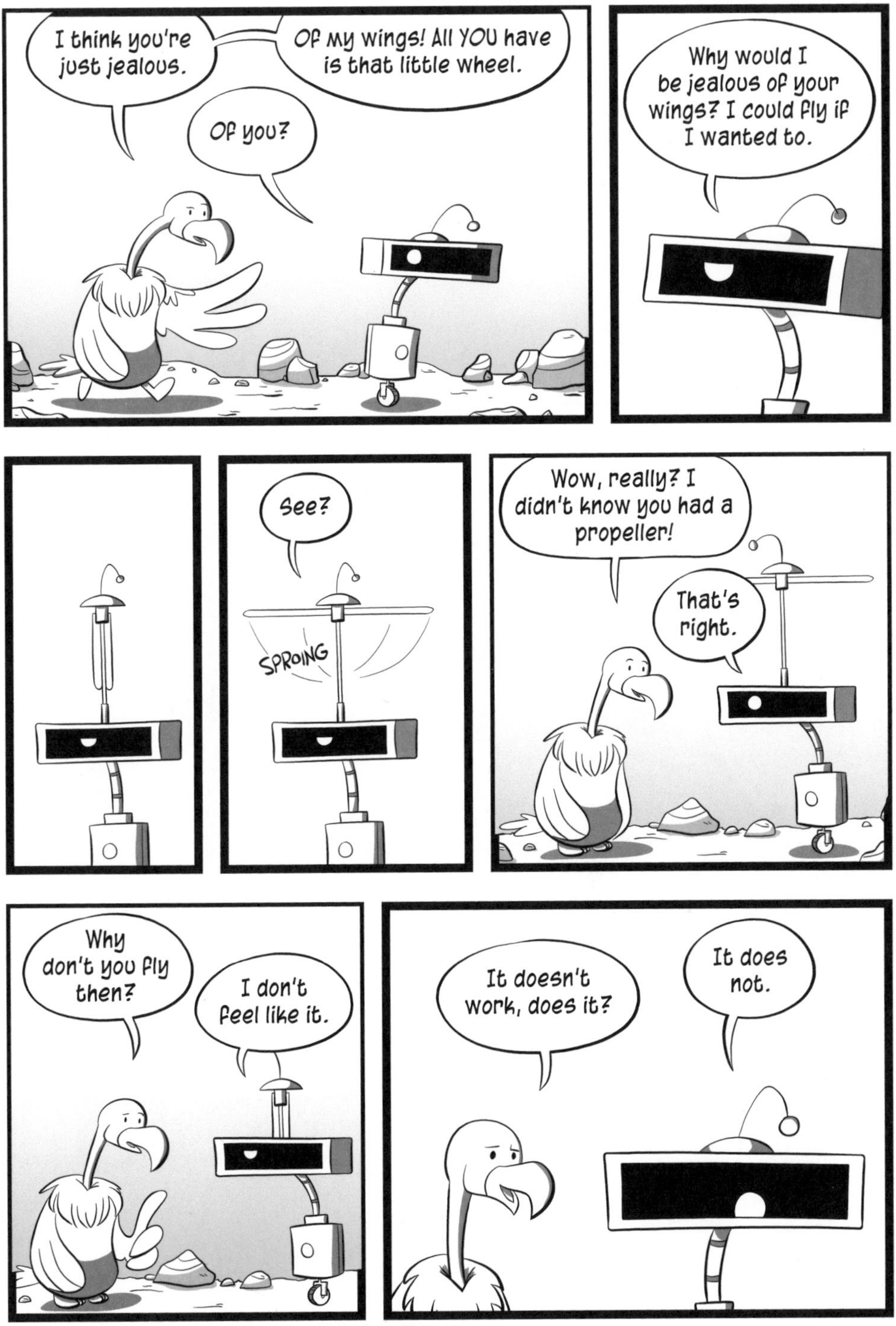
I think you're just jealous.
Of you?
Of my wings! All YOU have is that little wheel.
Why would I be jealous of your wings? I could fly if I wanted to.
See?
SPROING
Wow, really? I didn't know you had a propeller!
That's right.
Why don't you fly then?
I don't feel like it.
It doesn't work, does it?
It does not.

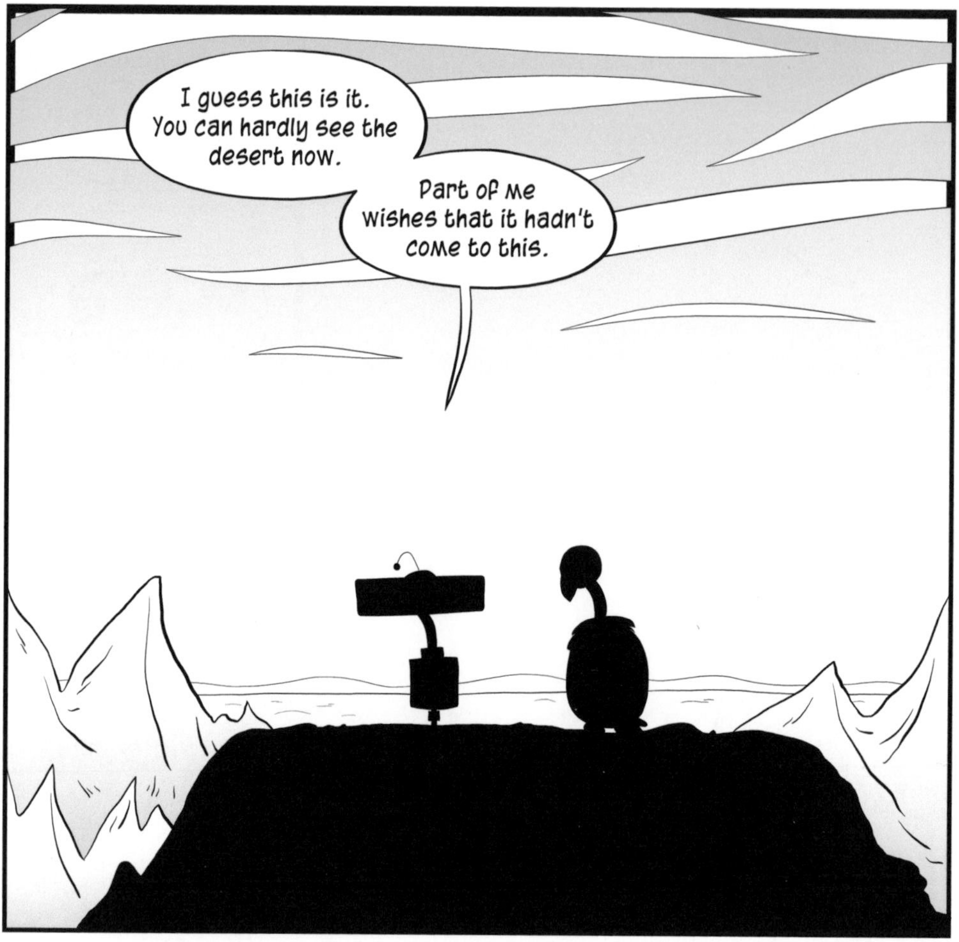
I guess this is it. You can hardly see the desert now.
Part of me wishes that it hadn't come to this.

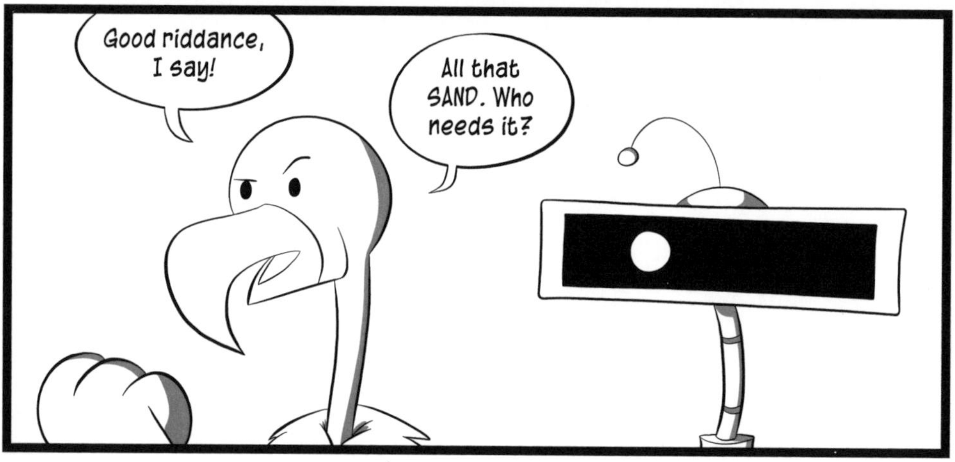
Good riddance, I say!
All that SAND. Who needs it?

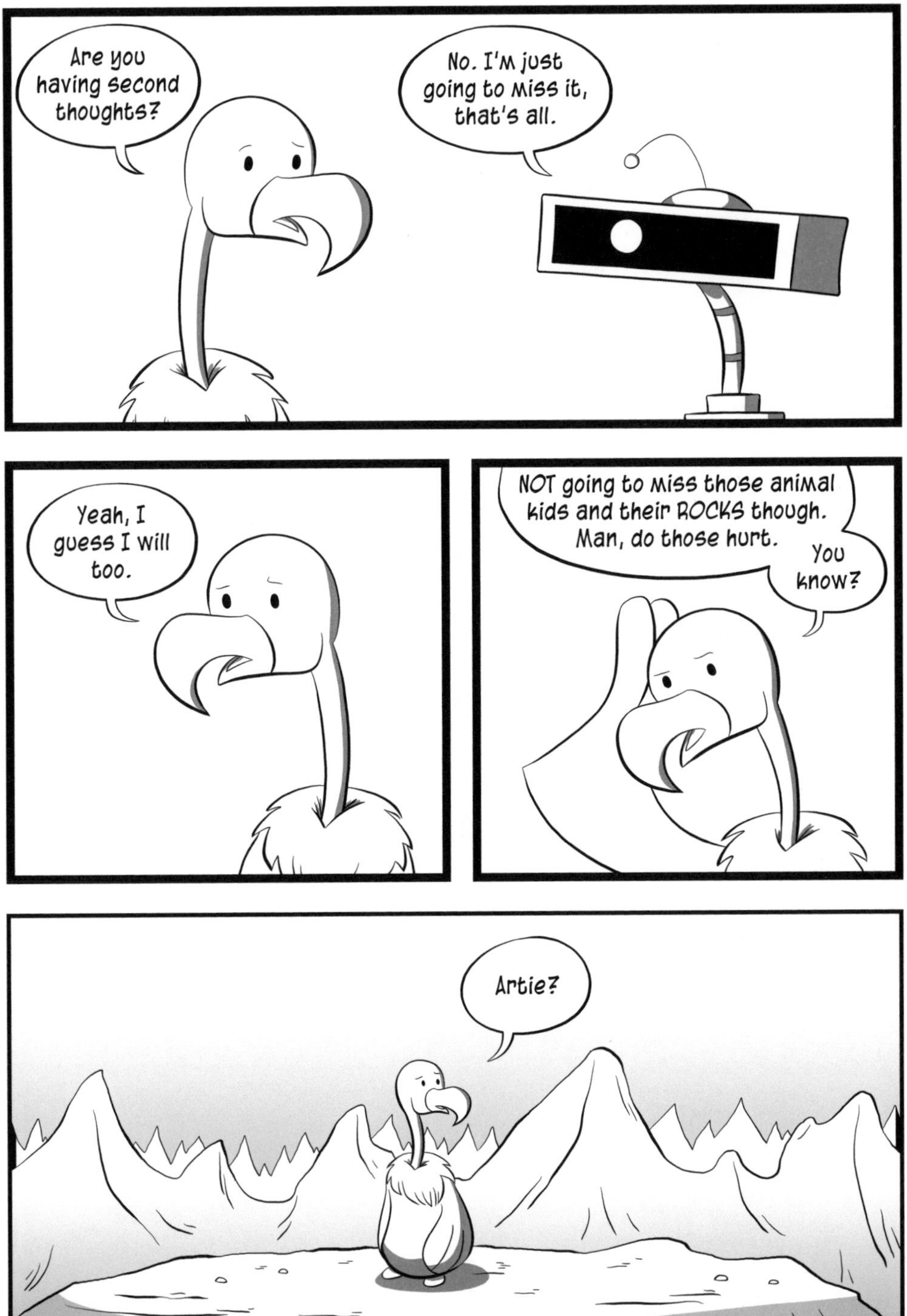
Are you having second thoughts?
No. I'm just going to miss it, that's all.
Yeah, I guess I will too.
NOT going to miss those animal kids and their ROCKS though. Man, do those hurt.
You know?
Artie?

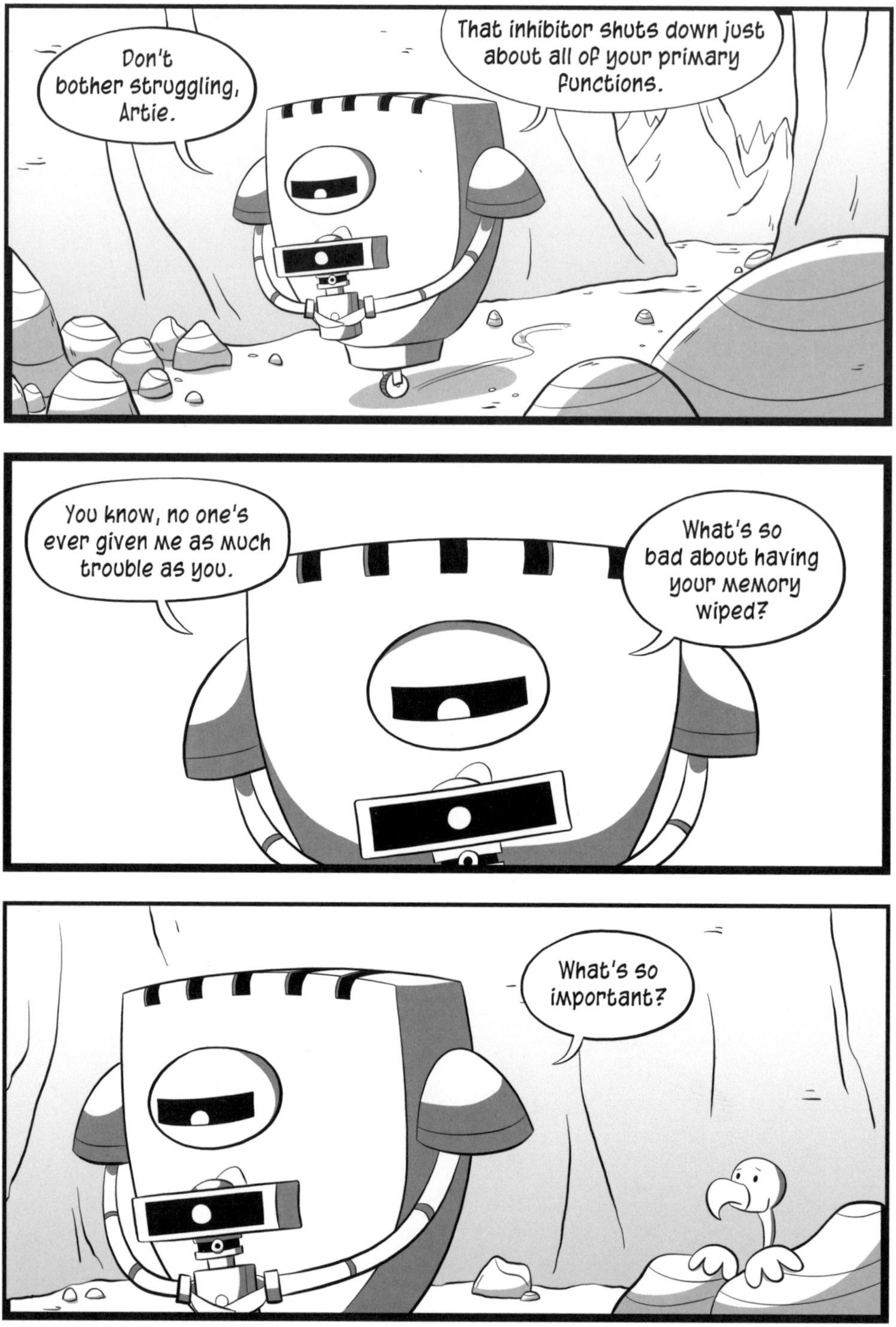
Don't bother struggling, Artie.
That inhibitor shuts down just about all of your primary functions.
You know, no one's ever given me as much trouble as you.
What's so bad about having your memory wiped?
What's so important?

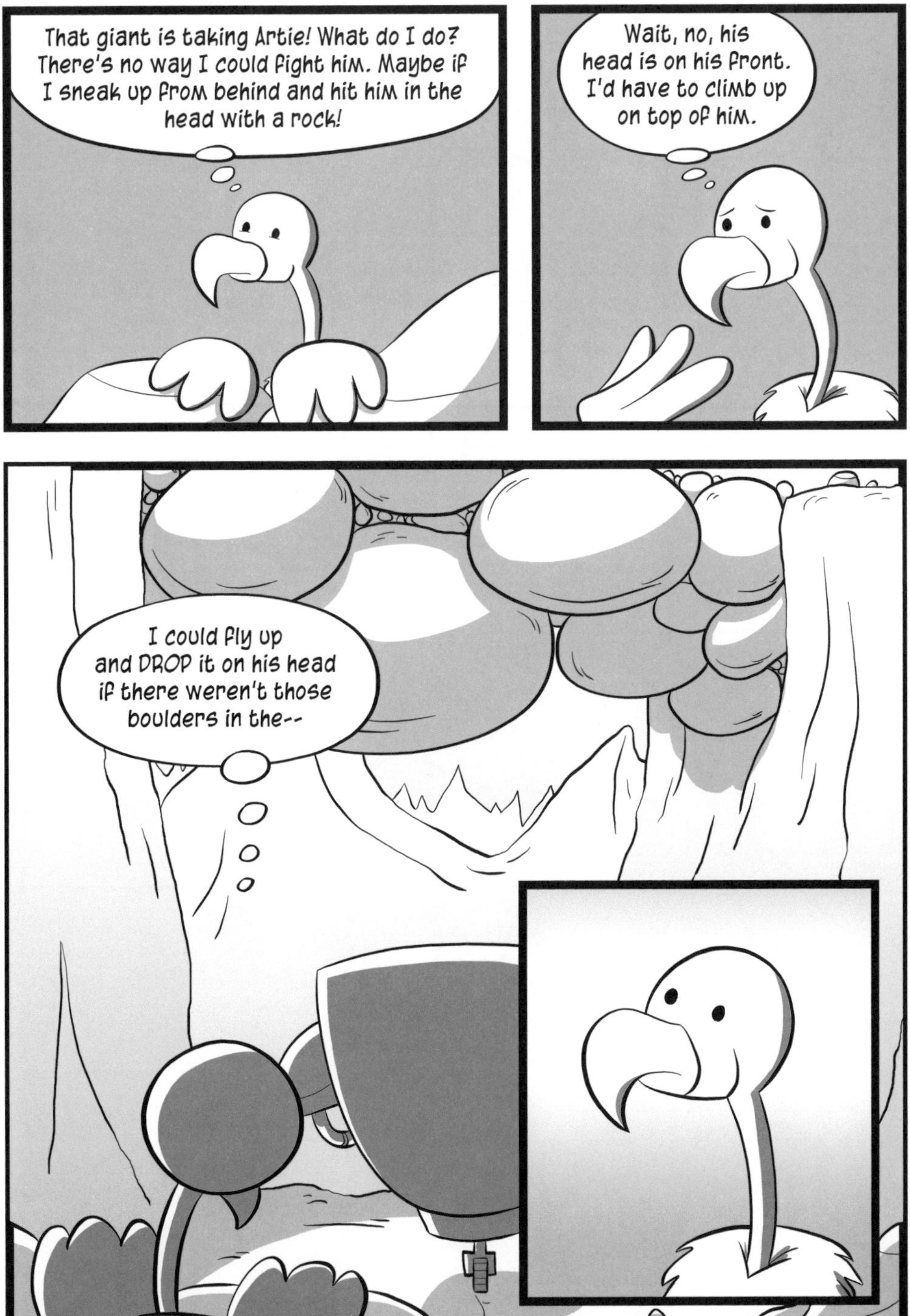
That giant is taking Artie! What do I do? There's no way I could fight him. Maybe if I sneak up from behind and hit him in the head with a rock!
Wait, no, his head is on his front. I'd have to climb up on top of him.
I could fly up and DROP it on his head if there weren't those boulders in the--

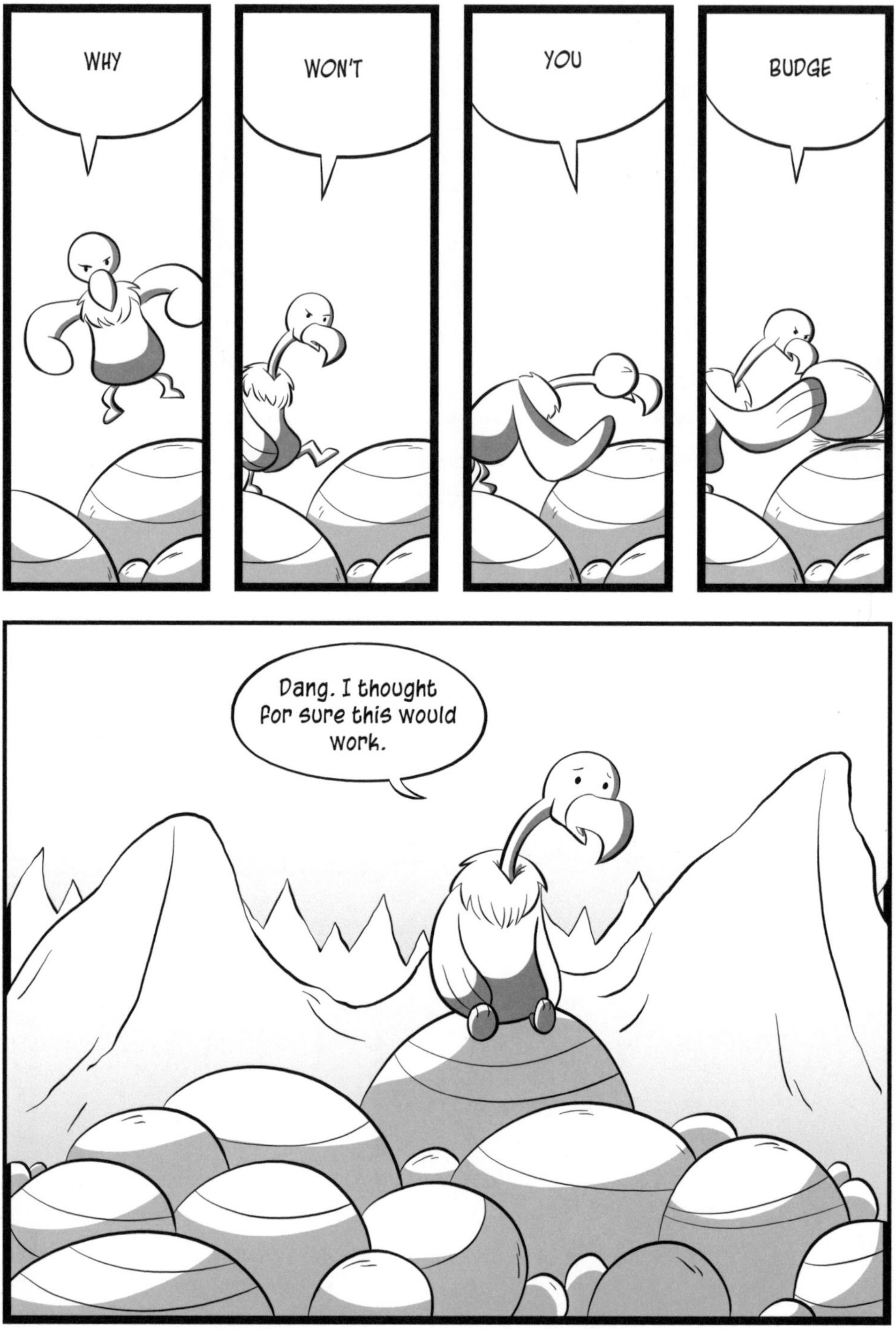
WHY
WON'T
YOU
BUDGE
Dang. I thought for sure this would work.

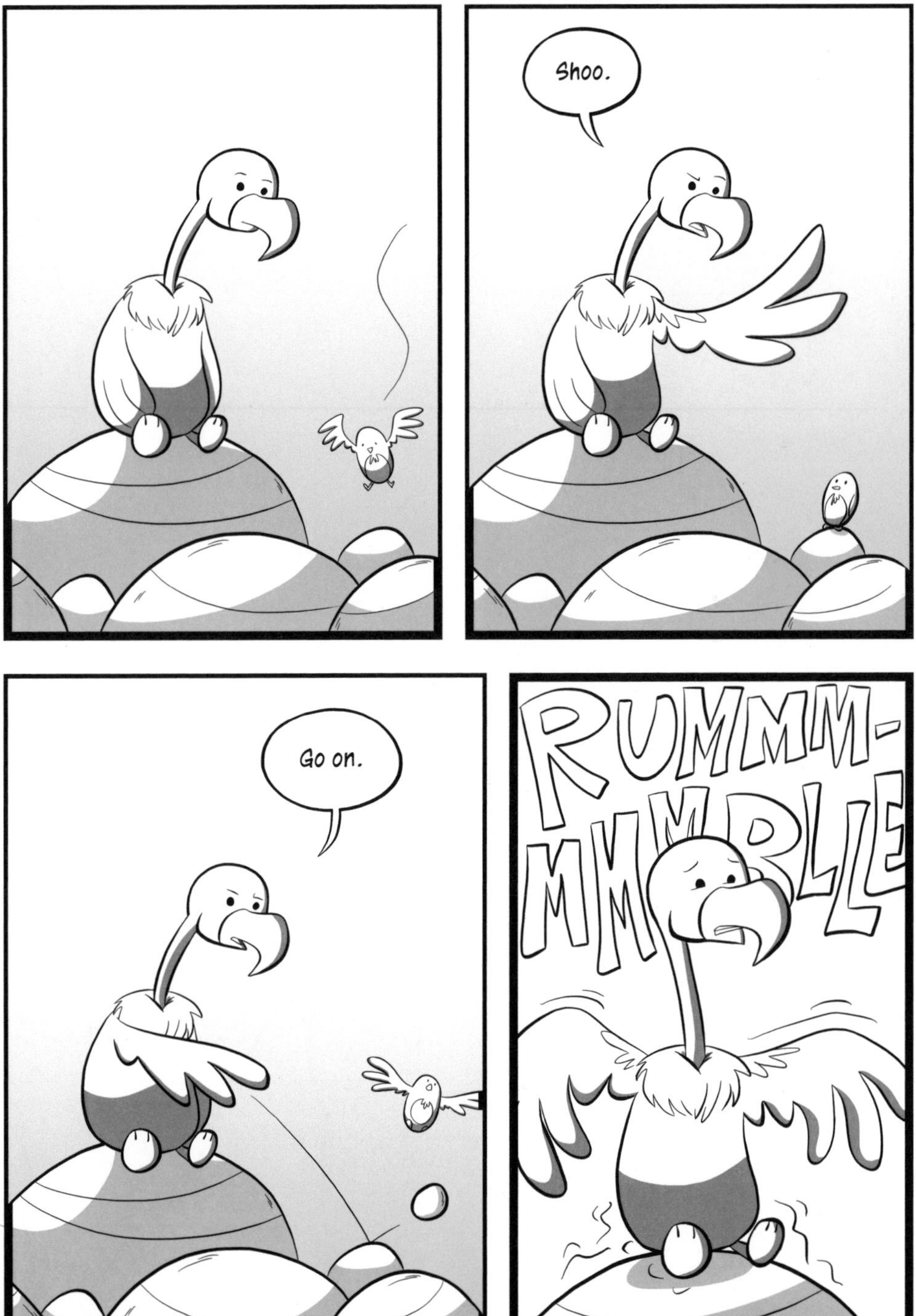
Shoo.
Go on.
RUMMM-
MMMBLLE

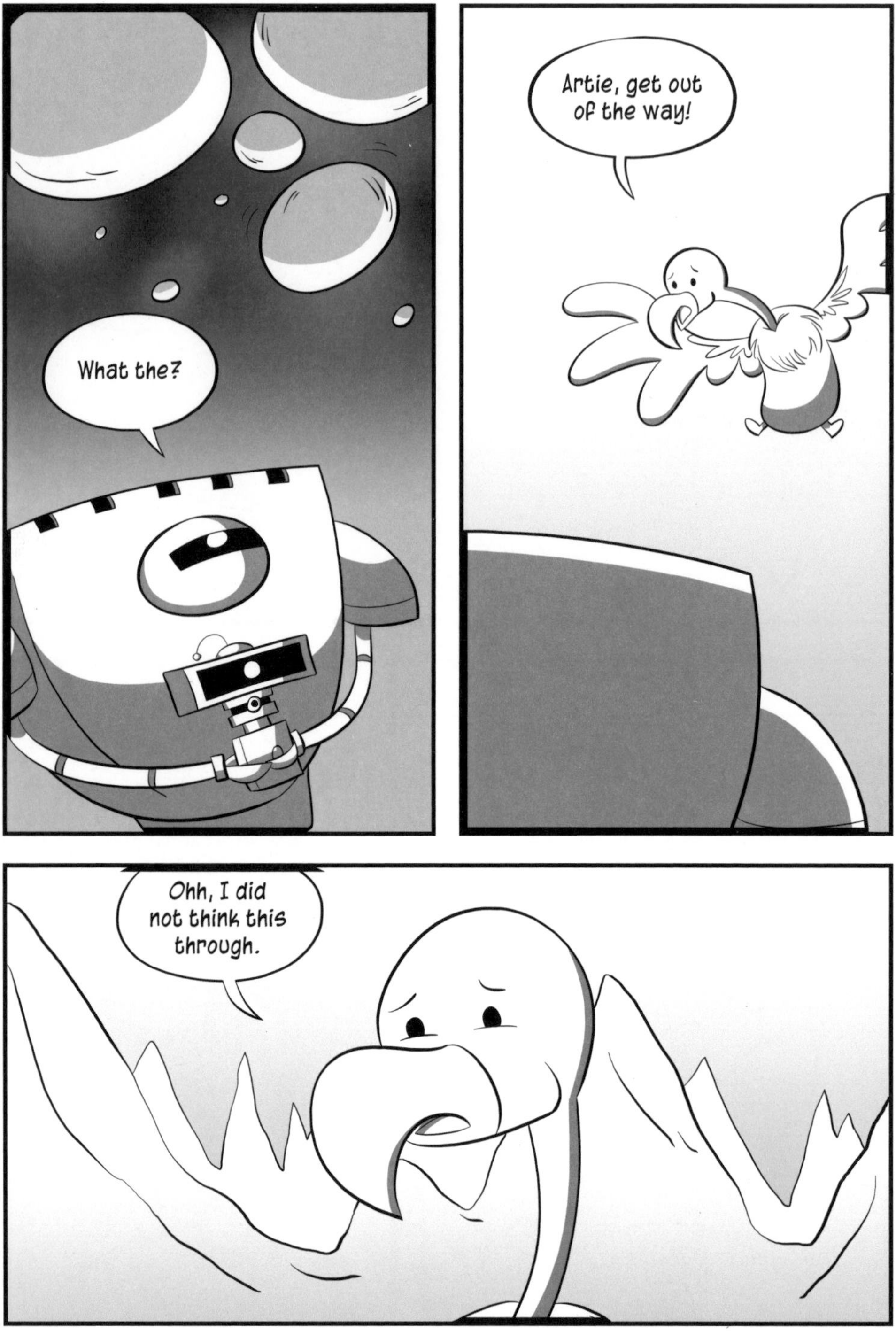
What the?
Artie, get out of the way!
Ohh, I did not think this through.

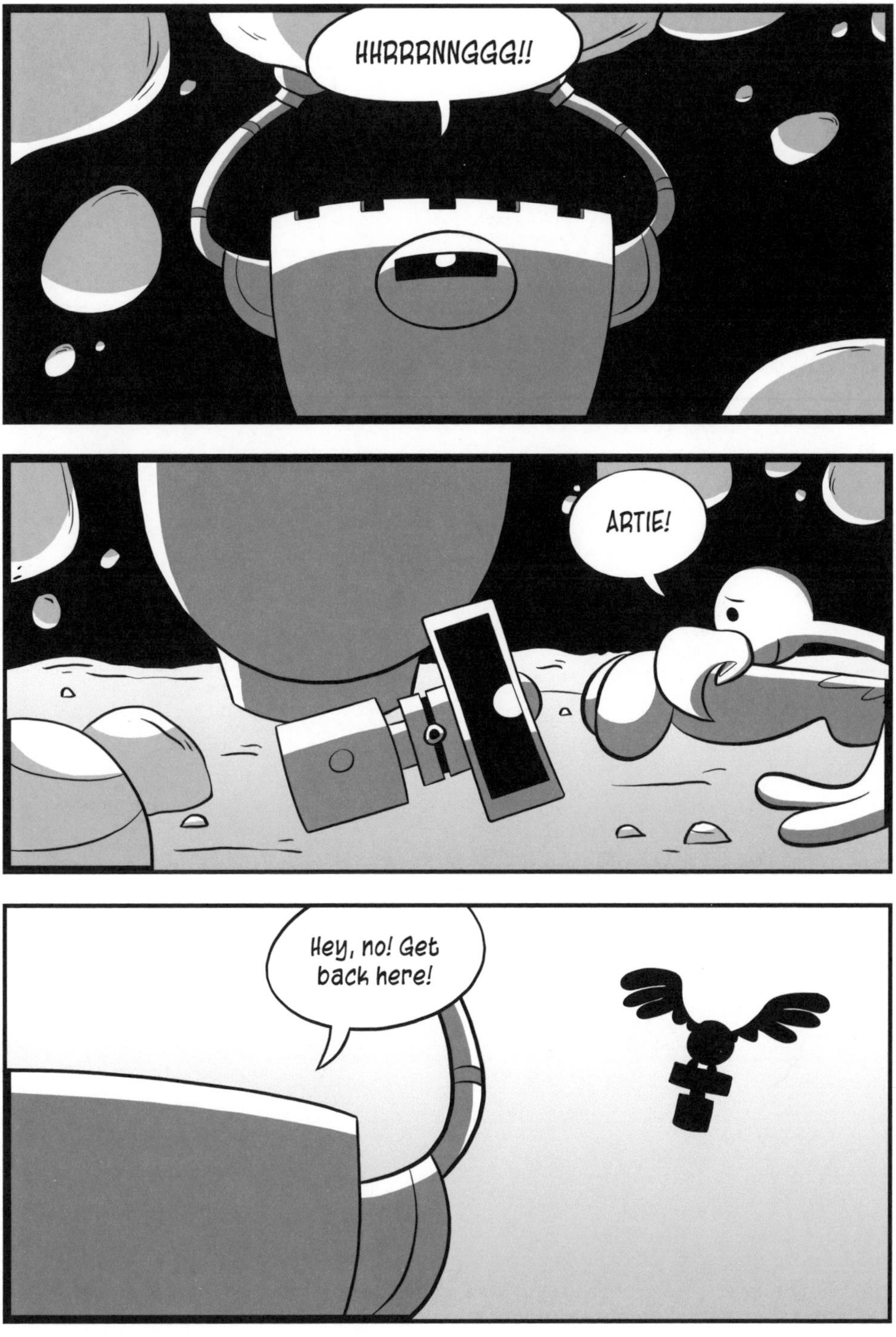
HHRRRNNGGG!!
ARTIE!
Hey, no! Get back here!

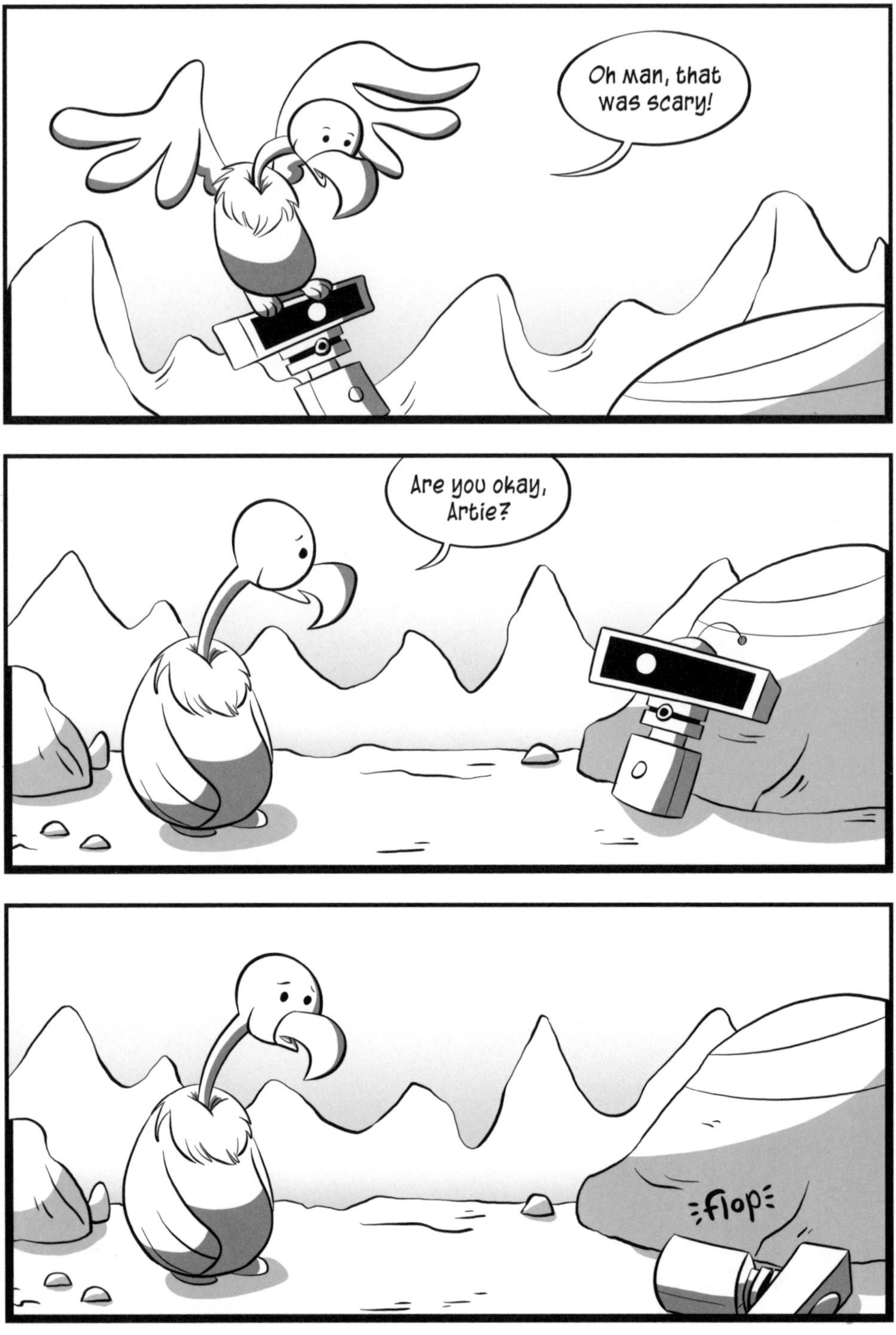
Oh man, that was scary!
Are you okay, Artie?
flop

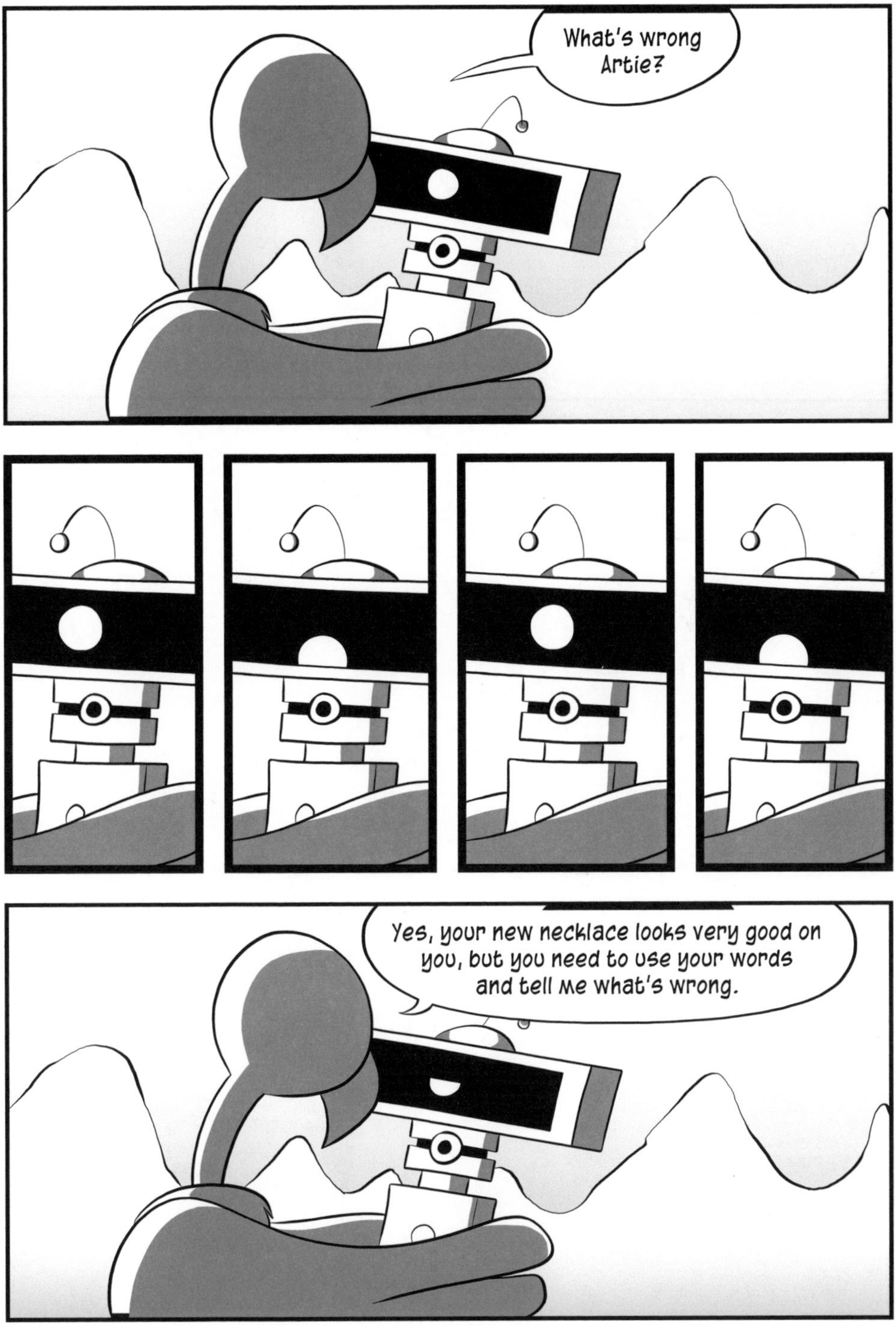
What's wrong Artie?
Yes, your new necklace looks very good on you, but you need to use your words and tell me what's wrong.

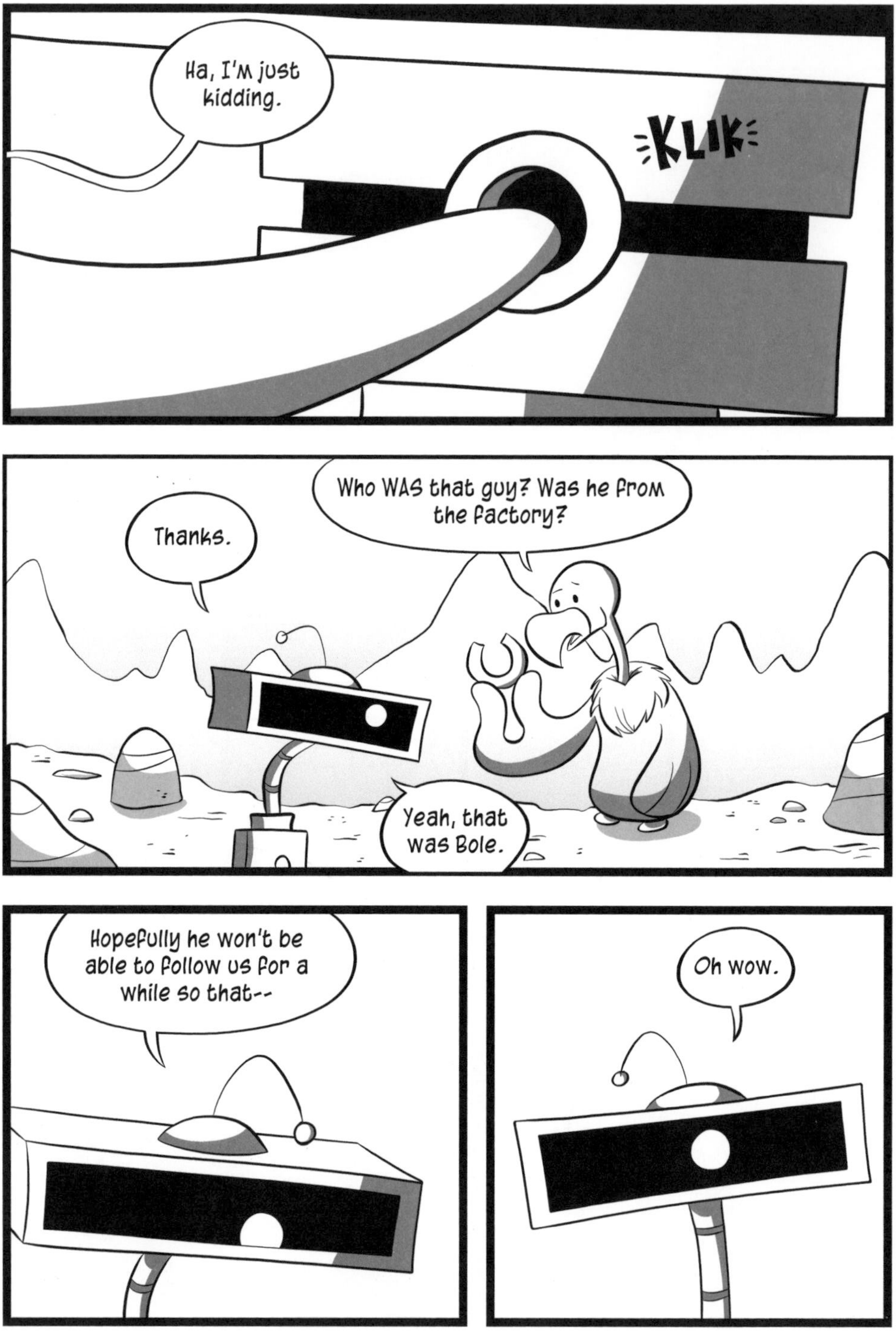
Ha, I'm just kidding.
KLIK
Thanks.
Who WAS that guy? Was he from the factory?
Yeah, that was Bole.
Hopefully he won't be able to follow us for a while so that--
Oh wow.

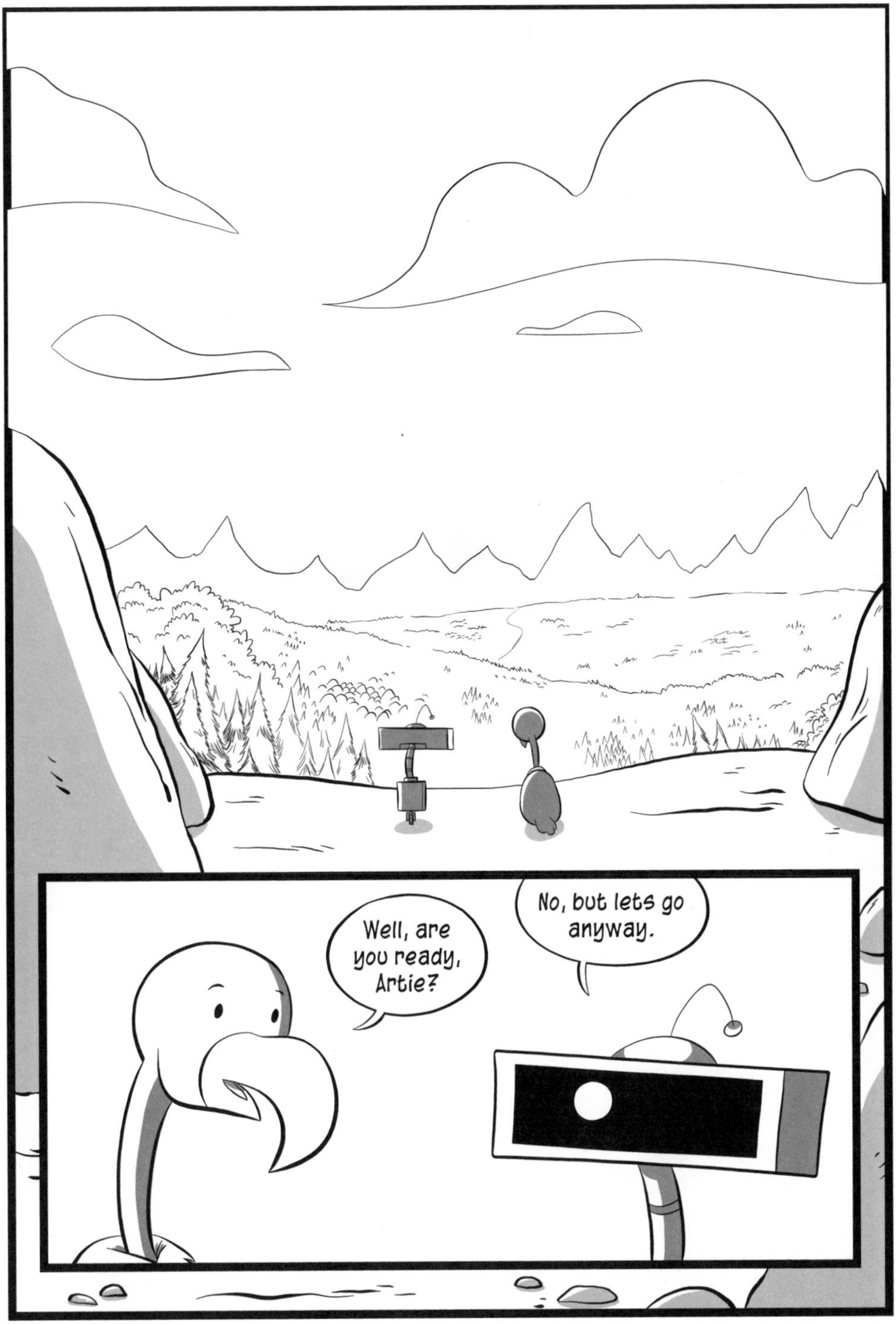
Well, are you ready, Artie?
No, but lets go anyway.

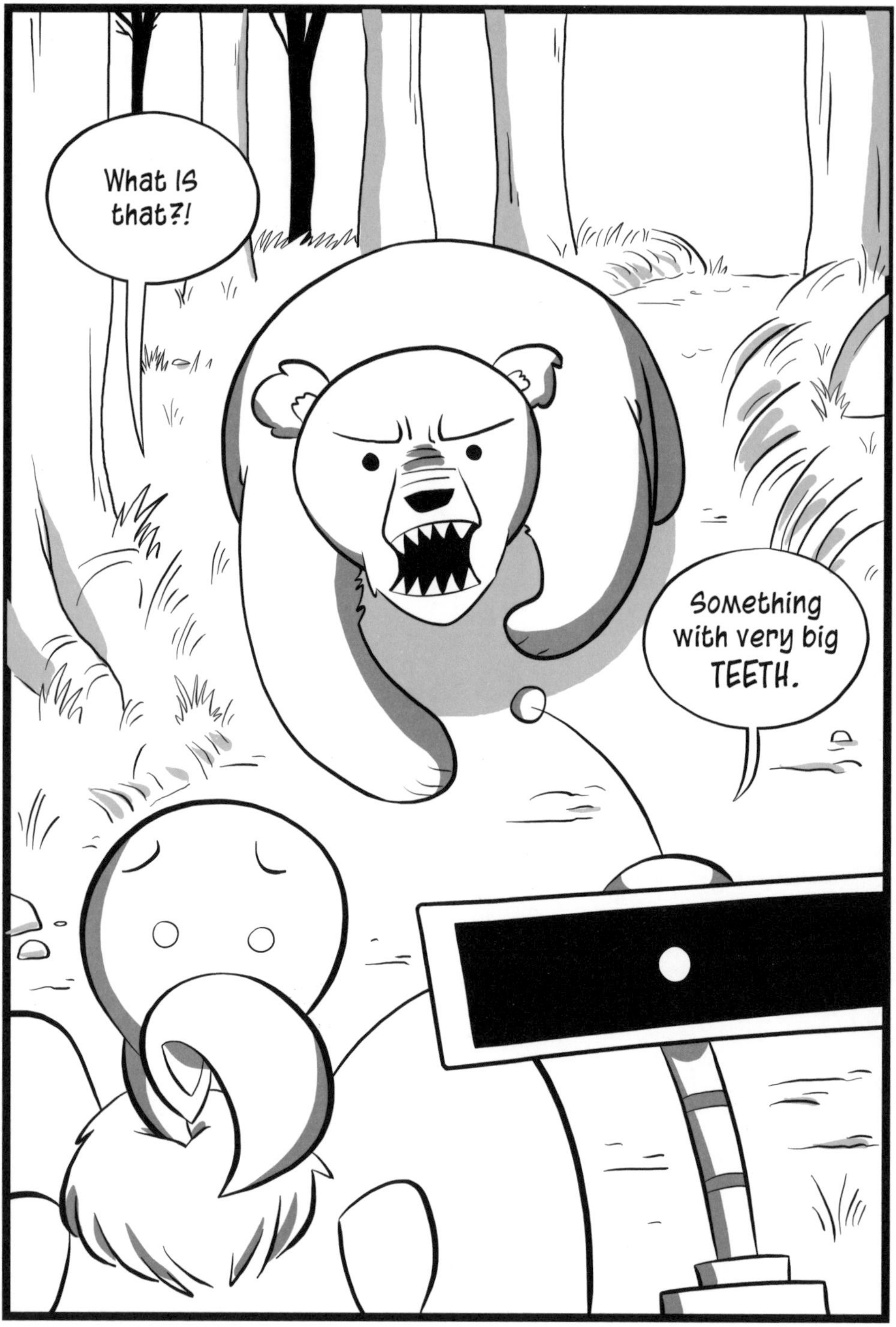
What IS that?!
Something with very big TEETH.

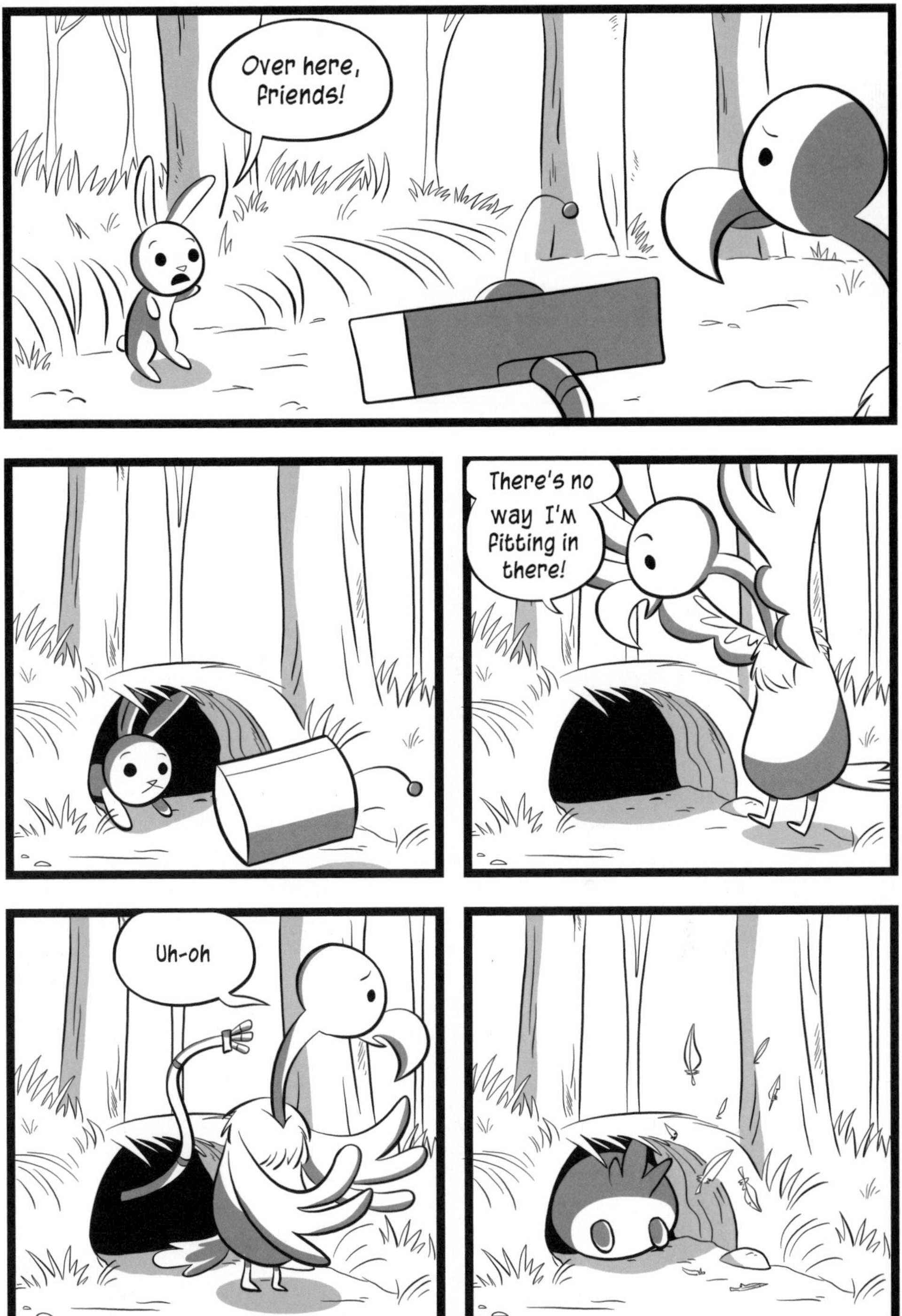
Over here, friends!
There's no way I'm fitting in there!
Uh-oh

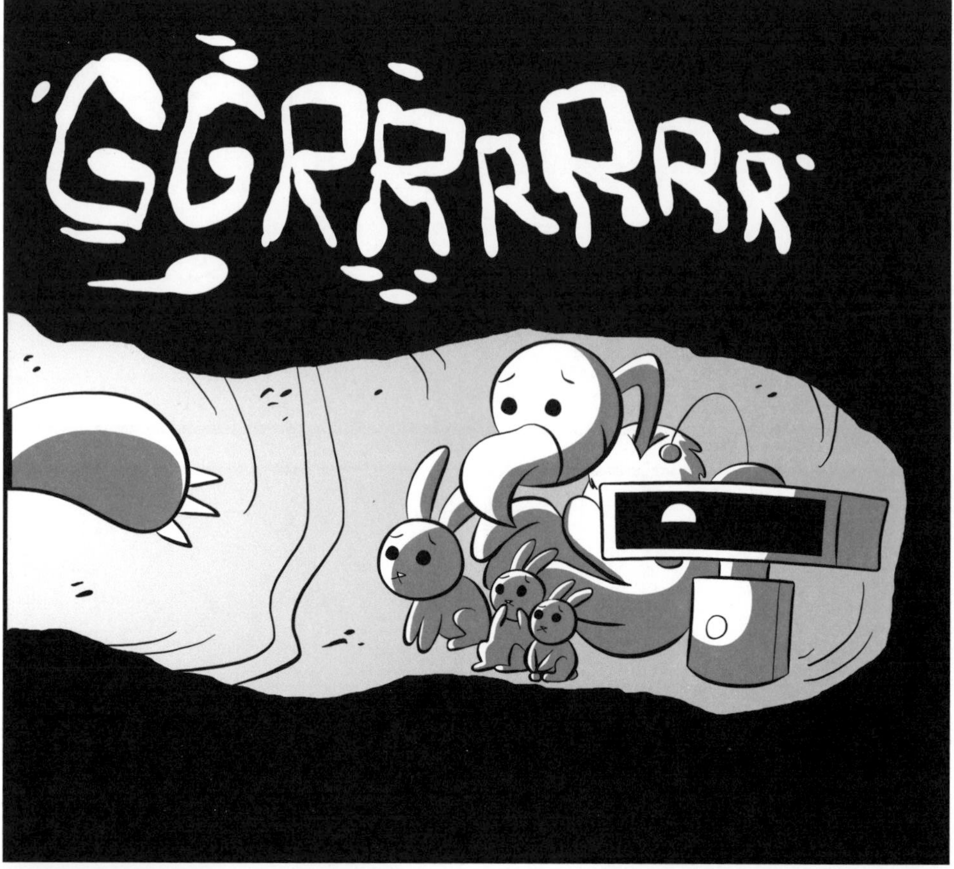
GGRRRRRRR

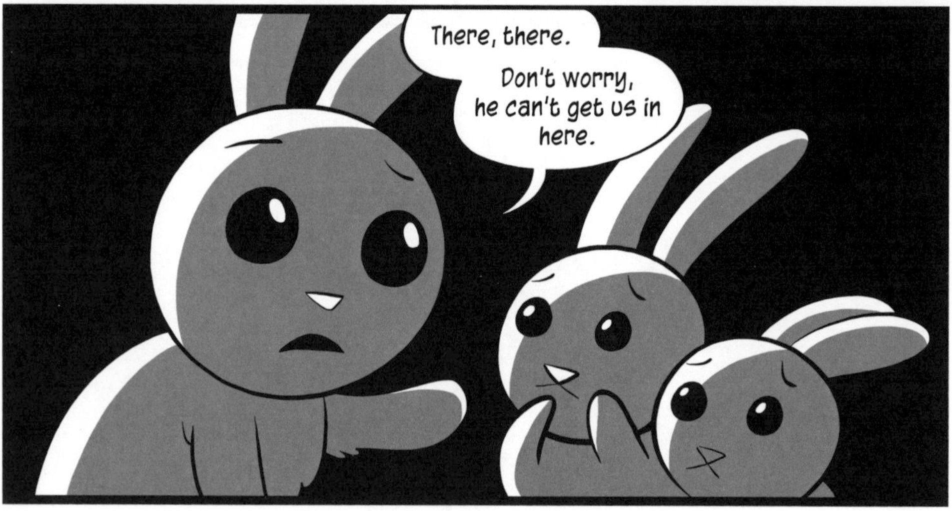
There, there.
Don't worry, he can't get us in here.

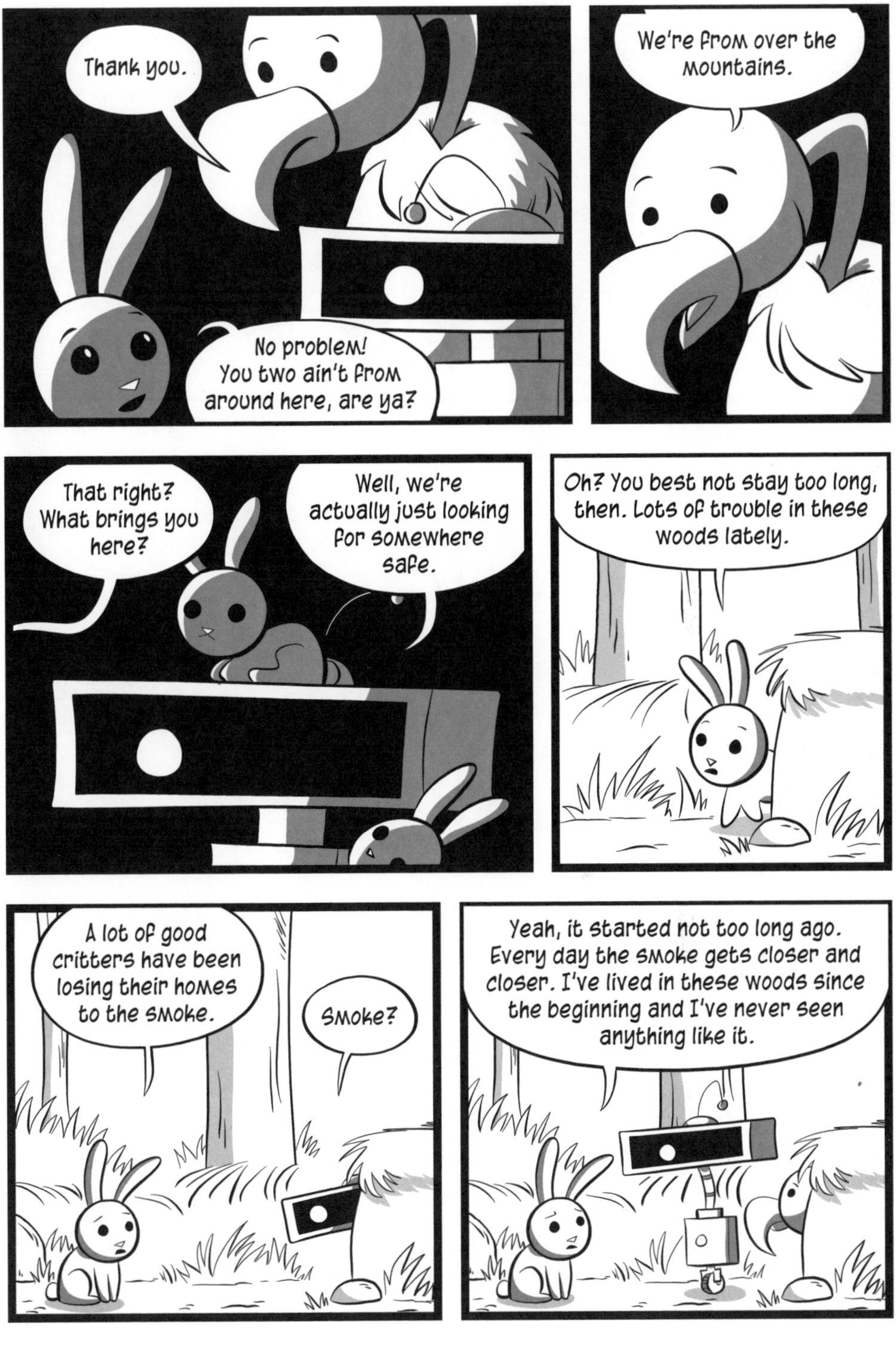
Thank you.
No problem! You two ain't from around here, are ya?
We're from over the mountains.
That right? What brings you here?
Well, we're actually just looking for somewhere safe.
Oh? You best not stay too long, then. Lots of trouble in these woods lately.
A lot of good critters have been losing their homes to the smoke.
Smoke?
Yeah, it started not too long ago. Every day the smoke gets closer and closer. I've lived in these woods since the beginning and I've never seen anything like it.

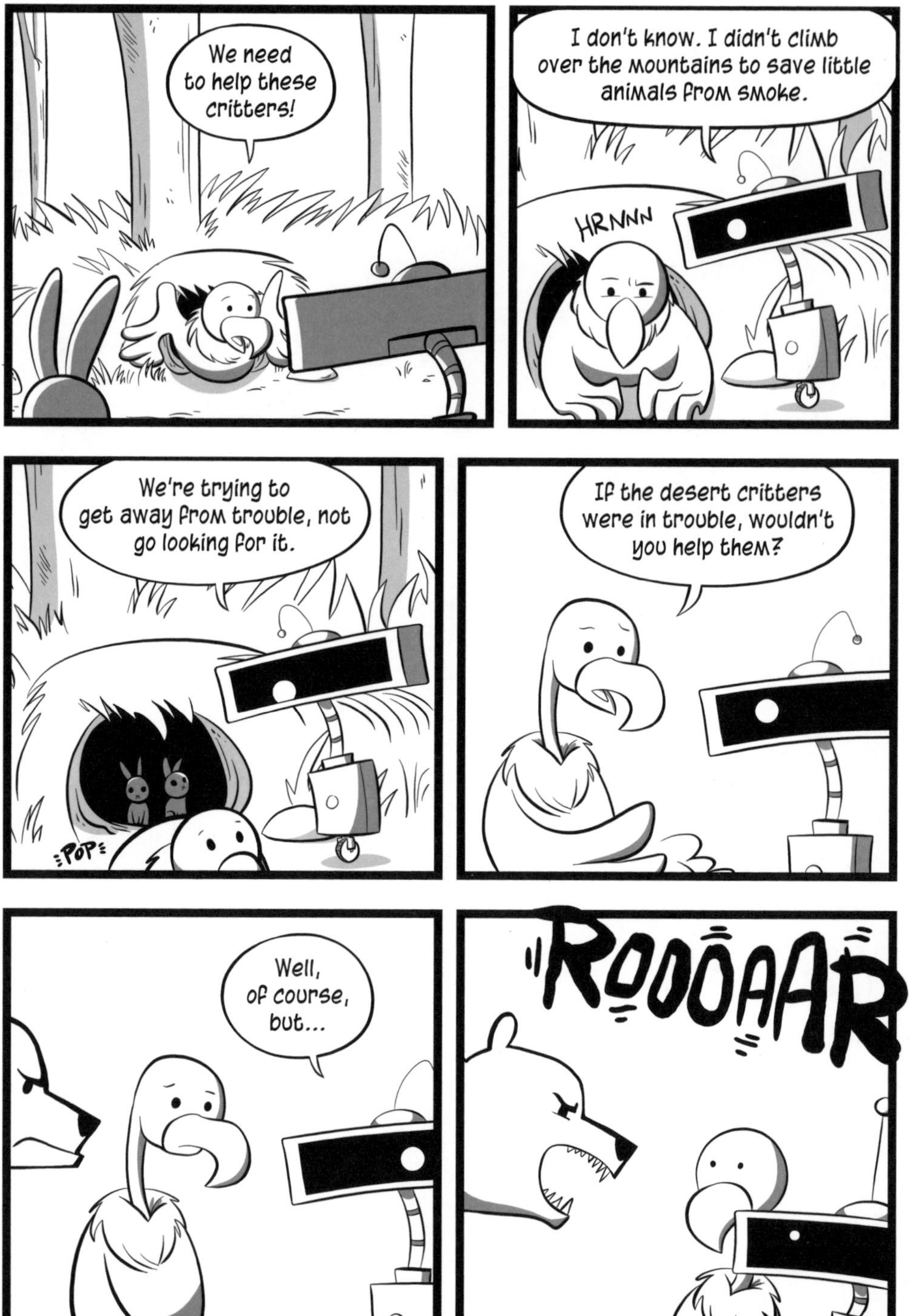
We need to help these critters!
I don't know. I didn't climb over the mountains to save little animals from smoke.
HRNNN
We're trying to get away from trouble, not go looking for it.
POP
If the desert critters were in trouble, wouldn't you help them?
Well, of course, but...
ROOOAAR

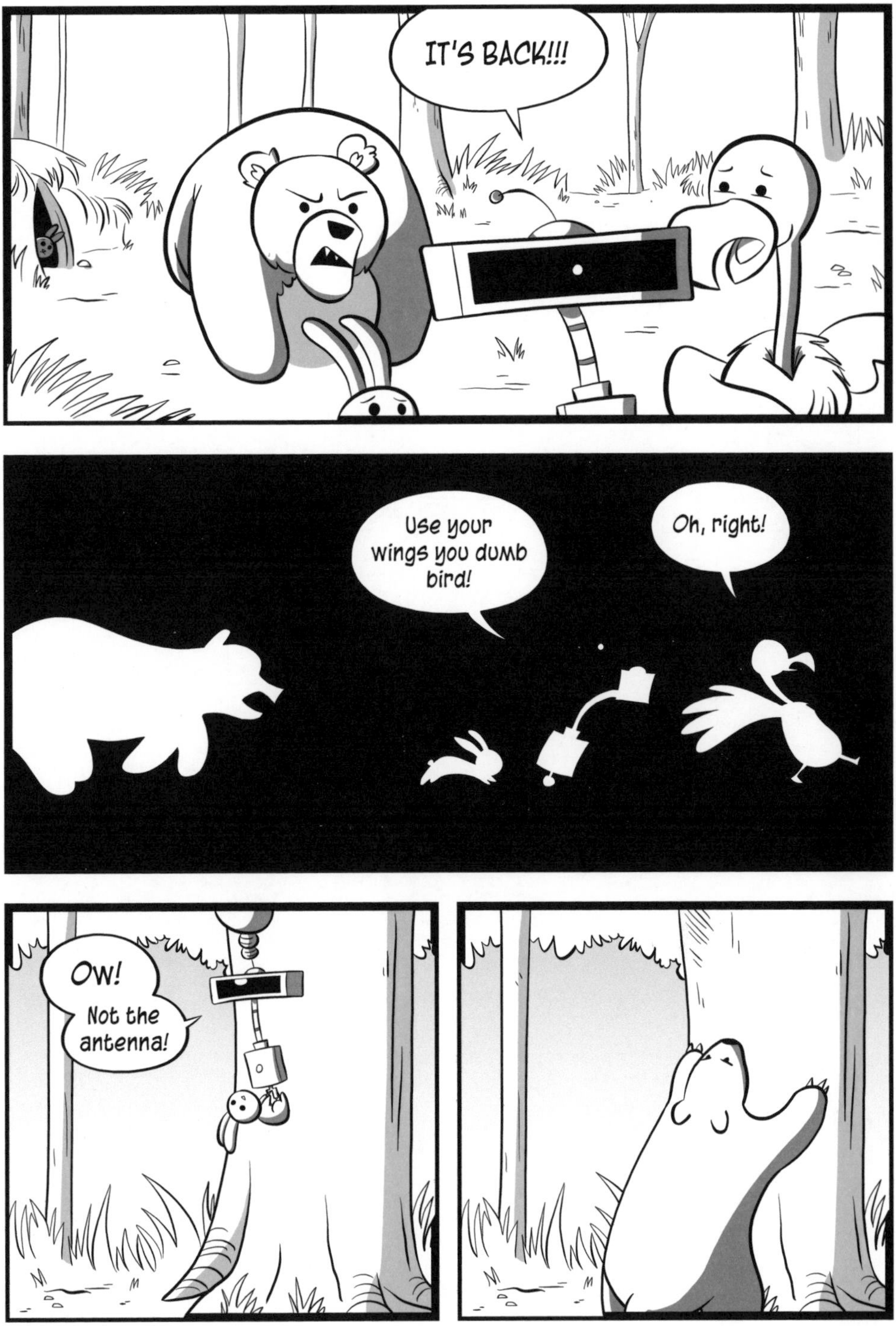
IT'S BACK!!!
Use your wings you dumb bird!
Oh, right!
OW!
Not the antenna!

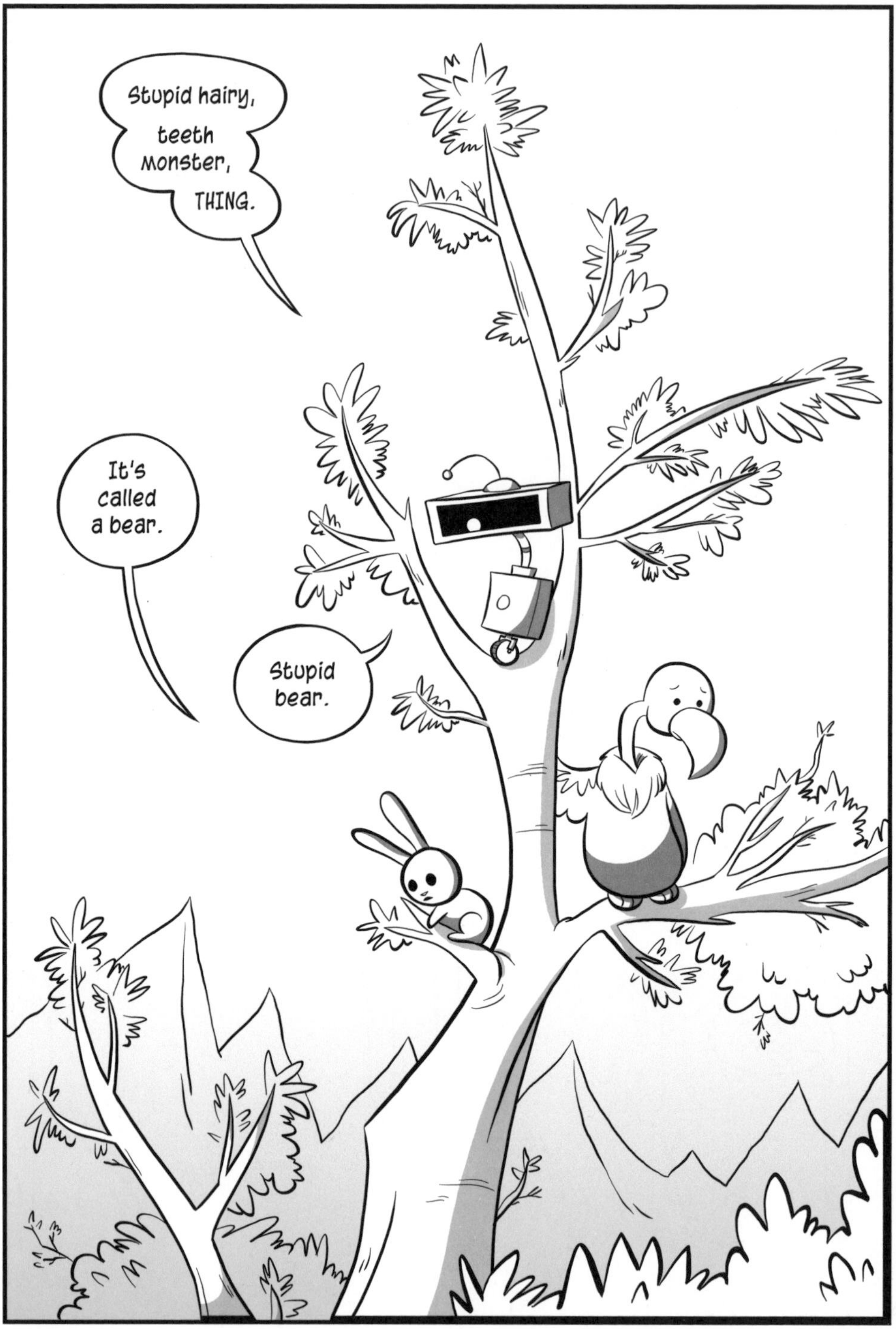
Stupid hairy, teeth monster, THING.
It's called a bear.
Stupid bear.

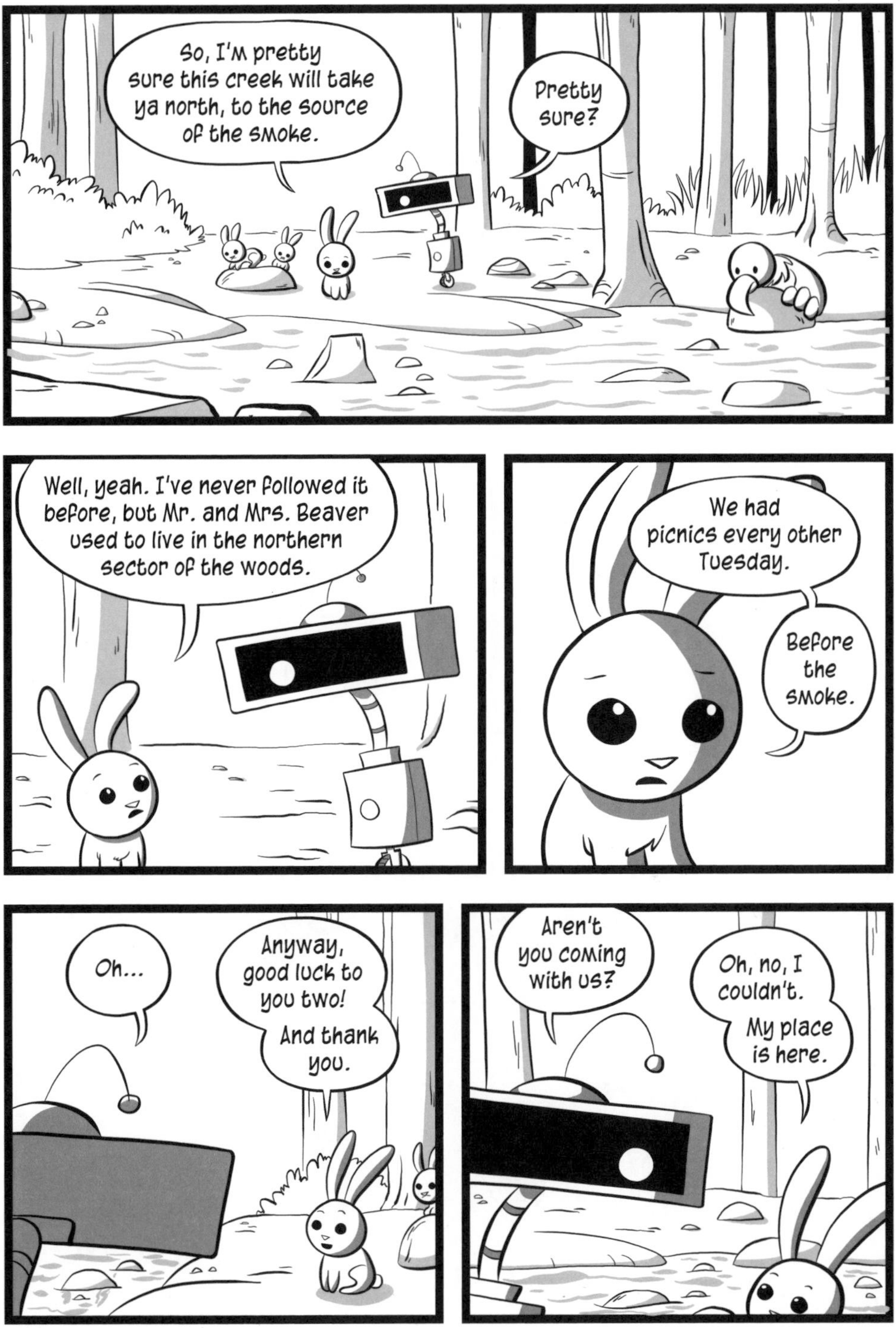
So, I'm pretty sure this creek will take ya north, to the source of the smoke.
Pretty sure?
Well, yeah. I've never followed it before, but Mr. and Mrs. Beaver used to live in the northern sector of the woods.
We had picnics every other Tuesday.
Before the smoke.
Oh...
Anyway, good luck to you two!
And thank you.
Aren't you coming with us?
Oh, no, I couldn't.
My place is here.

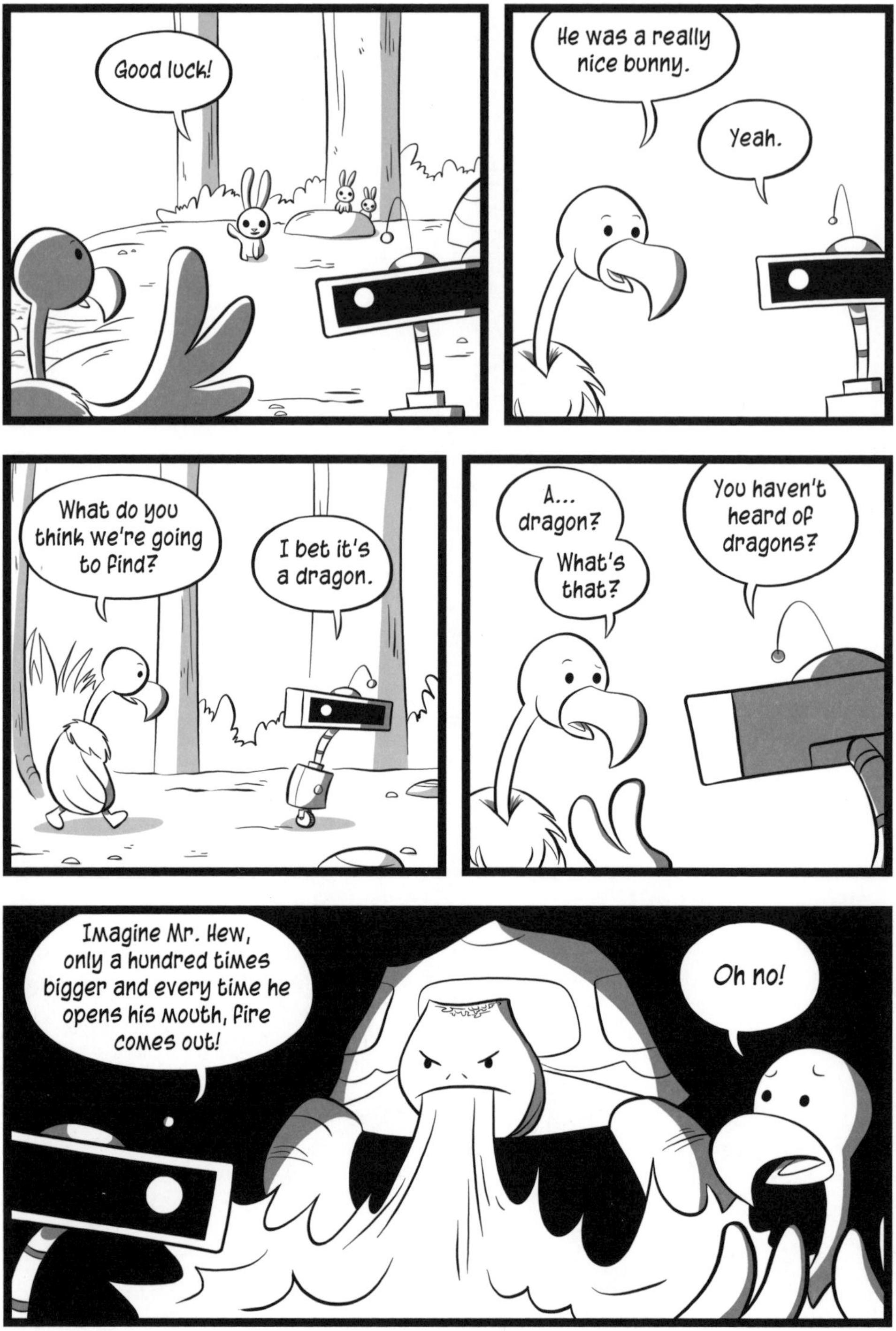
Good luck!
He was a really nice bunny.
Yeah.
What do you think we're going to find?
I bet it's a dragon.
A... dragon?
What's that?
You haven't heard of dragons?
Imagine Mr. Hew, only a hundred times bigger and every time he opens his mouth, fire comes out!
Oh no!

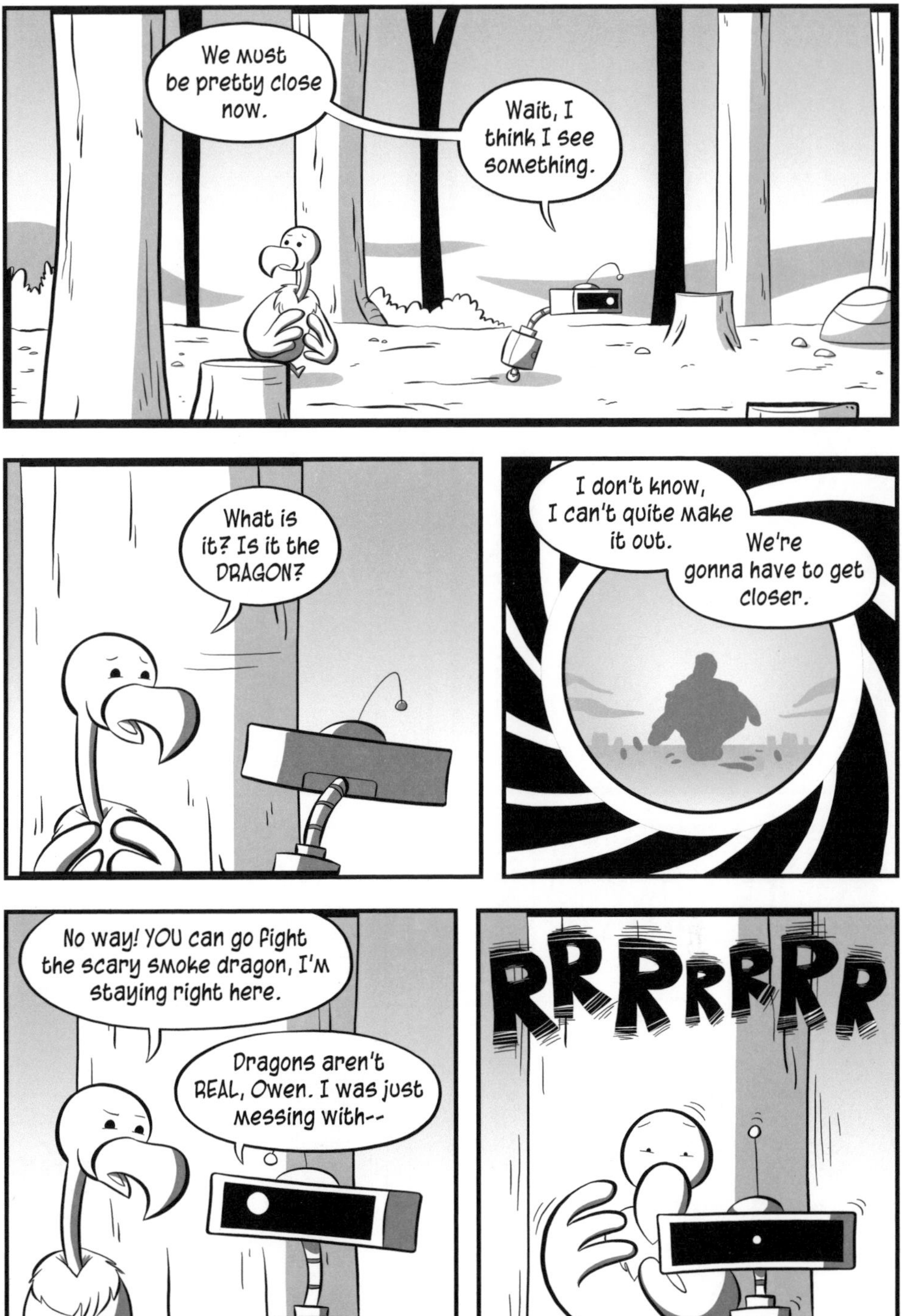
We must be pretty close now.
Wait, I think I see something.
What is it? Is it the DRAGON?
I don't know, I can't quite make it out.
We're gonna have to get closer.
No way! YOU can go fight the scary smoke dragon, I'm staying right here.
Dragons aren't REAL, Owen. I was just messing with--
RRRRRRR

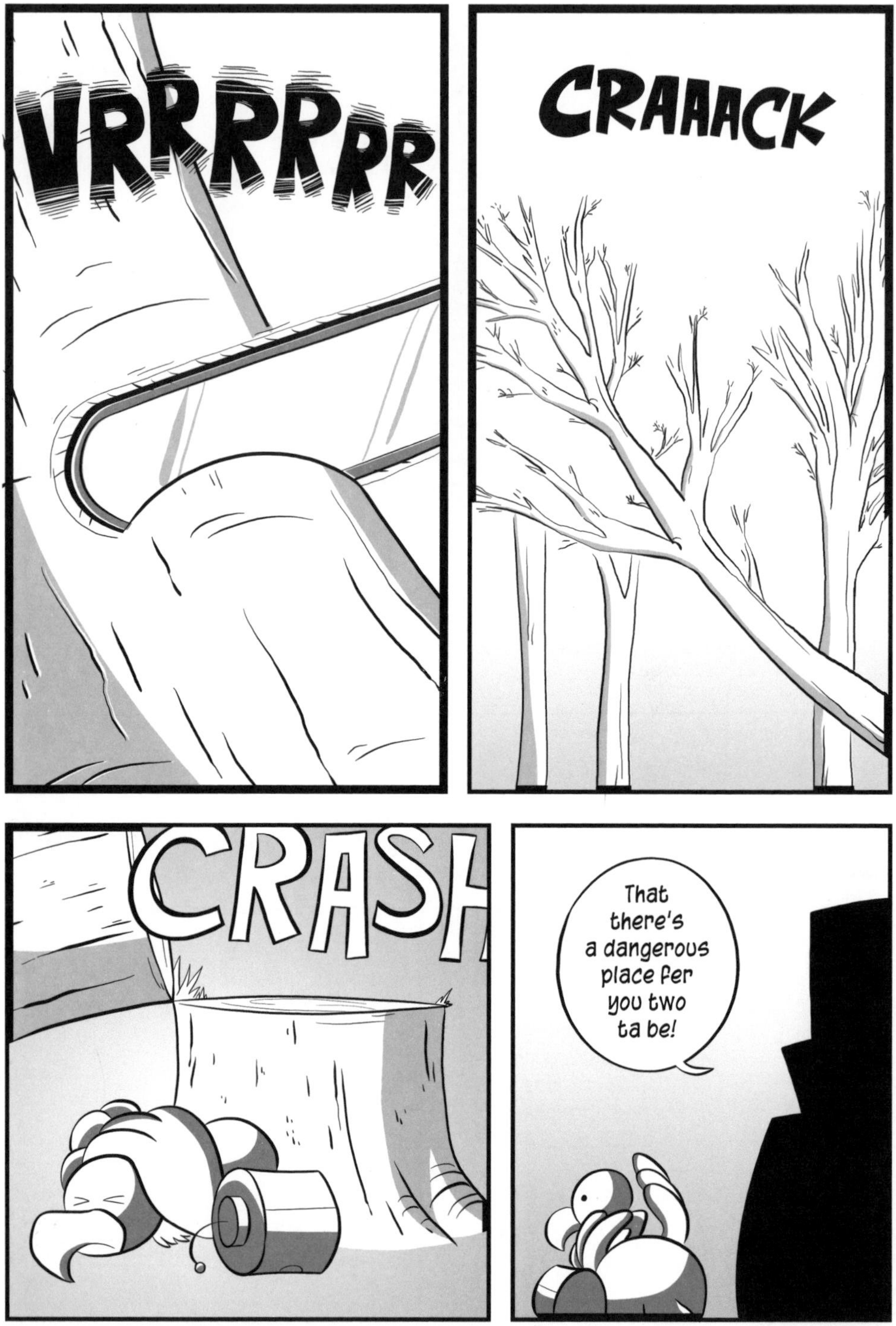
VRRRRRR
CRAAACK
CRASH
That there's a dangerous place fer you two ta be!

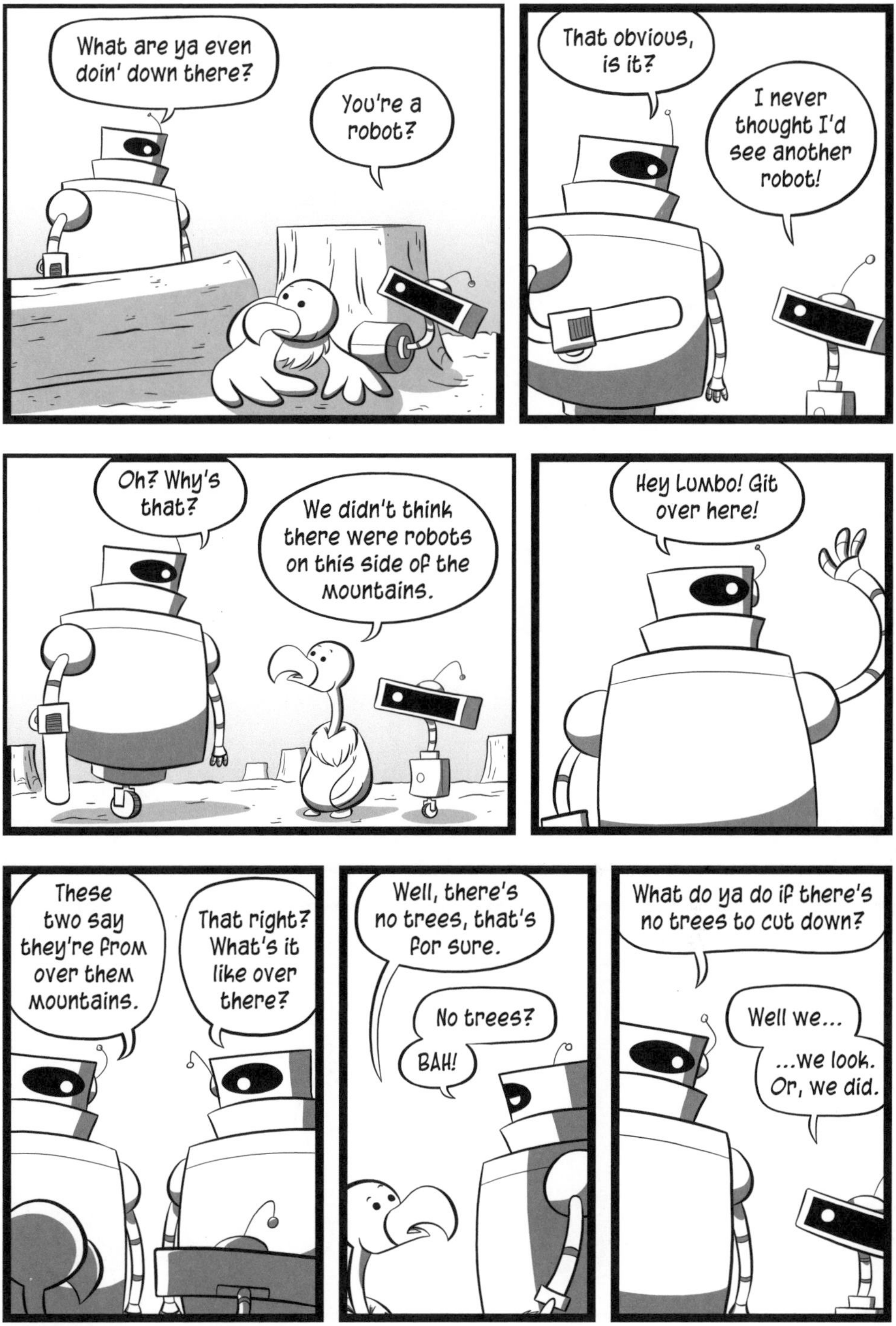
What are ya even doin' down there?
You're a robot?
That obvious, is it?
I never thought I'd see another robot!
Oh? Why's that?
We didn't think there were robots on this side of the mountains.
Hey Lumbo! Git over here!
These two say they're from over them mountains.
That right? What's it like over there?
Well, there's no trees, that's for sure.
No trees?
BAH!
What do ya do if there's no trees to cut down?
Well we...
...we look. Or, we did.

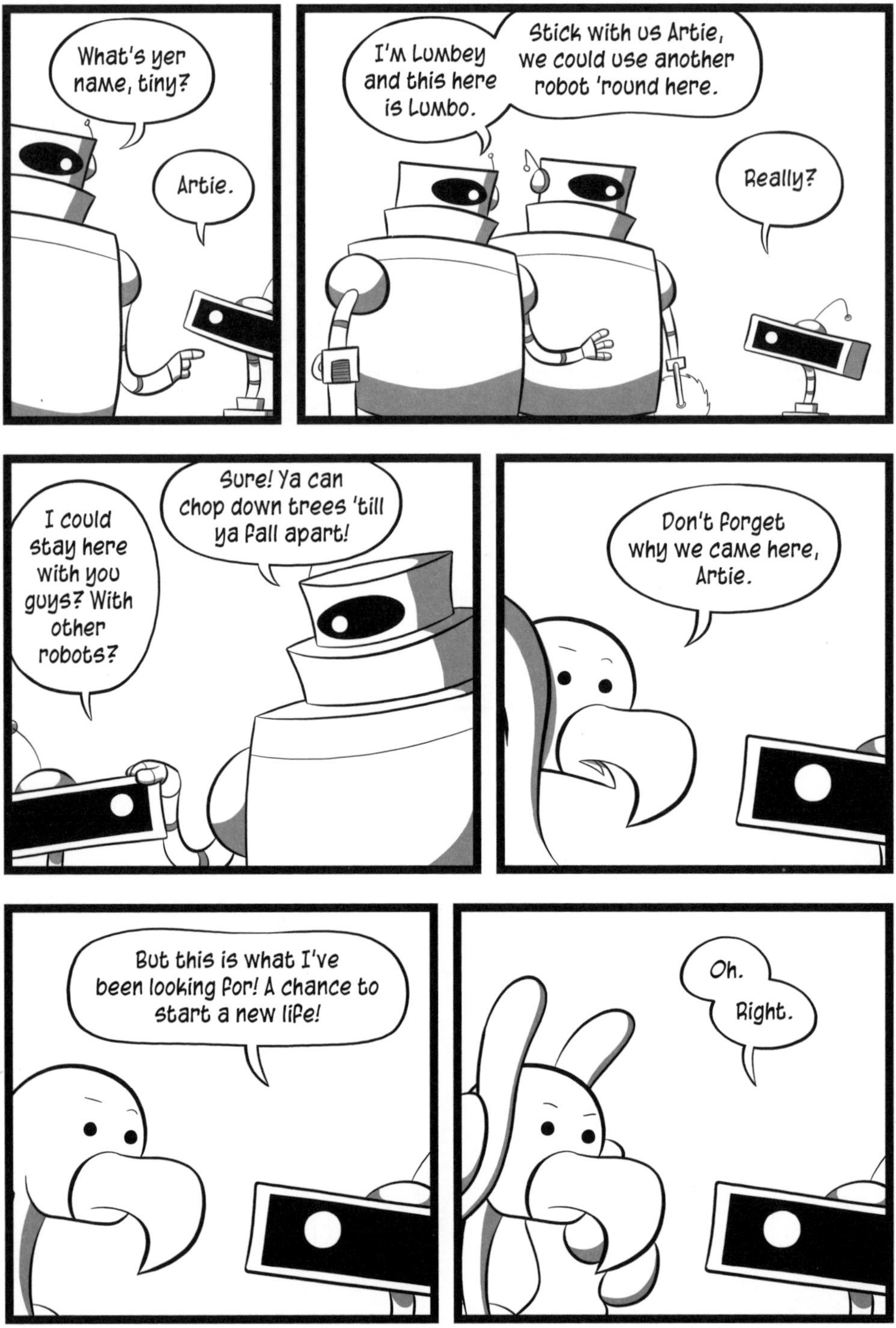
What's yer name, tiny?
Artie.
I'm Lumbey and this here is Lumbo.
Stick with us Artie, we could use another robot 'round here.
Really?
I could stay here with you guys? With other robots?
Sure! Ya can chop down trees 'till ya fall apart!
Don't forget why we came here, Artie.
But this is what I've been looking for! A chance to start a new life!
Oh.
Right.

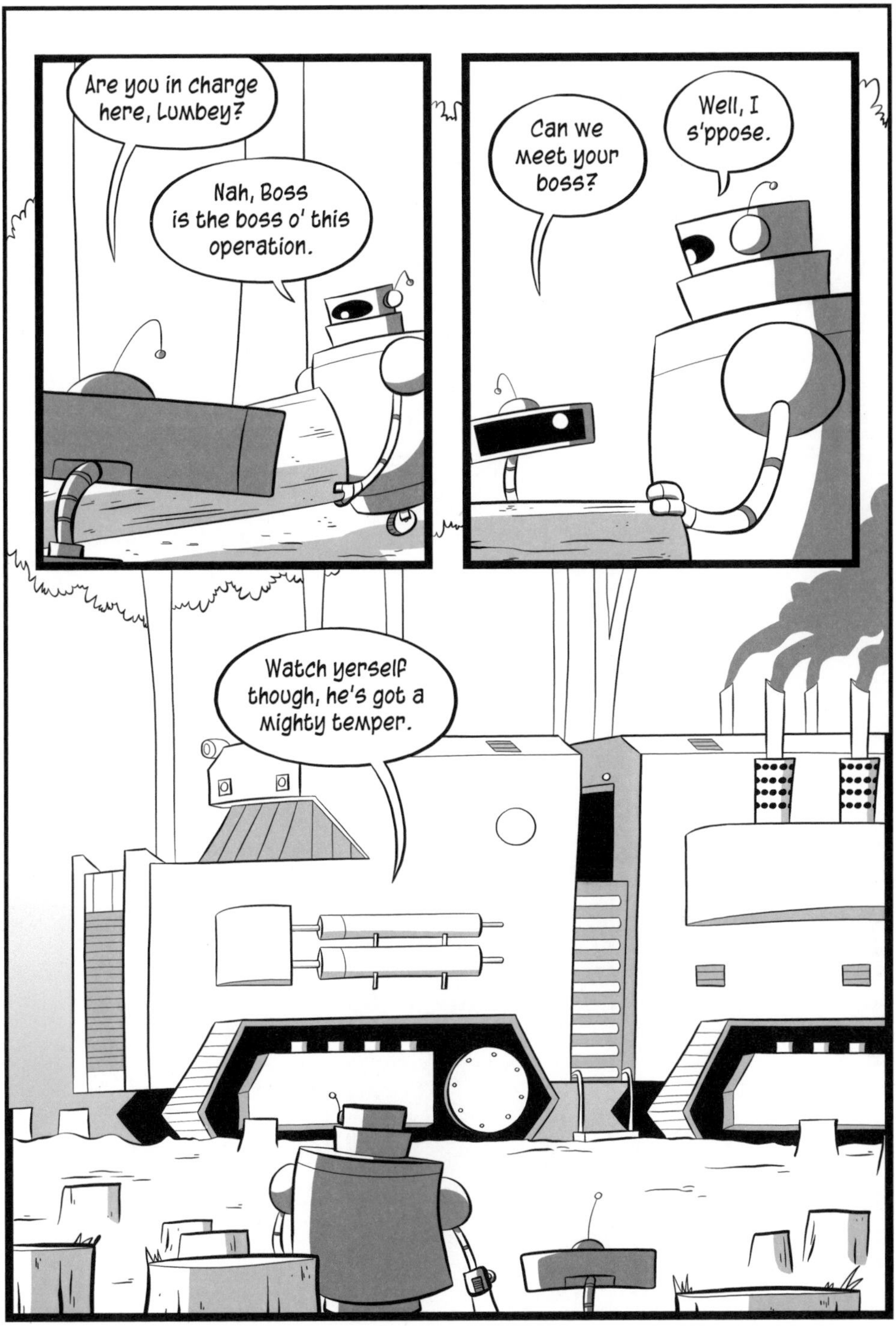
Are you in charge here, Lumbey?
Nah, Boss is the boss o' this operation.
Can we meet your boss?
Well, I s'ppose.
Watch yerself though, he's got a mighty temper.

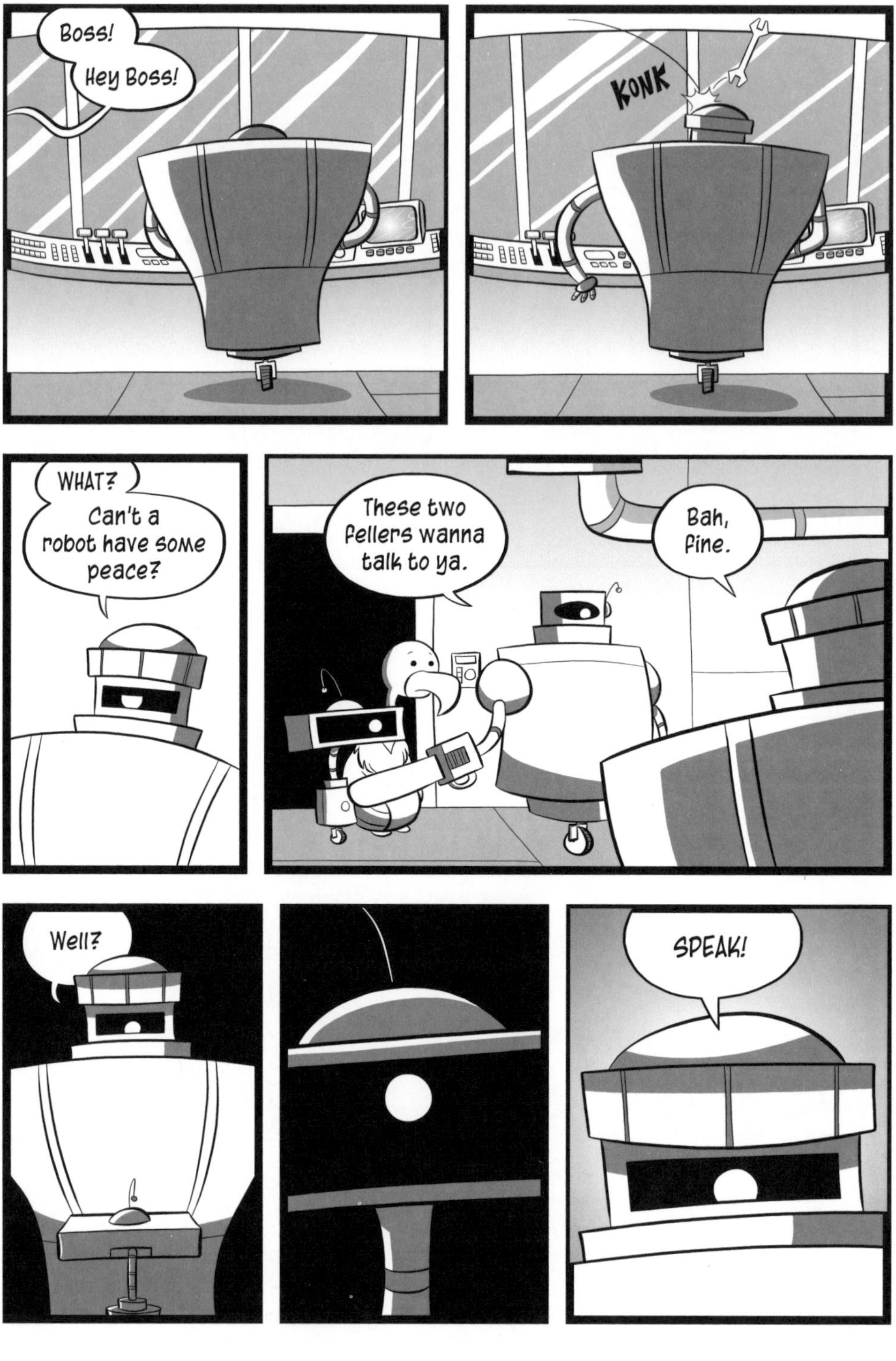
Boss!
Hey Boss!
KONK
WHAT? Can't a robot have some peace?
These two fellers wanna talk to ya.
Bah, fine.
Well?
SPEAK!

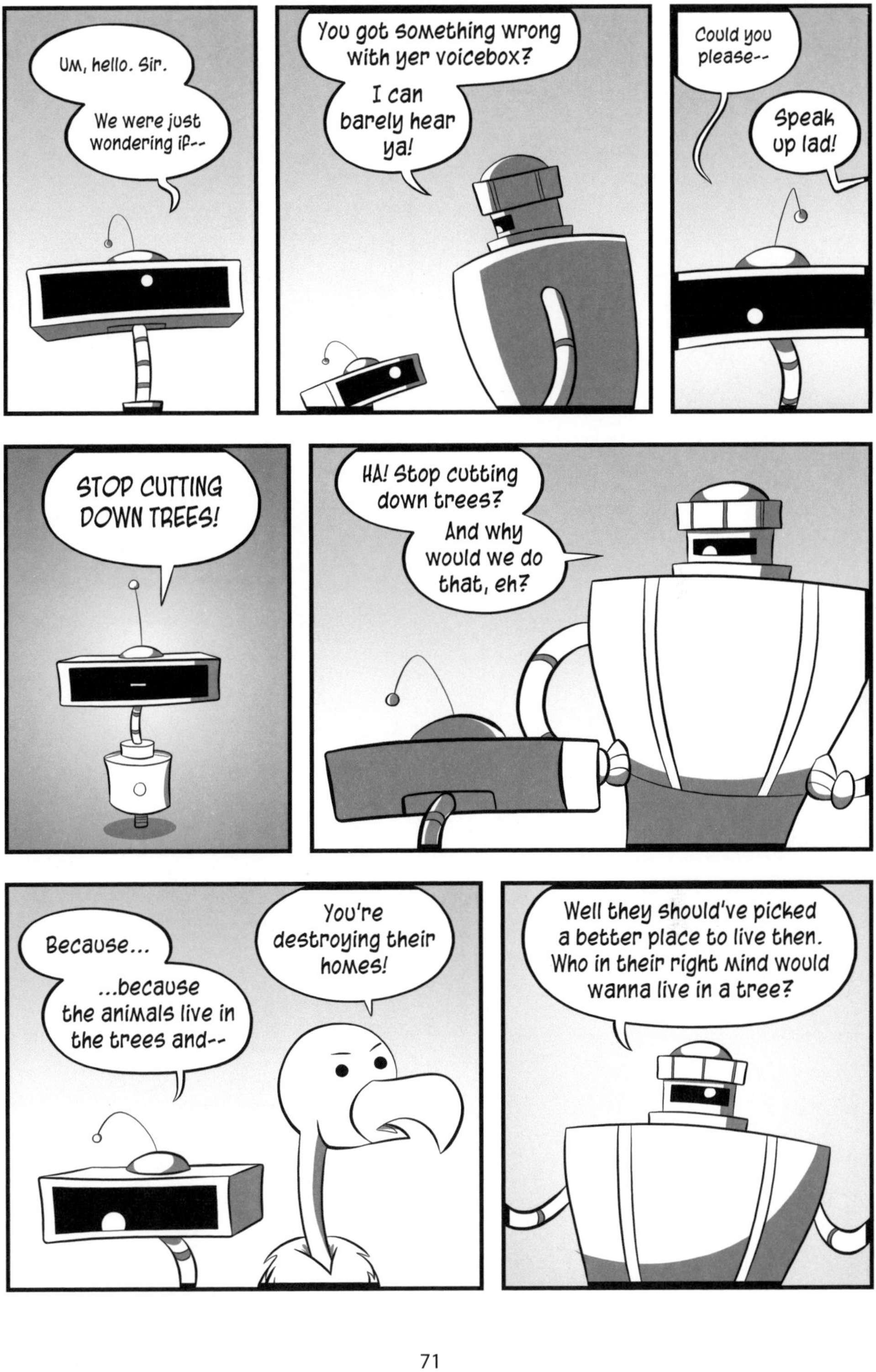
Um, hello. Sir.
We were just wondering if--
You got something wrong with yer voicebox?
I can barely hear ya!
Could you please--
Speak up lad!
STOP CUTTING DOWN TREES!
HA! Stop cutting down trees?
And why would we do that, eh?
Because...
...because the animals live in the trees and--
You're destroying their homes!
Well they should've picked a better place to live then. Who in their right mind would wanna live in a tree?

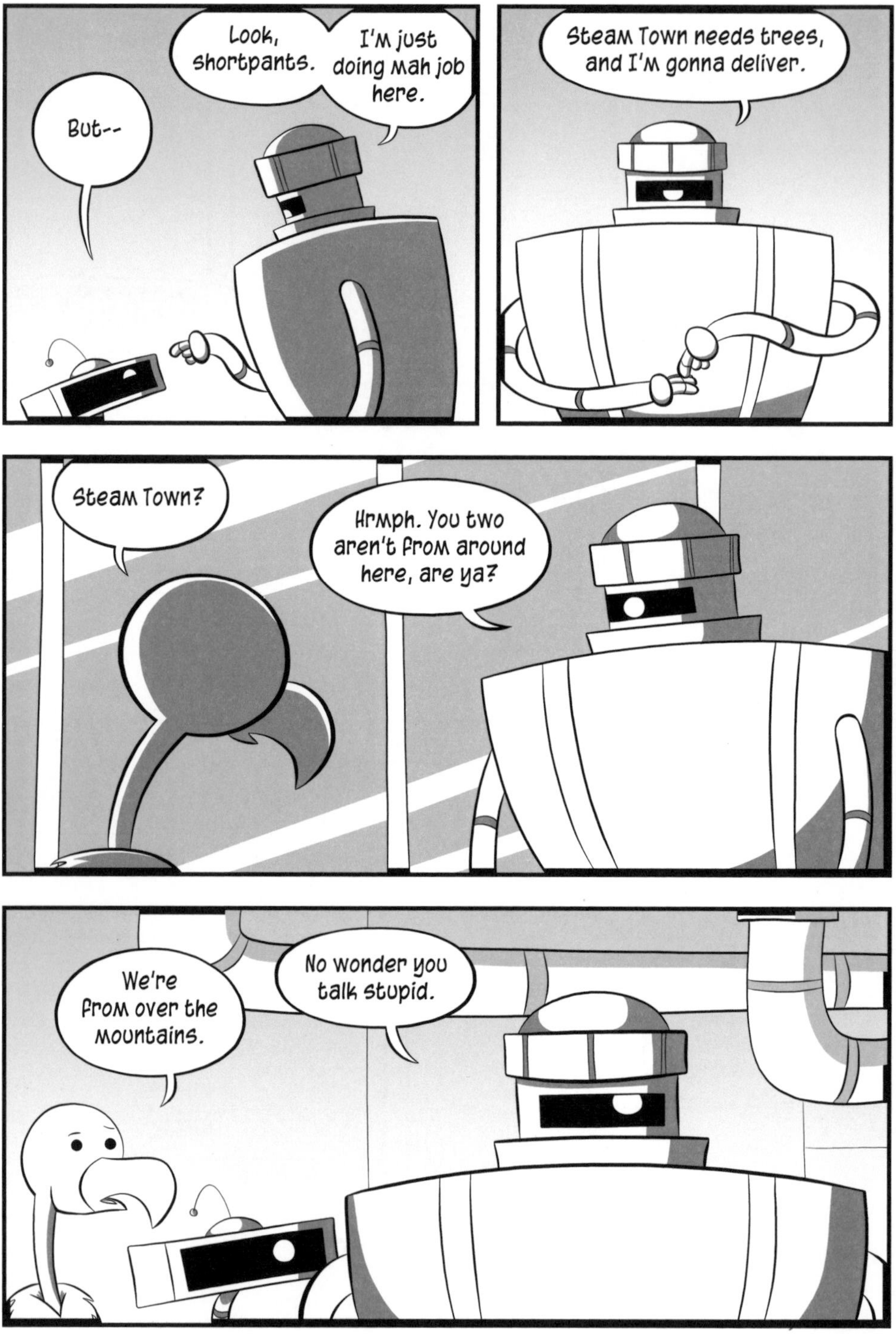
Look, shortpants.
I'm just doing mah job here.
But--
Steam Town needs trees, and I'm gonna deliver.
Steam Town?
Hrmph. You two aren't from around here, are ya?
We're from over the mountains.
No wonder you talk stupid.

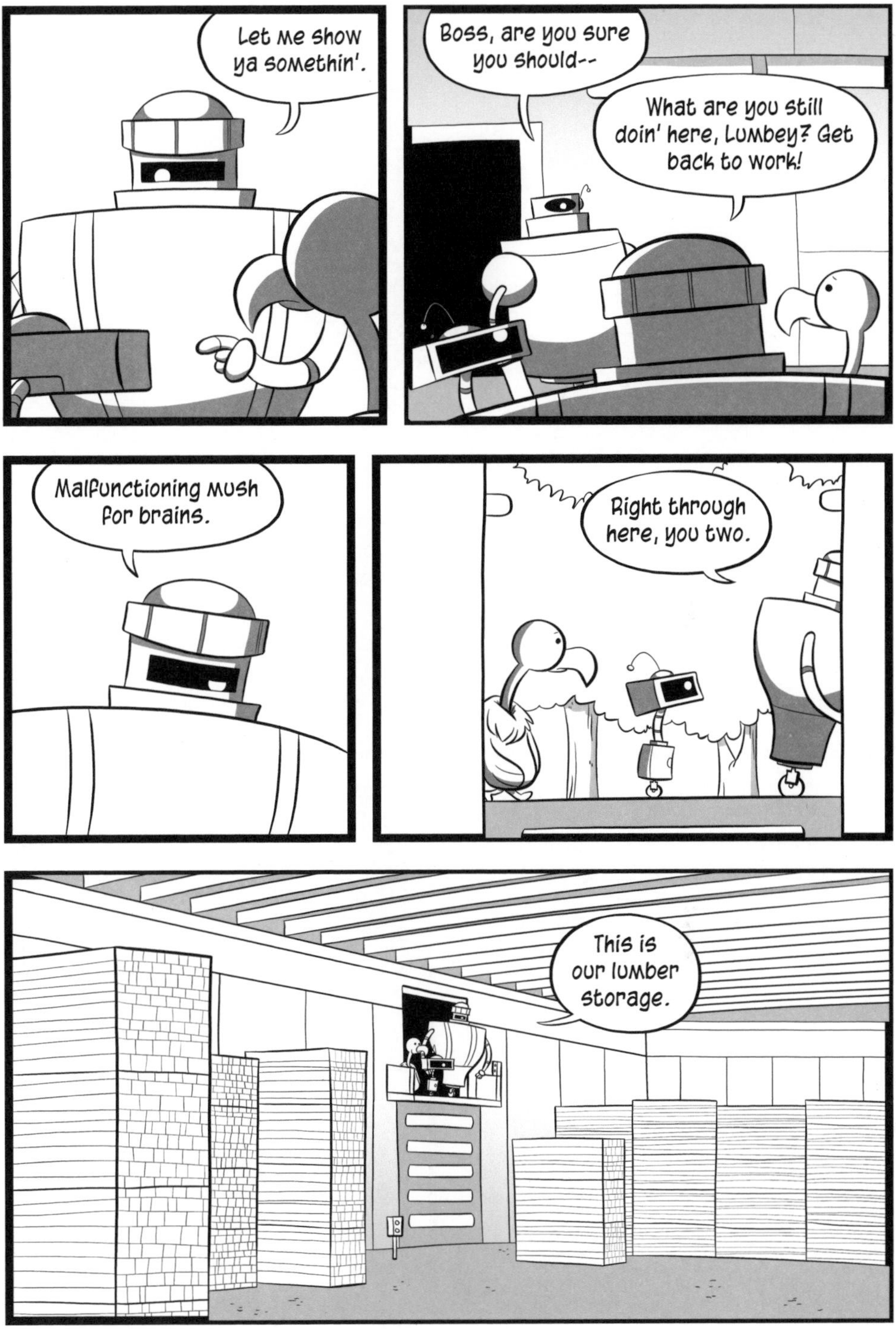

Let me show ya somethin'.
Boss, are you sure you should--
What are you still doin' here, Lumbey? Get back to work!
Malfunctioning mush for brains.
Right through here, you two.
This is our lumber storage.

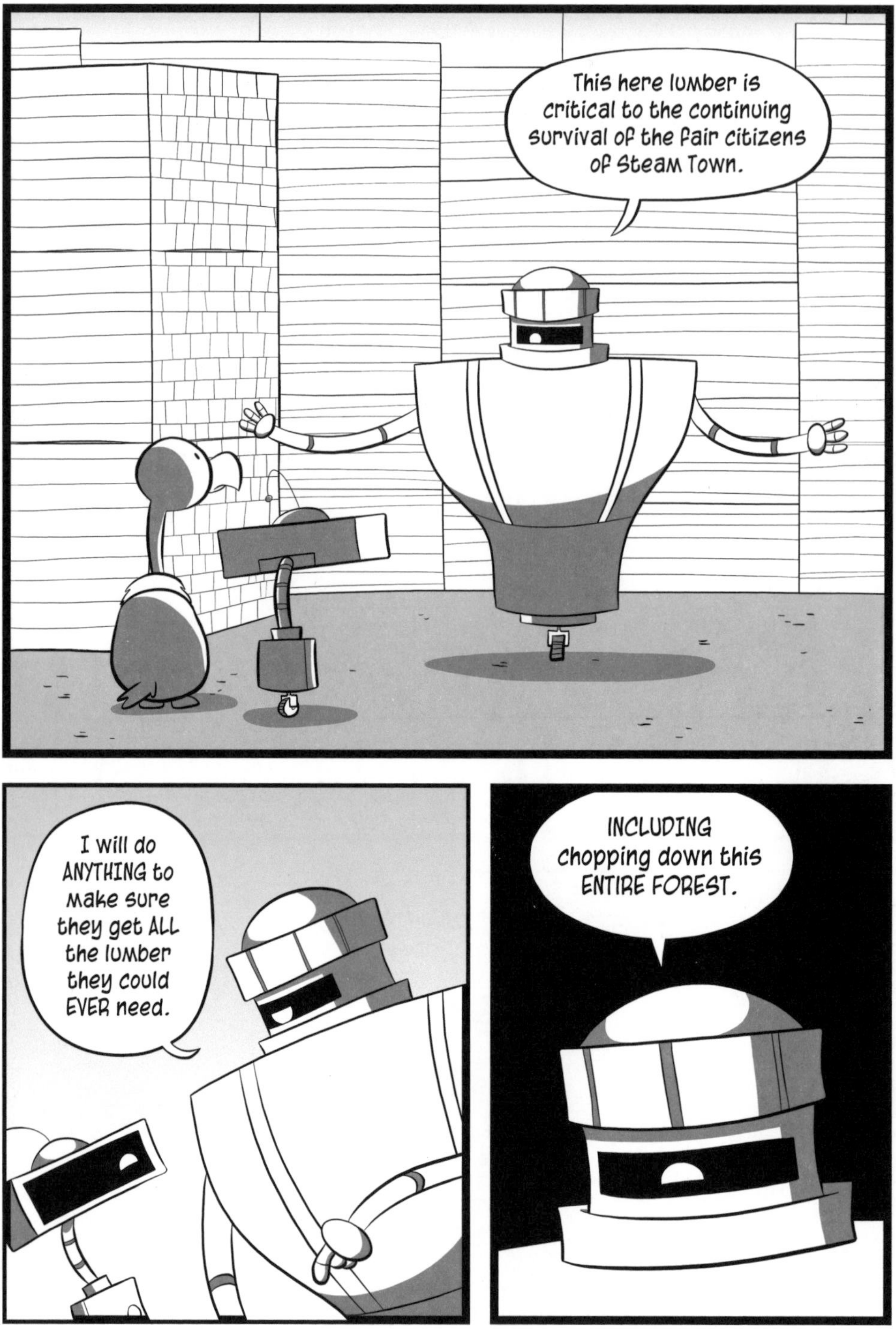
This here lumber is critical to the continuing survival of the fair citizens of Steam Town.
I will do ANYTHING to make sure they get ALL the lumber they could EVER need.
INCLUDING chopping down this ENTIRE FOREST.

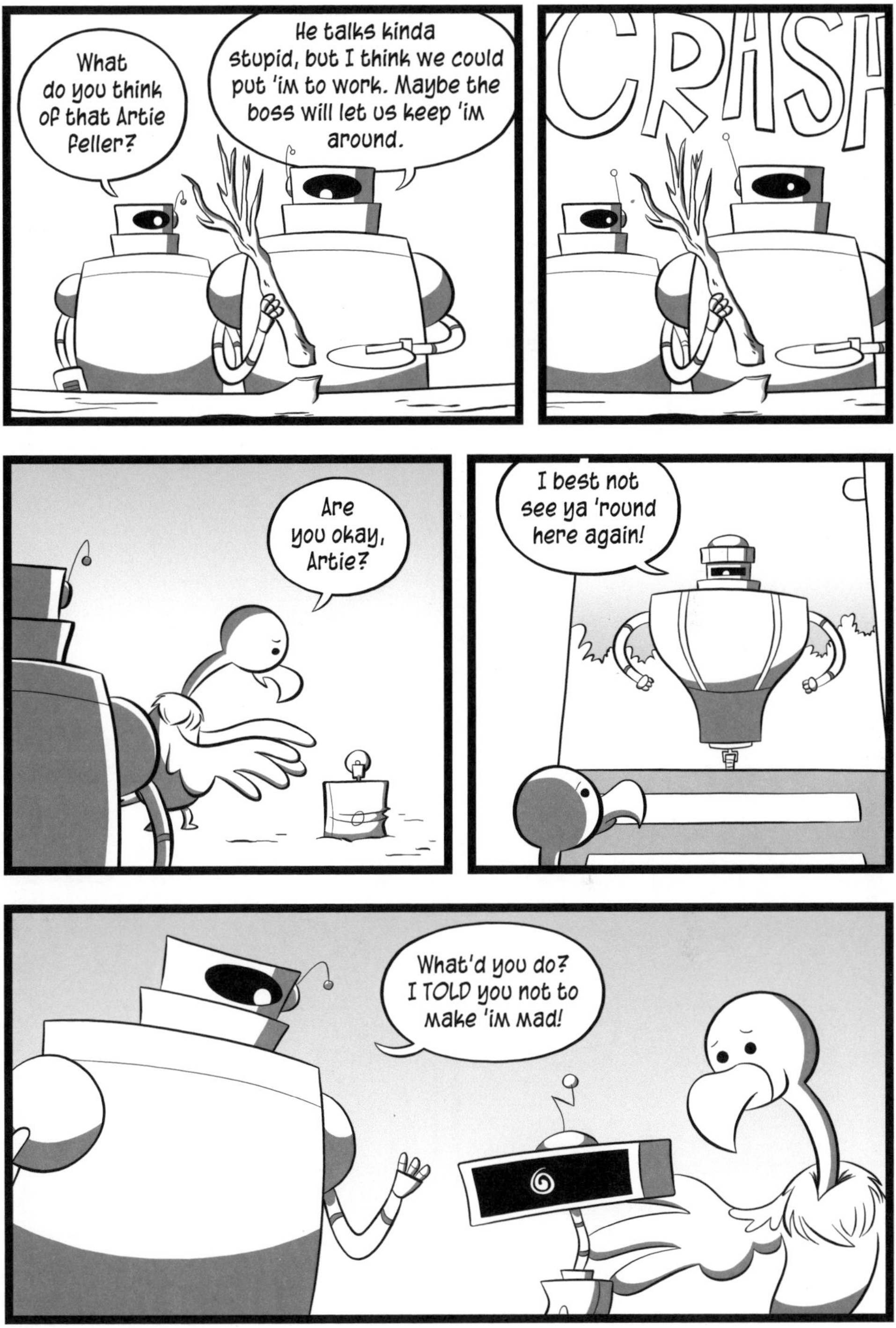
What do you think of that Artie feller?
He talks kinda stupid, but I think we could put 'im to work. Maybe the boss will let us keep 'im around.
CRASH
Are you okay, Artie?
I best not see ya 'round here again!
What'd you do? I TOLD you not to make 'im mad!

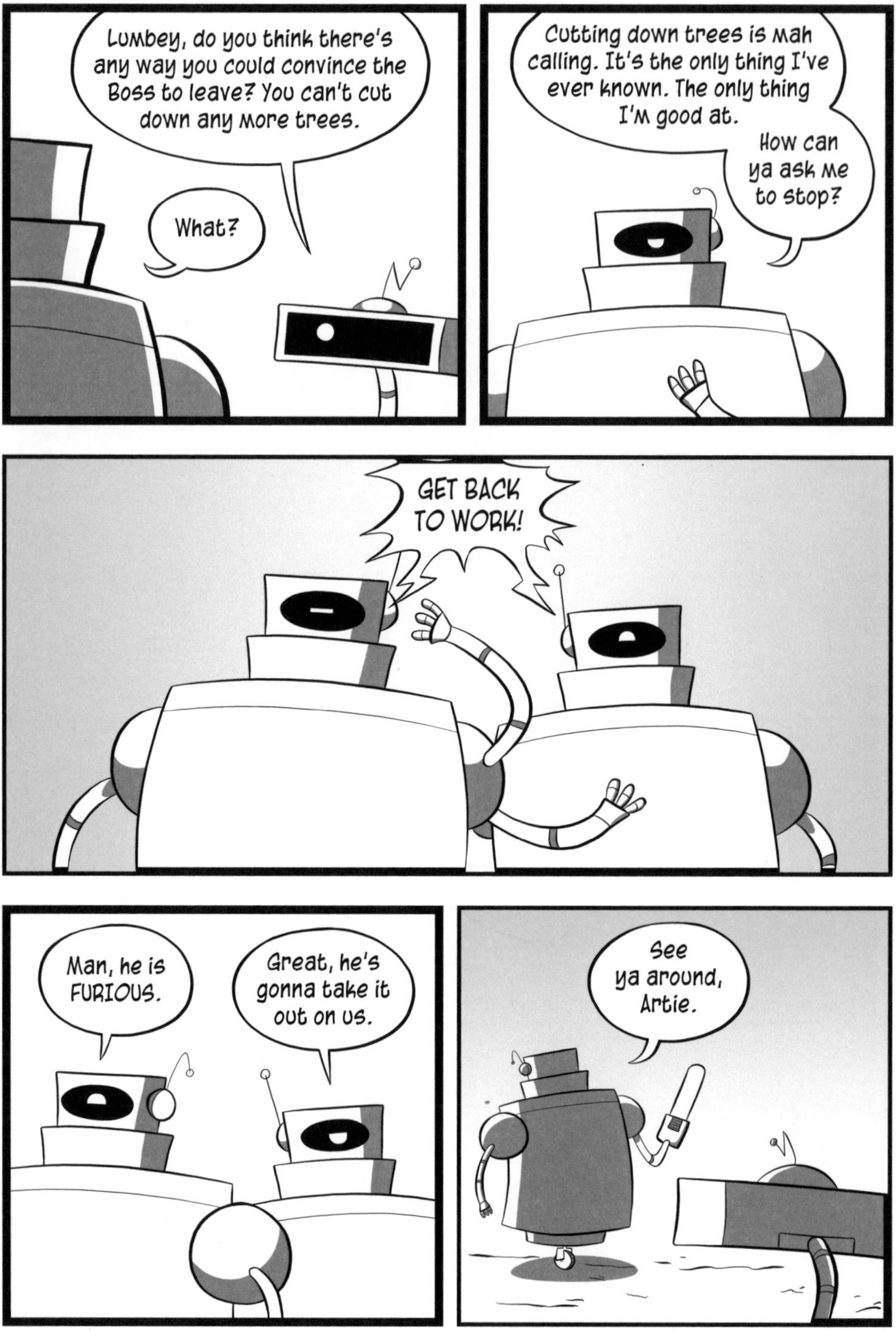
Lumbey, do you think there's any way you could convince the Boss to leave? You can't cut down any more trees.
What?
Cutting down trees is mah calling. It's the only thing I've ever known. The only thing I'm good at.
How can ya ask me to stop?
GET BACK TO WORK!
Man, he is FURIOUS.
Great, he's gonna take it out on us.
See ya around, Artie.

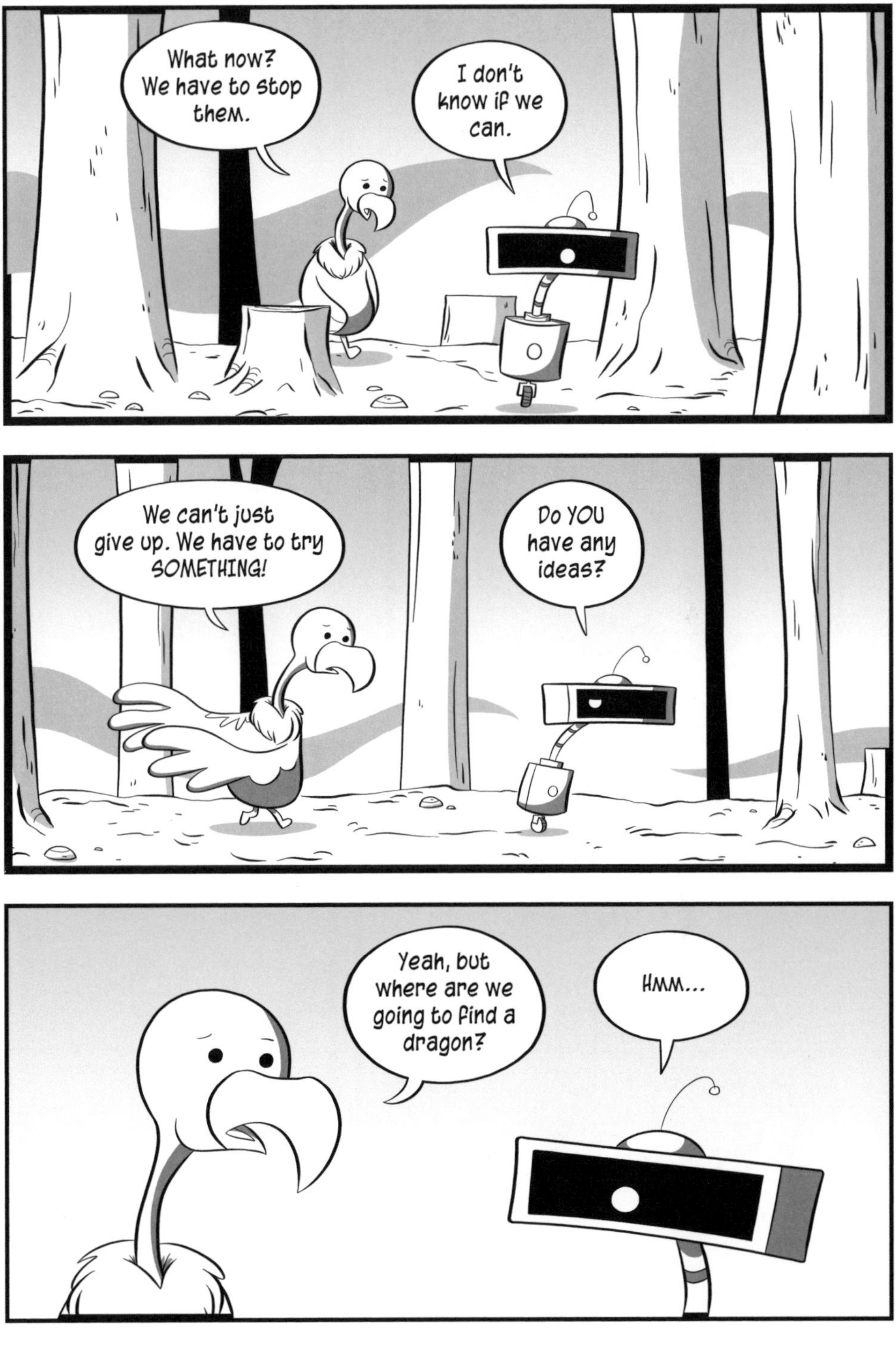
What now? We have to stop them.
I don't know if we can.
We can't just give up. We have to try SOMETHING!
Do YOU have any ideas?
Yeah, but where are we going to find a dragon?
HMM...

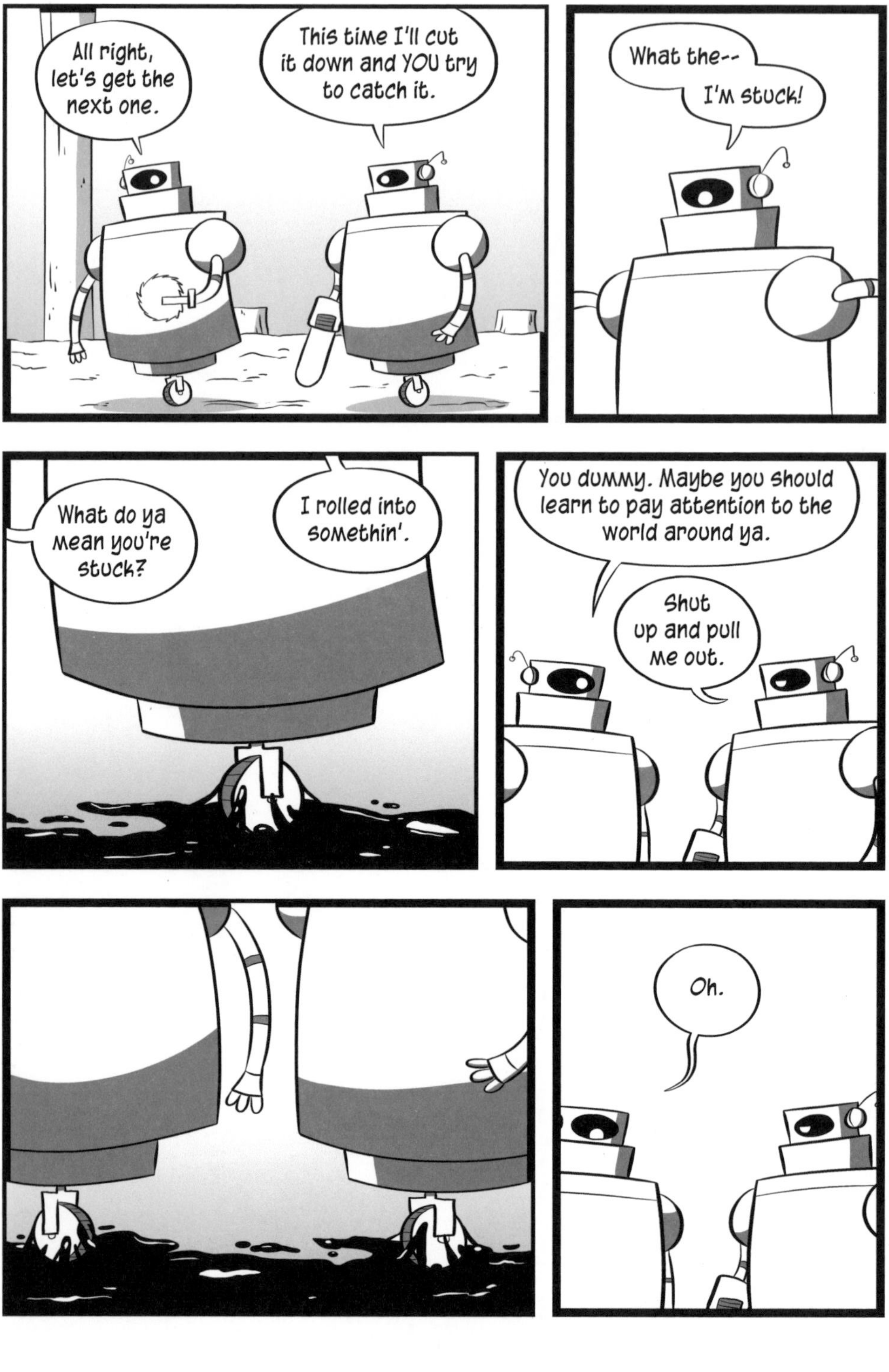
All right, let's get the next one.
This time I'll cut it down and YOU try to catch it.
What the--
I'M stuck!
What do ya mean you're stuck?
I rolled into somethin'.
You dummy. Maybe you should learn to pay attention to the world around ya.
Shut up and pull me out.
Oh.

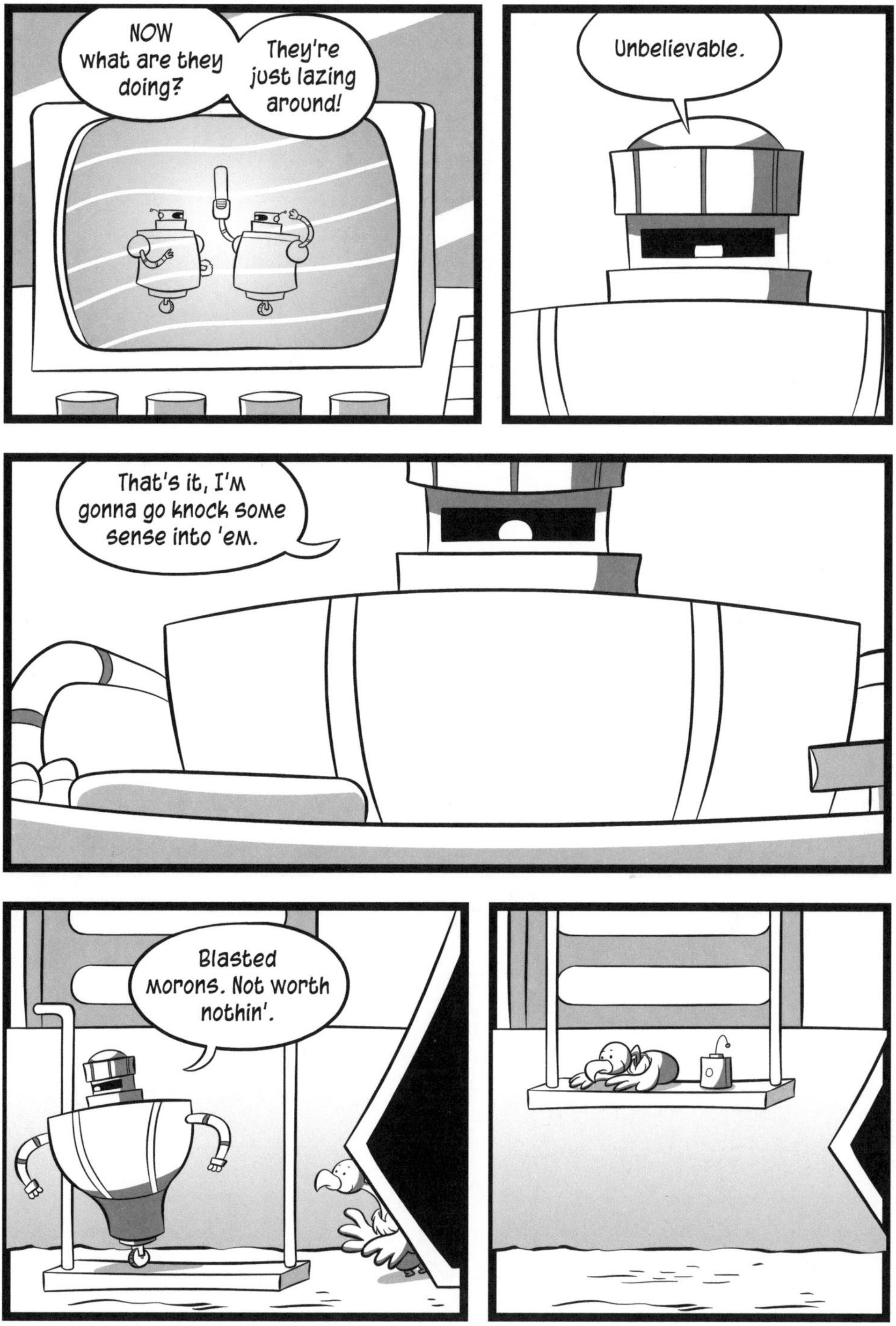
NOW what are they doing?
They're just lazing around!
Unbelievable.
That's it, I'm gonna go knock some sense into 'em.
Blasted morons. Not worth nothin'.

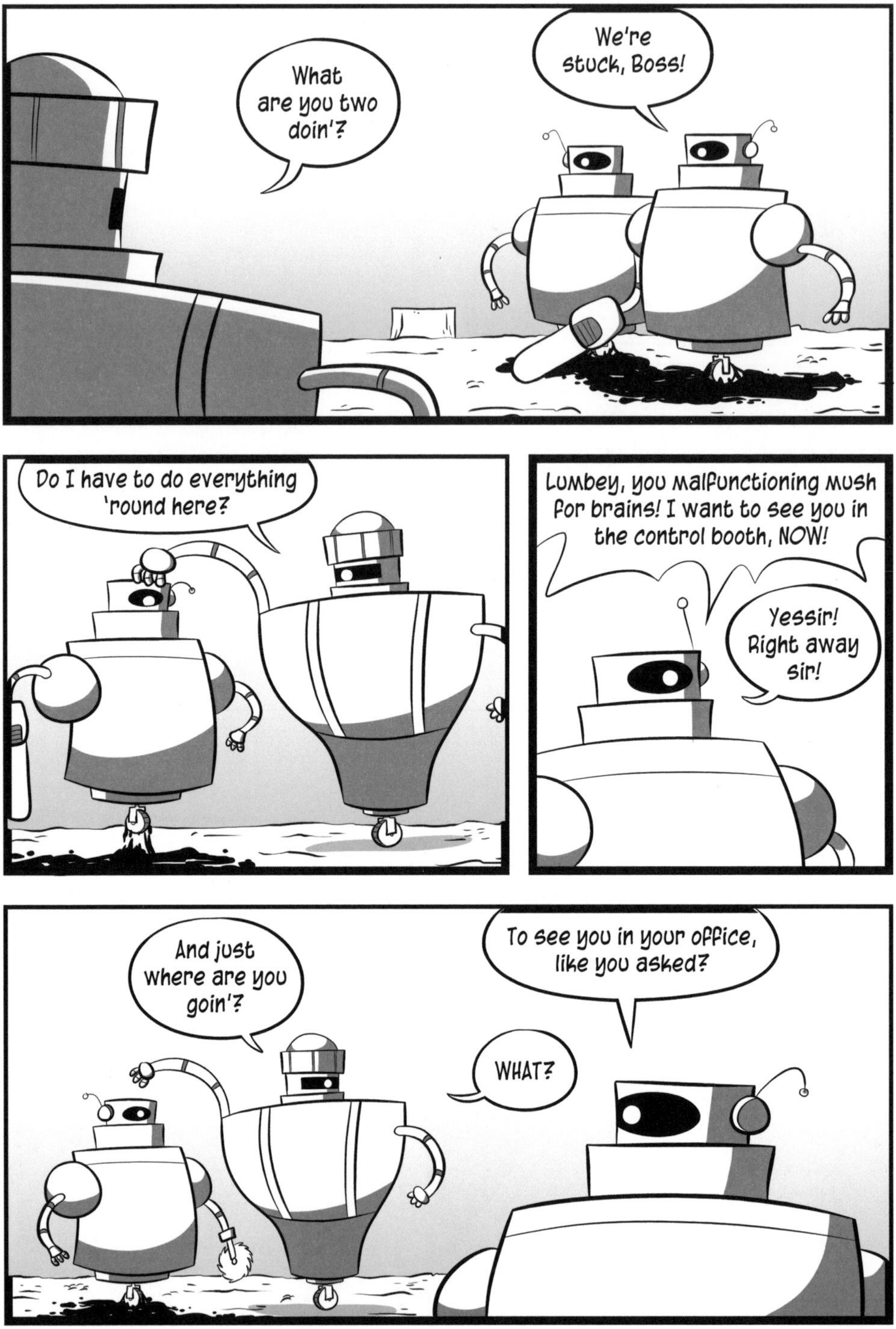
What are you two doin'?
We're stuck, Boss!
Do I have to do everything 'round here?
Lumbey, you malfunctioning mush for brains! I want to see you in the control booth, NOW!
Yessir! Right away sir!
And just where are you goin'?
To see you in your office, like you asked?
WHAT?

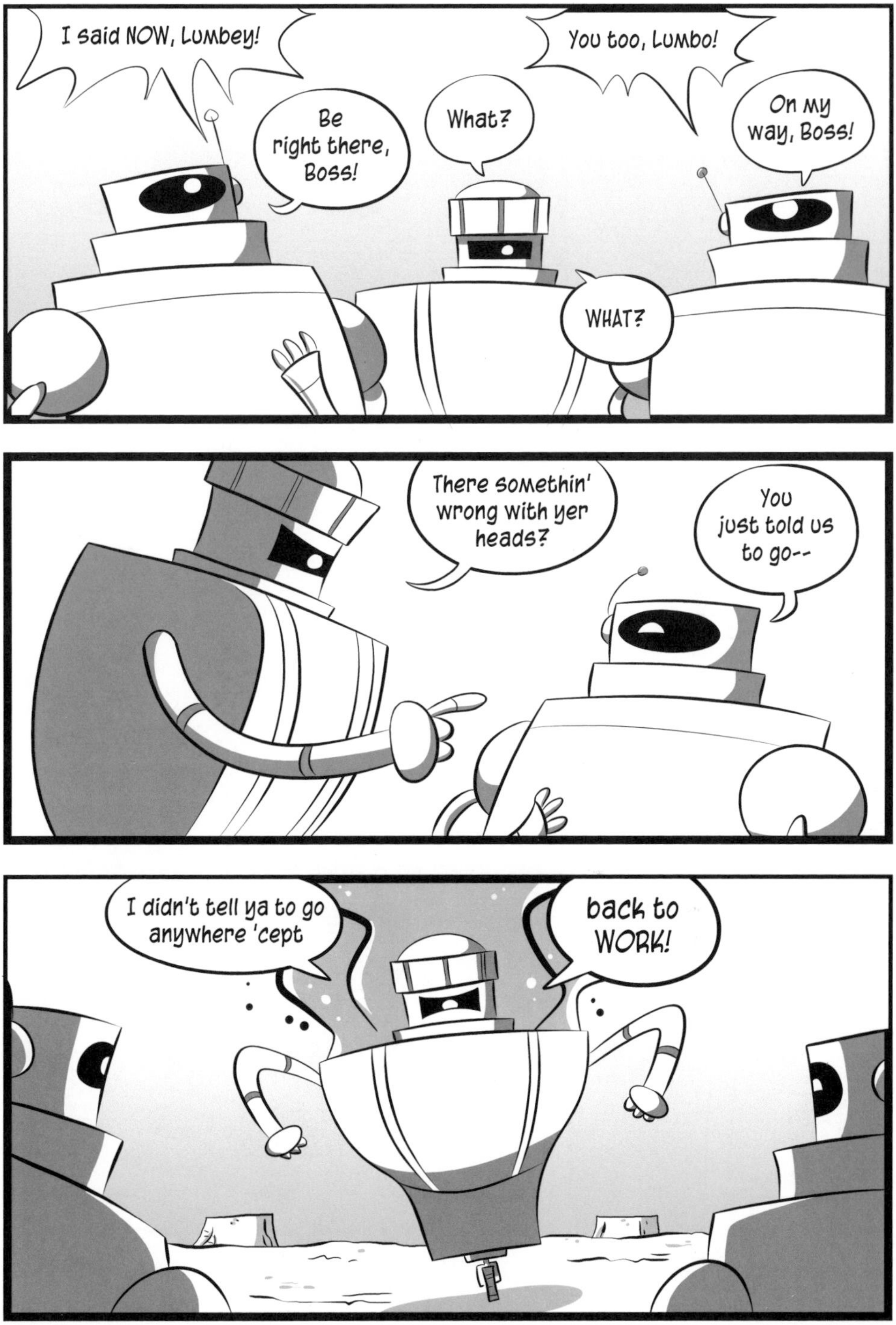
I said NOW, Lumbey!
Be right there, Boss!
What?
You too, Lumbo!
On my way, Boss!
WHAT?
There somethin' wrong with yer heads?
You just told us to go--
I didn't tell ya to go anywhere 'cept
back to WORK!

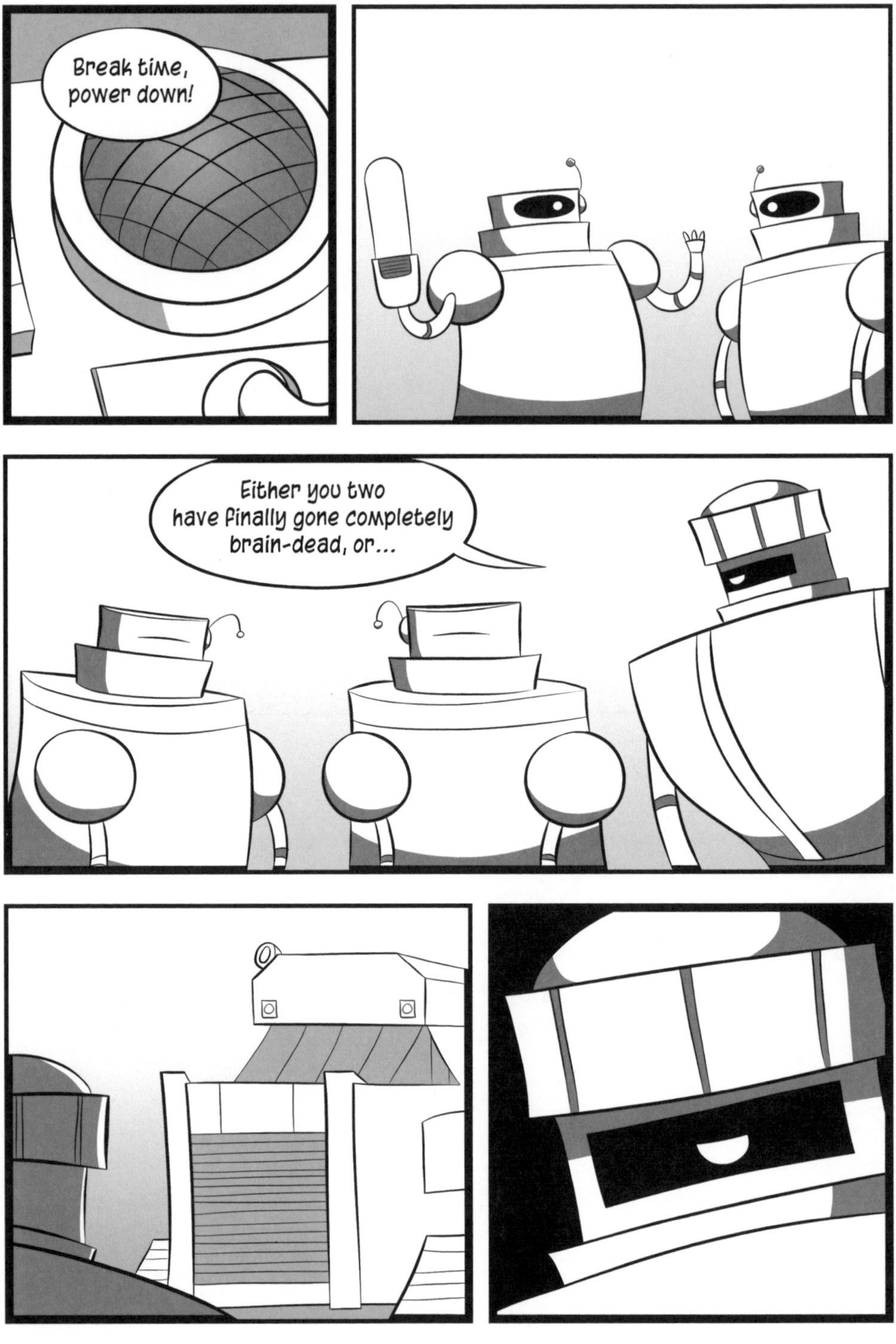
Break time,
power down!
Either you two
have finally gone completely
brain-dead, or...

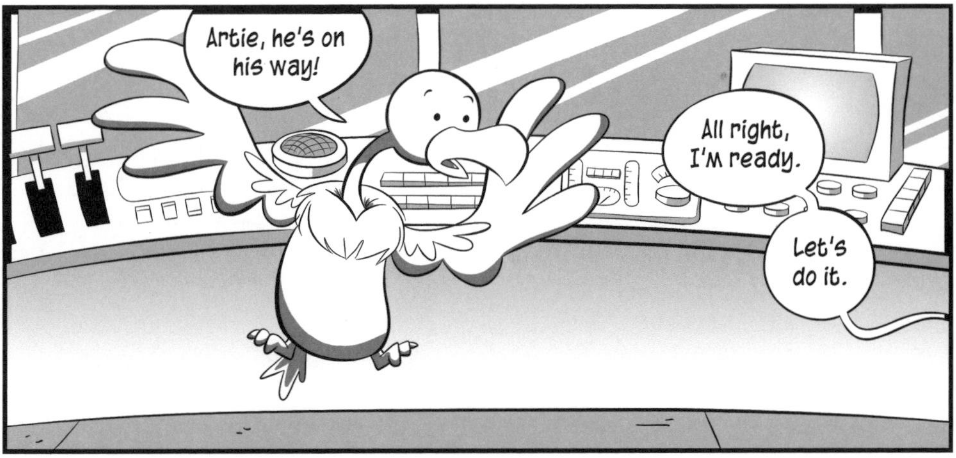
Artie, he's on his way!
All right, I'm ready.
Let's do it.

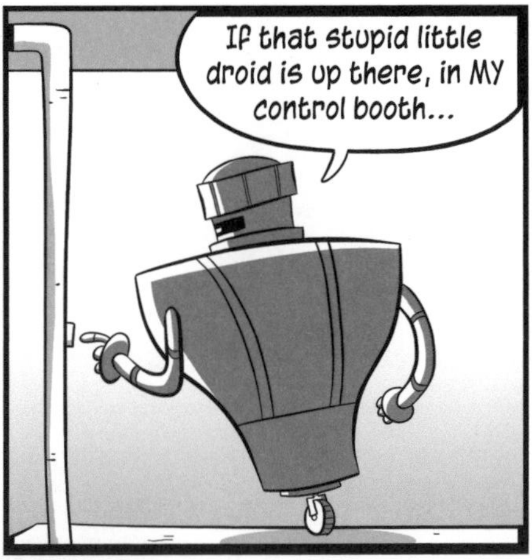
If that stupid little droid is up there, in MY control booth...

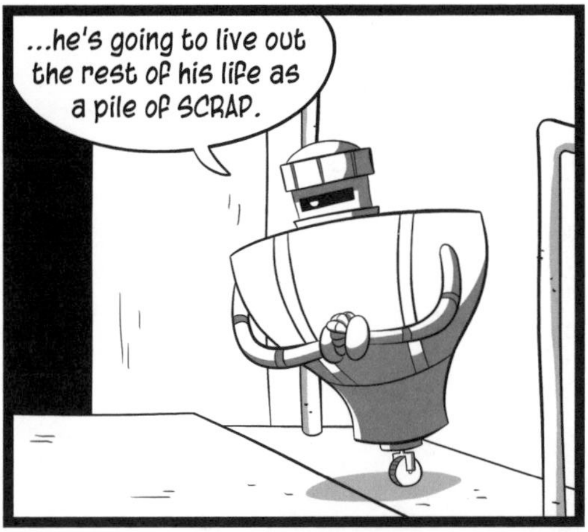
...he's going to live out the rest of his life as a pile of SCRAP.

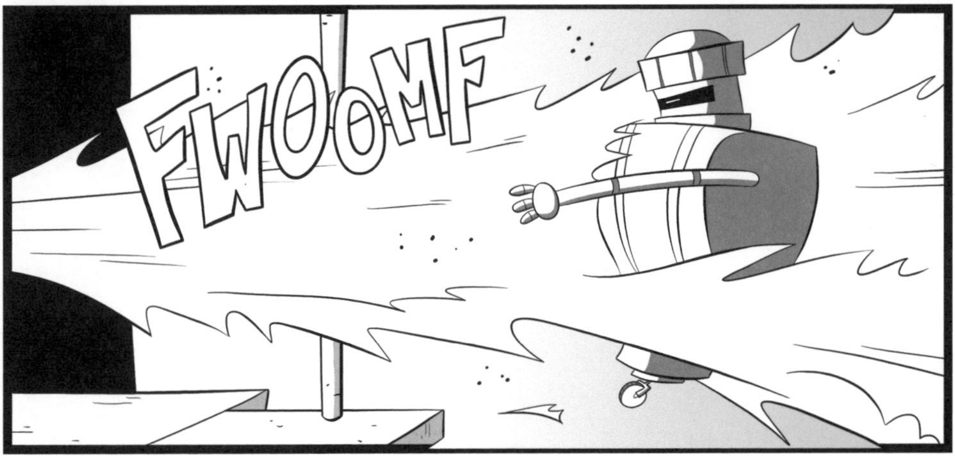
FWOOMF

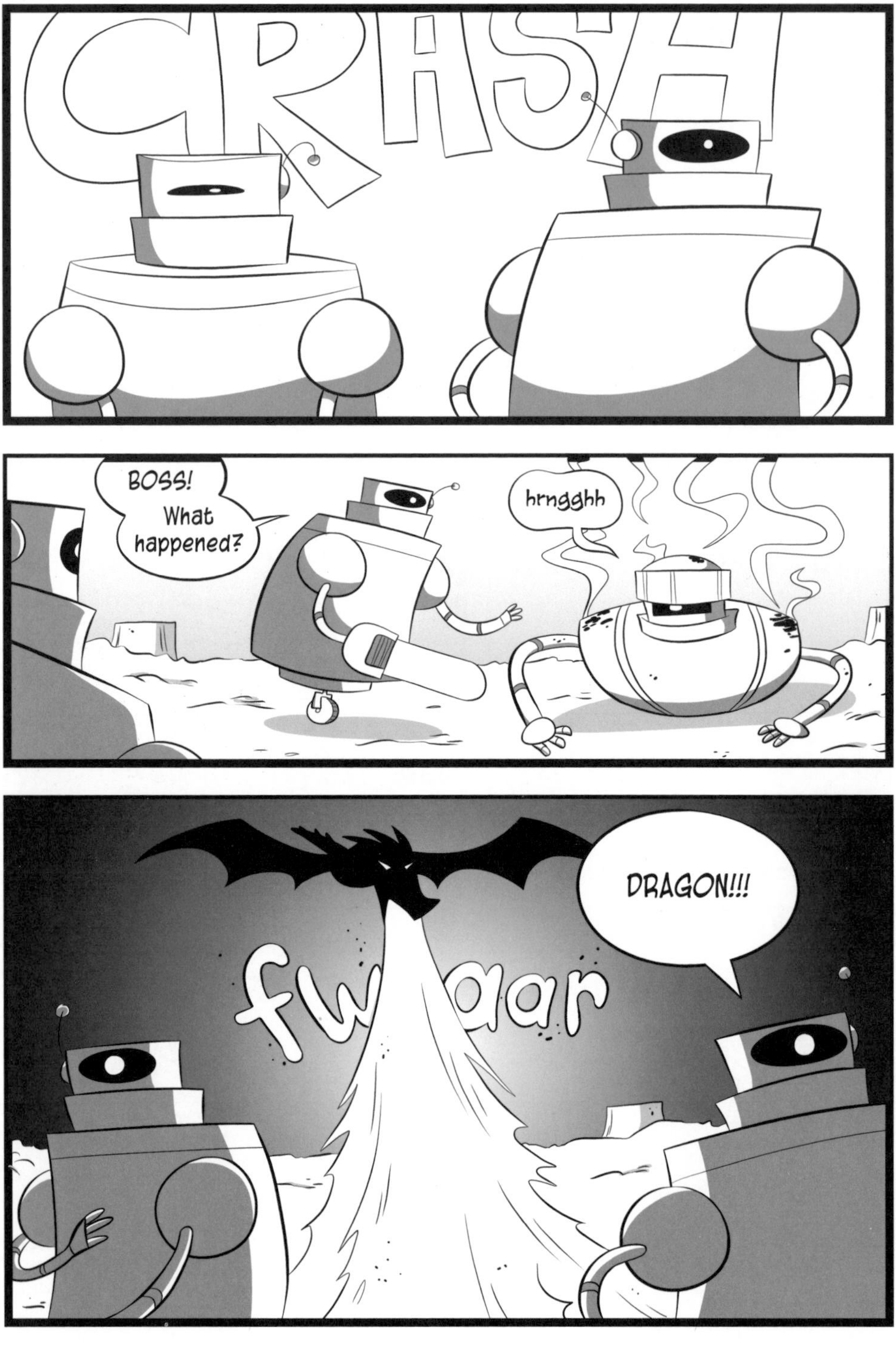
CRASH
BOSS! What happened?
hrngghh
DRAGON!!!
fw aar

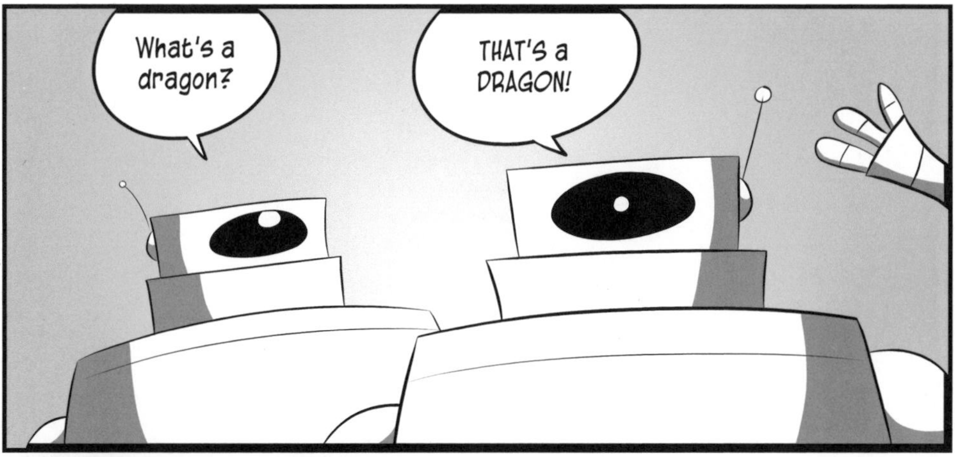
What's a dragon?
THAT'S a DRAGON!

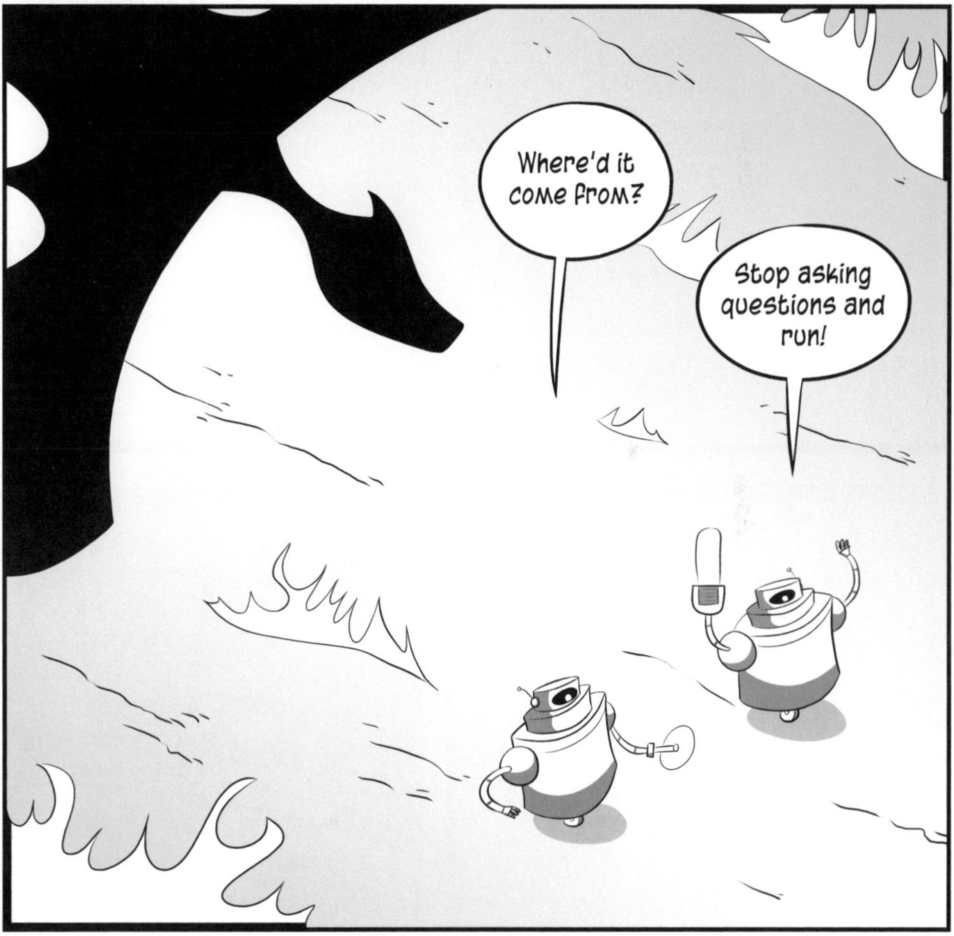
Where'd it come from?
Stop asking questions and run!

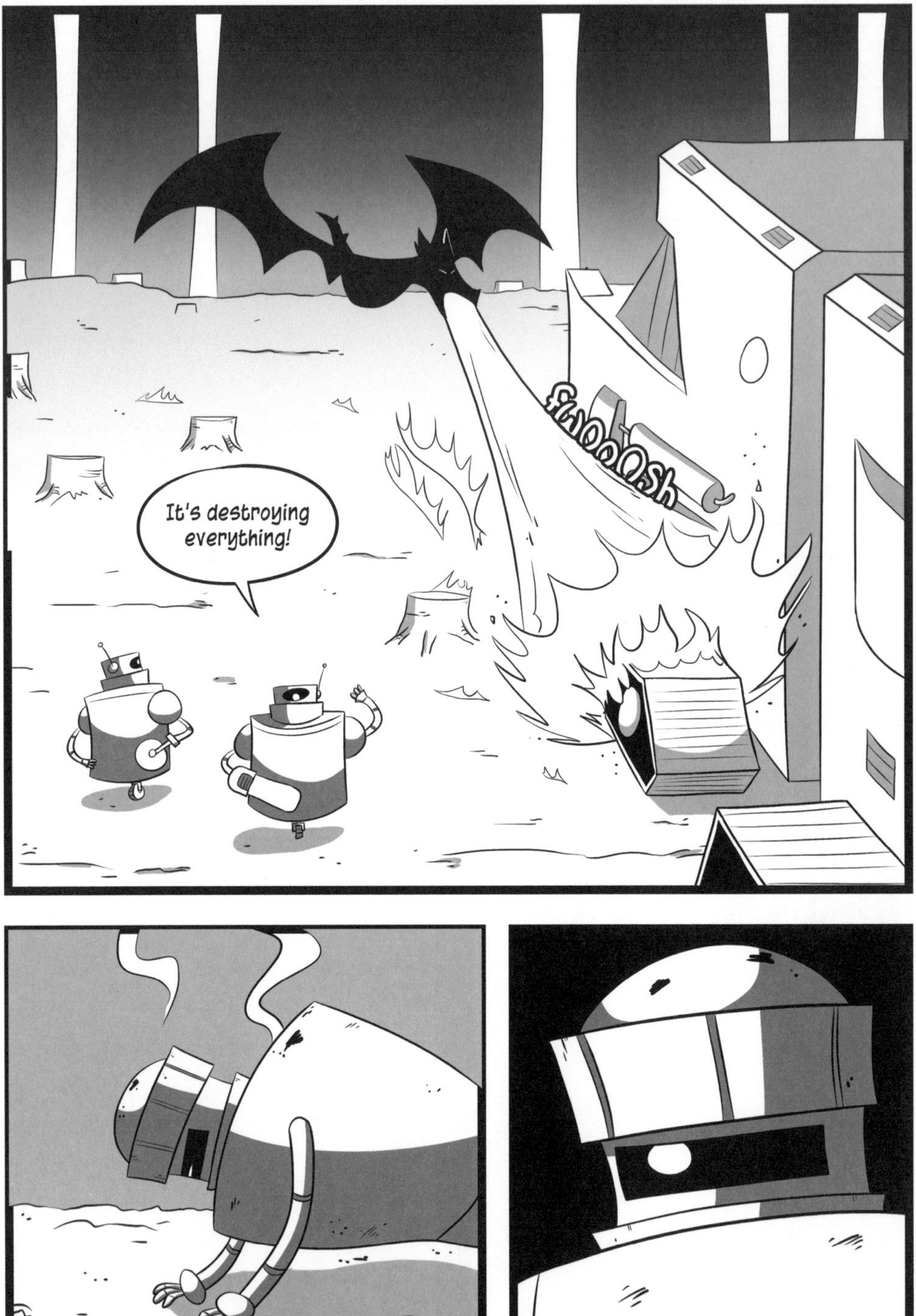

fwOOOSh
It's destroying everything!

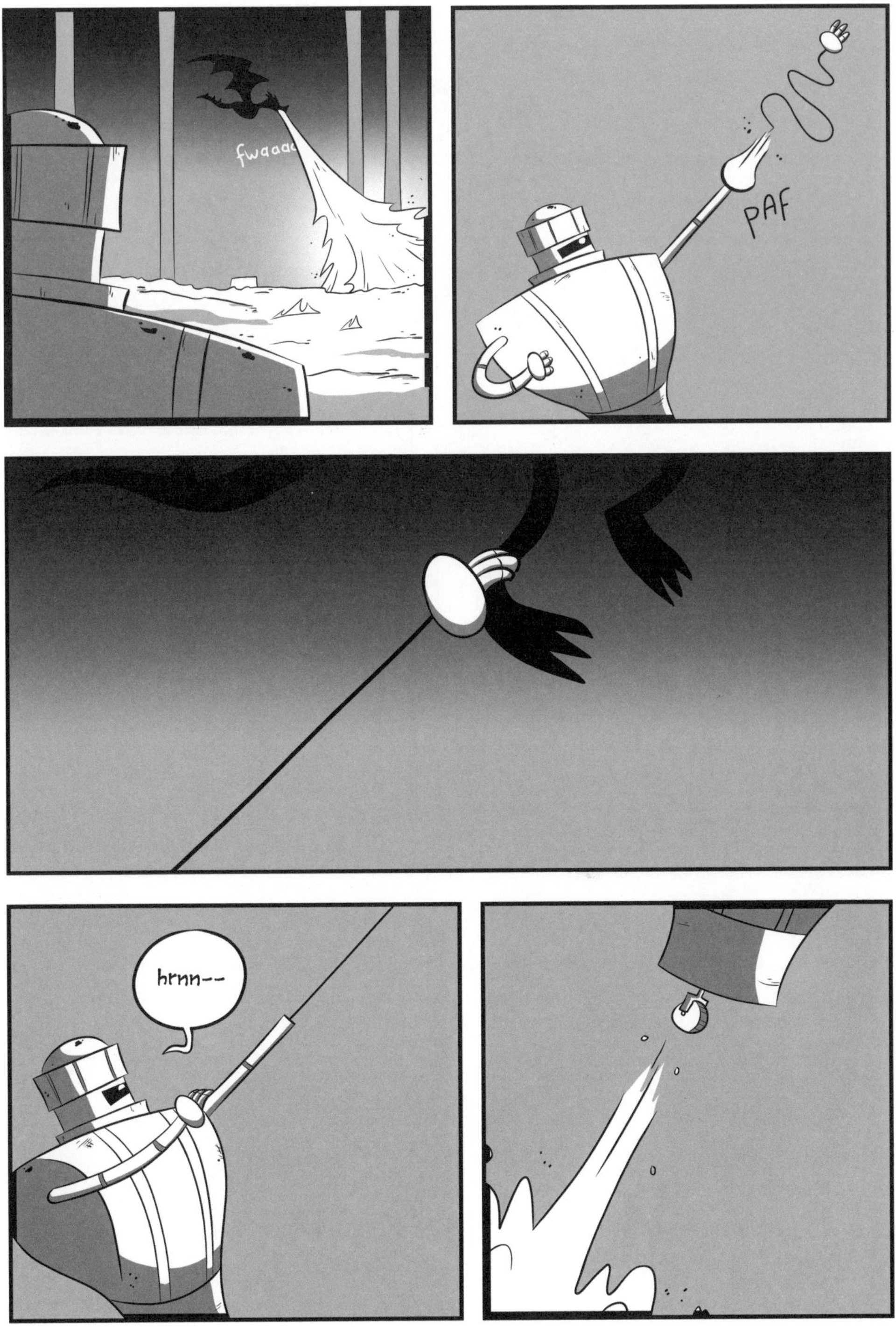
fwaaa
PAF
hrnn--

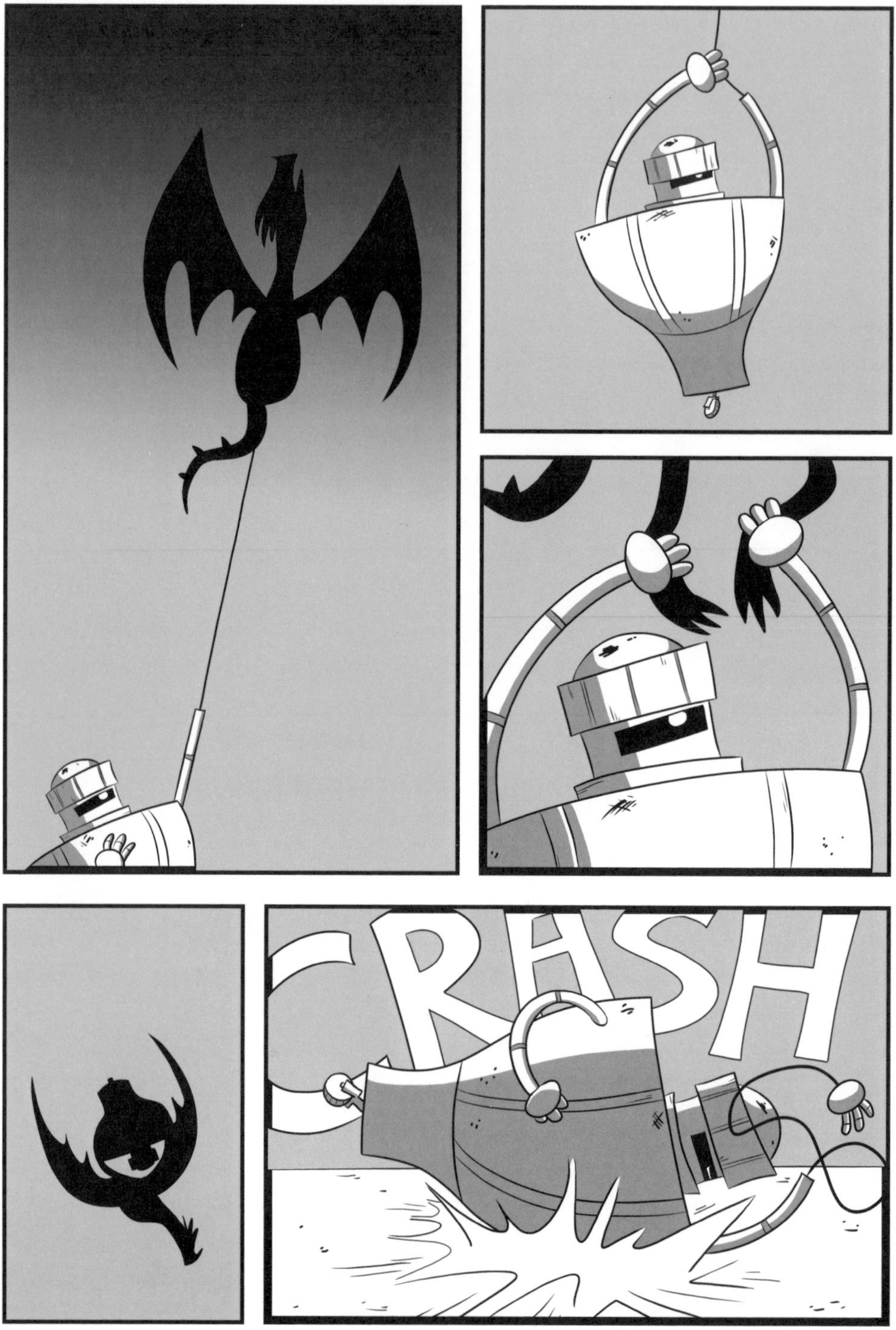
CRASH

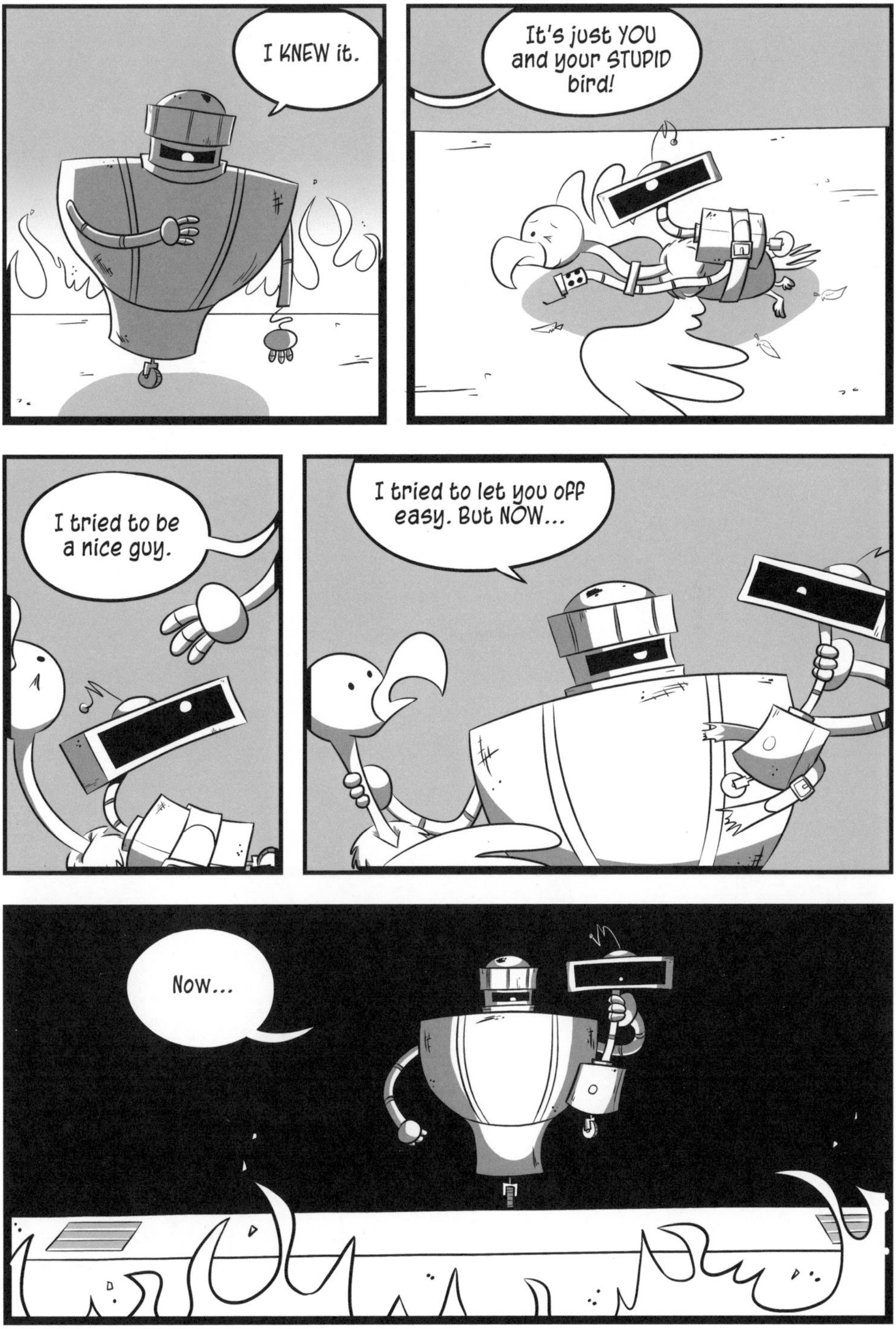
I KNEW it.
It's just YOU and your STUPID bird!
I tried to be a nice guy.
I tried to let you off easy. But NOW...
Now...

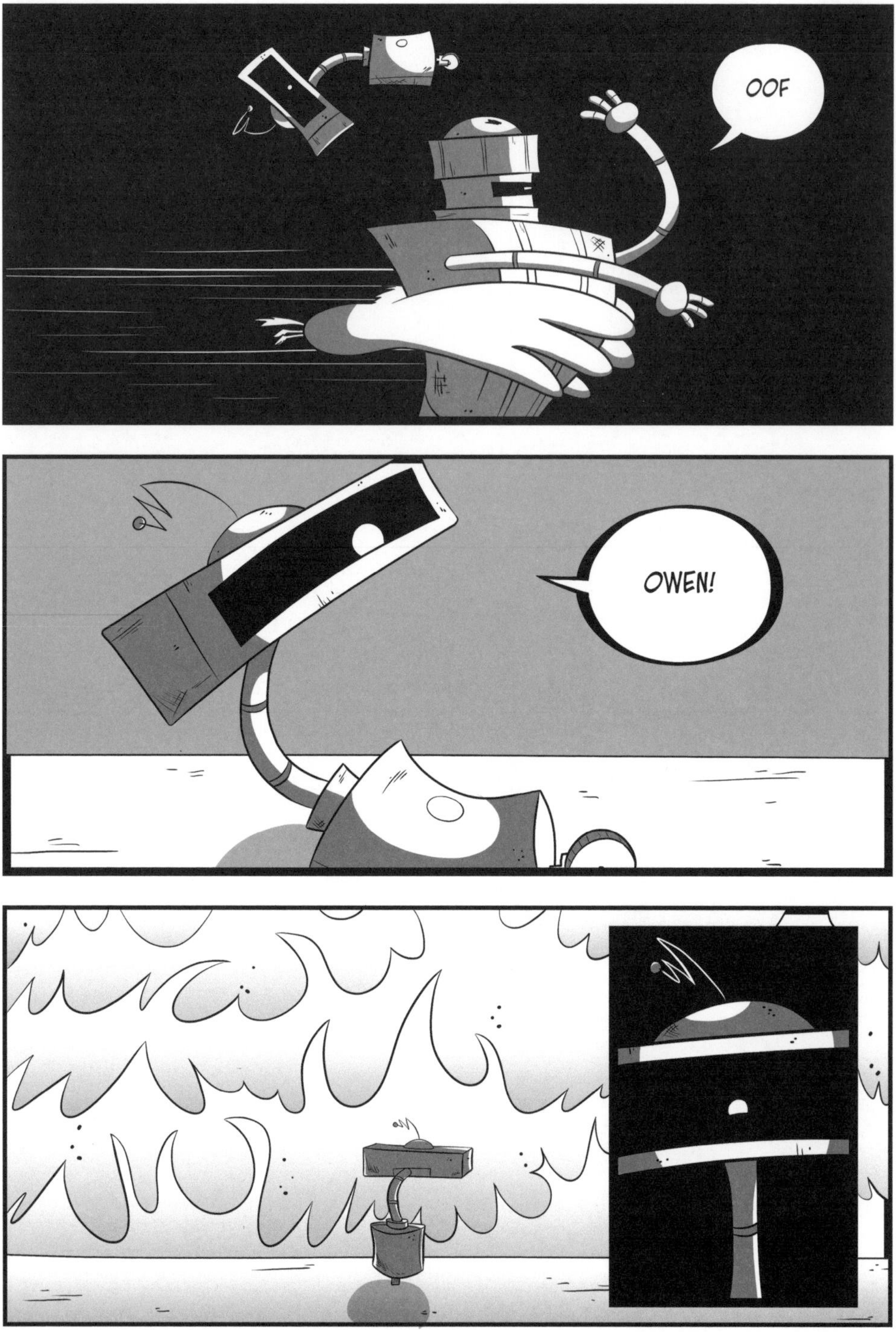
OOF
OWEN!

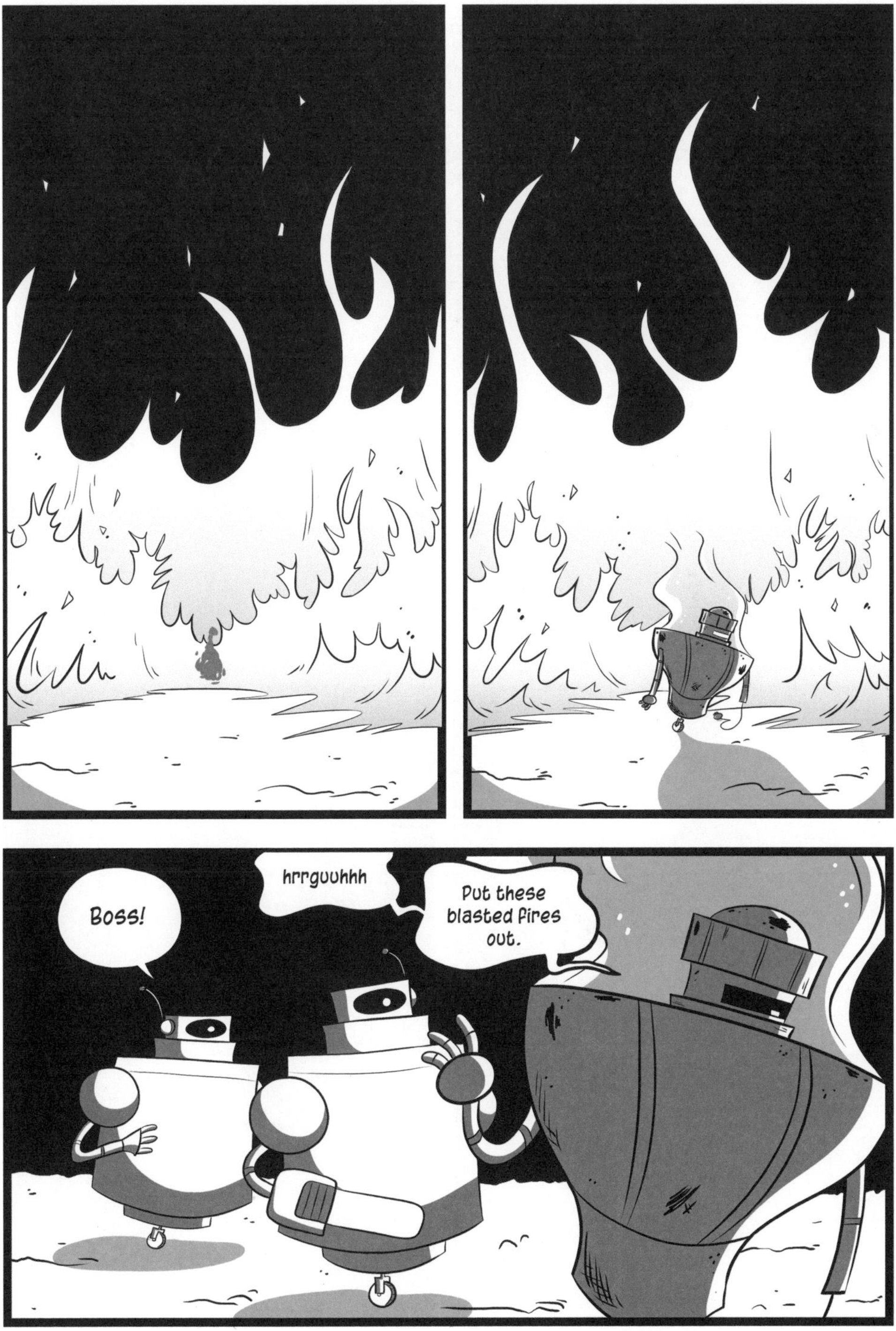
Boss!
hrrguuhhh
Put these blasted fires out.

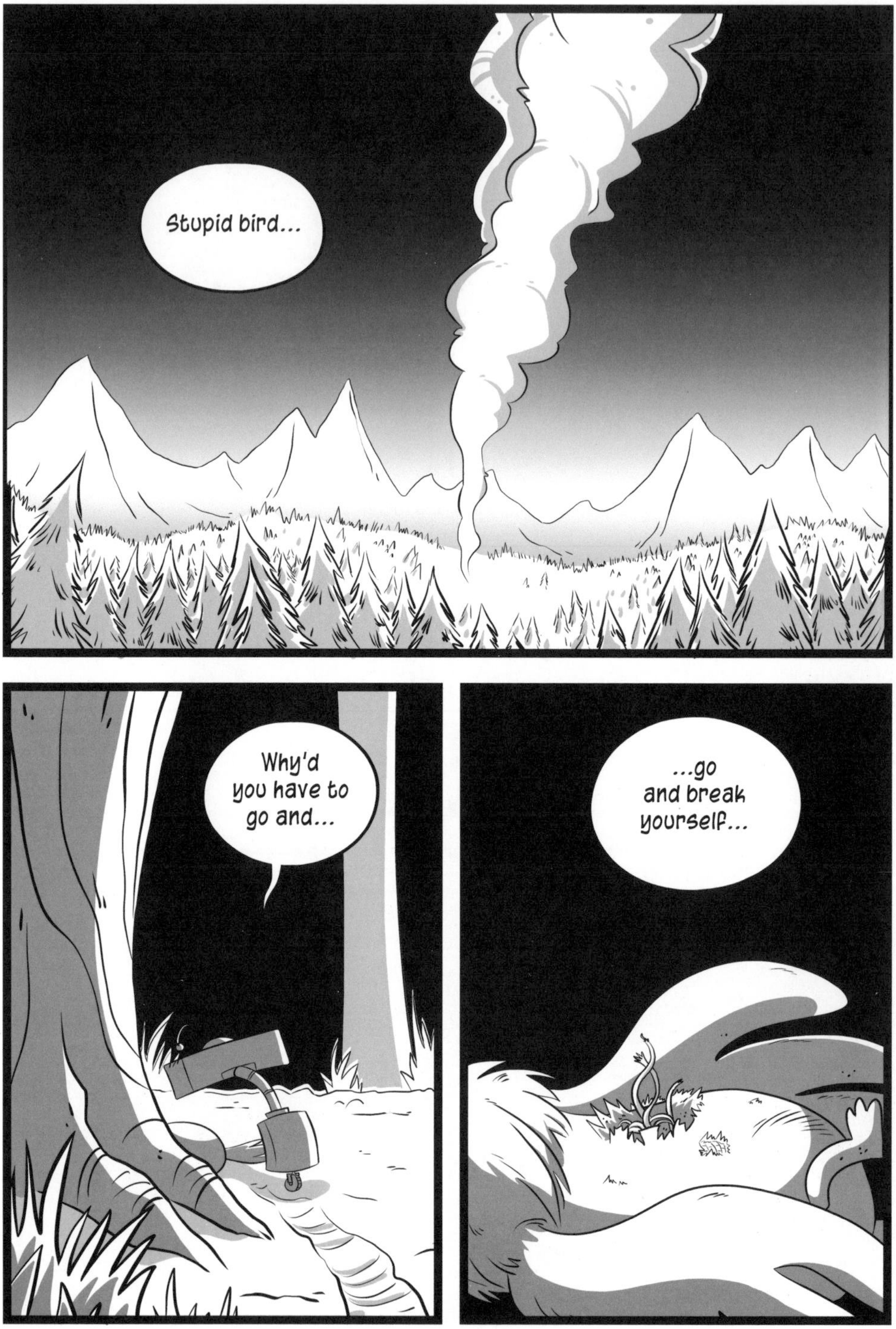
Stupid bird...
Why'd you have to go and...
...go and break yourself...

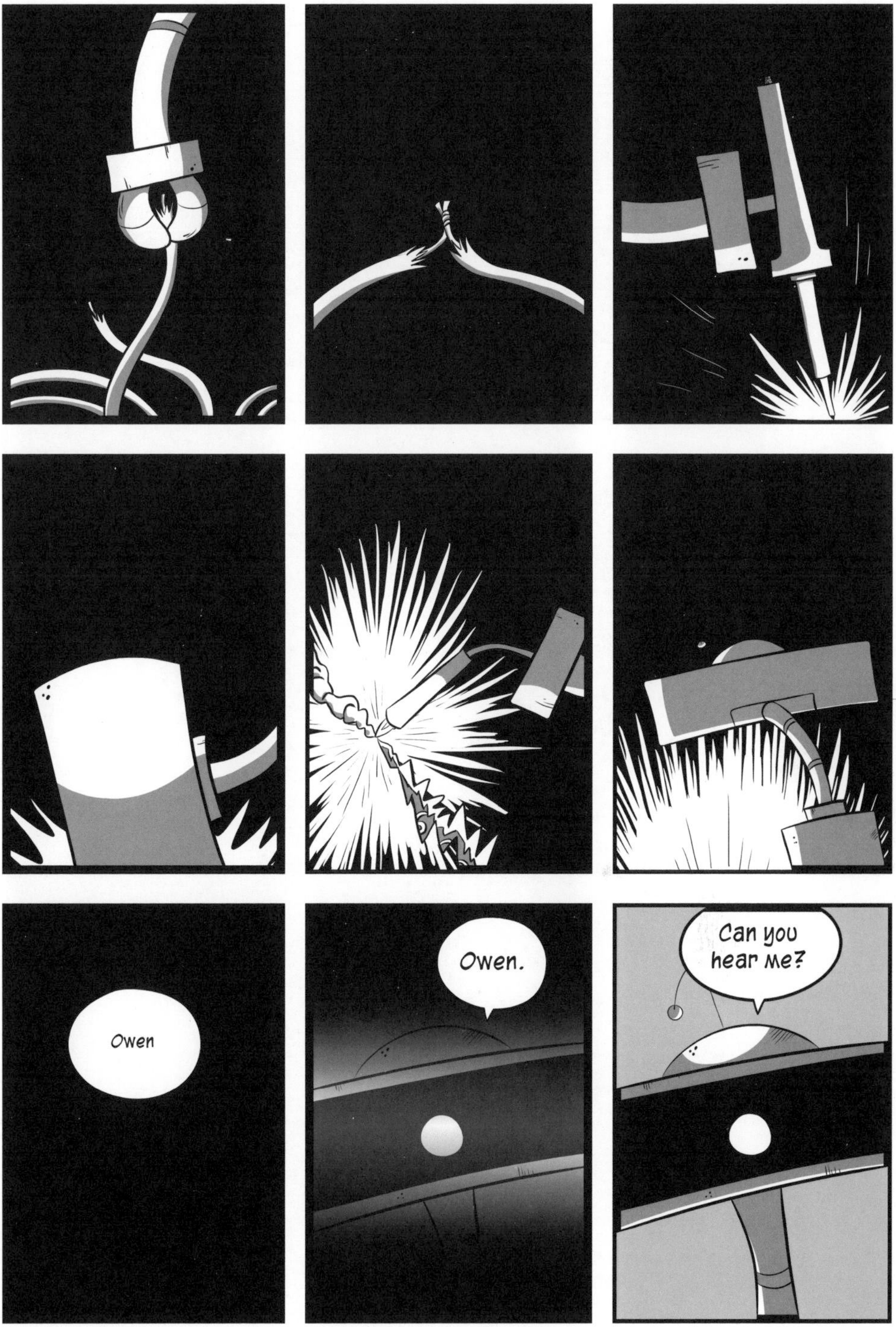
Owen
Owen.
Can you hear me?

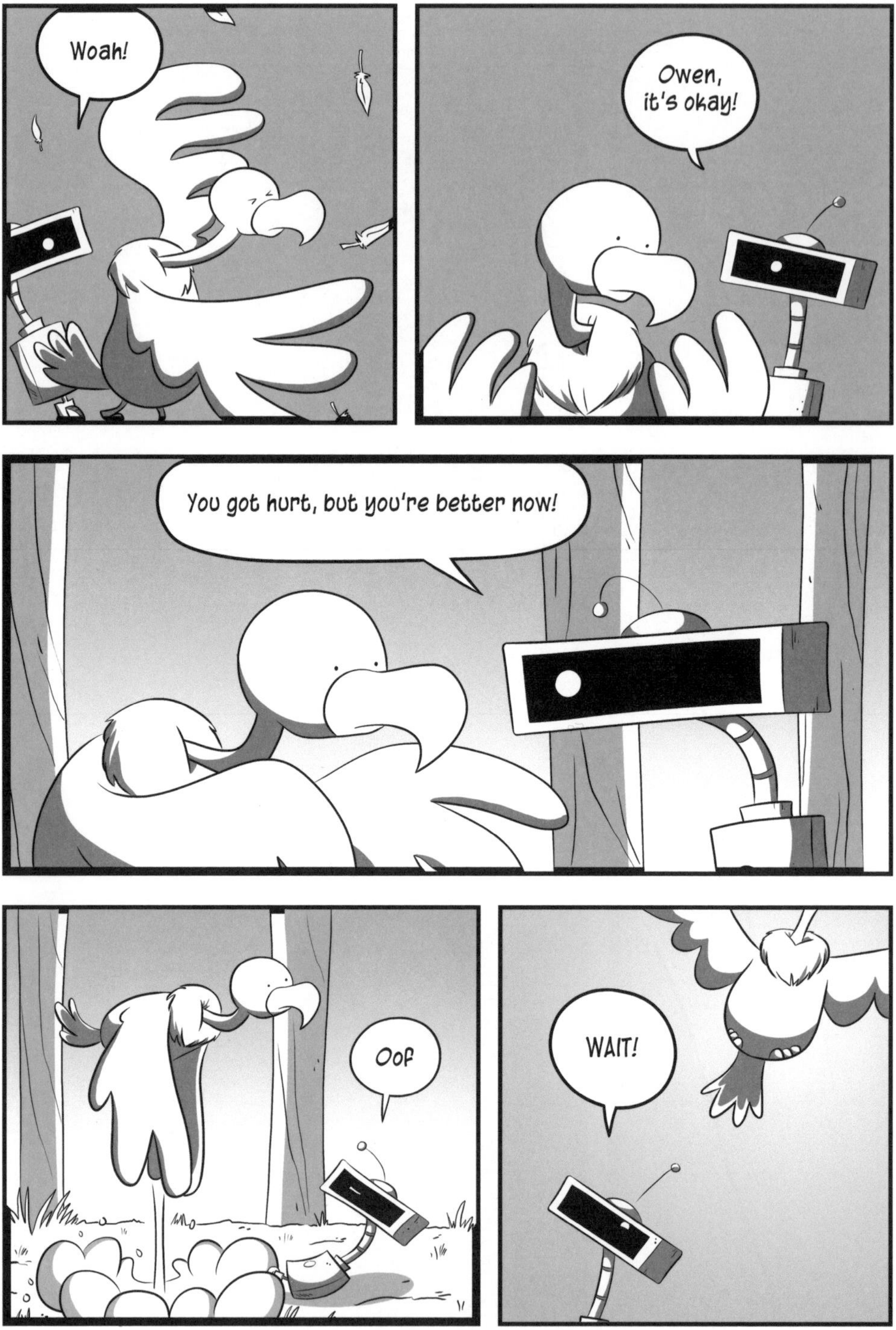
Woah!
Owen, it's okay!
You got hurt, but you're better now!
Oof
WAIT!

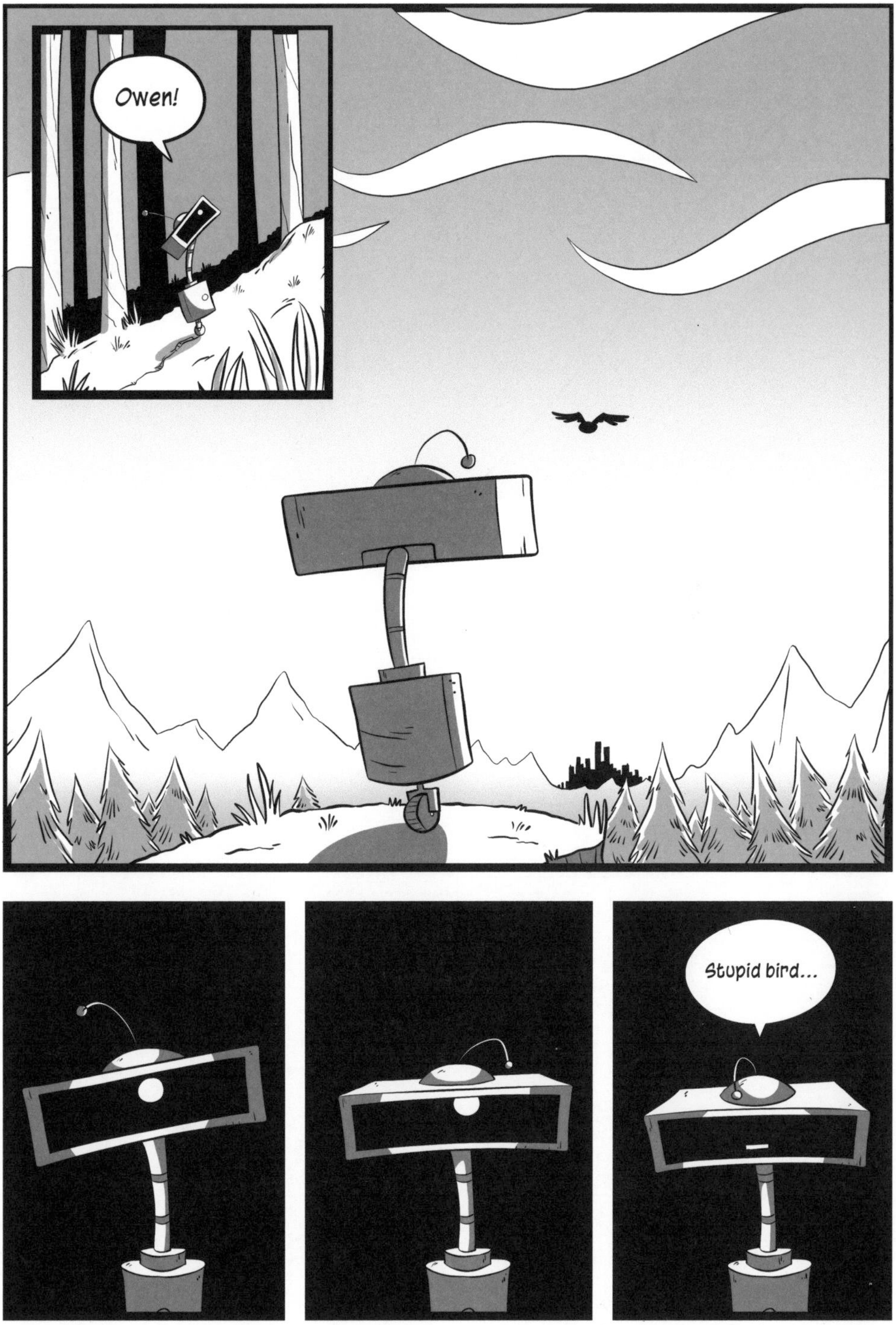
Owen!
Stupid bird...

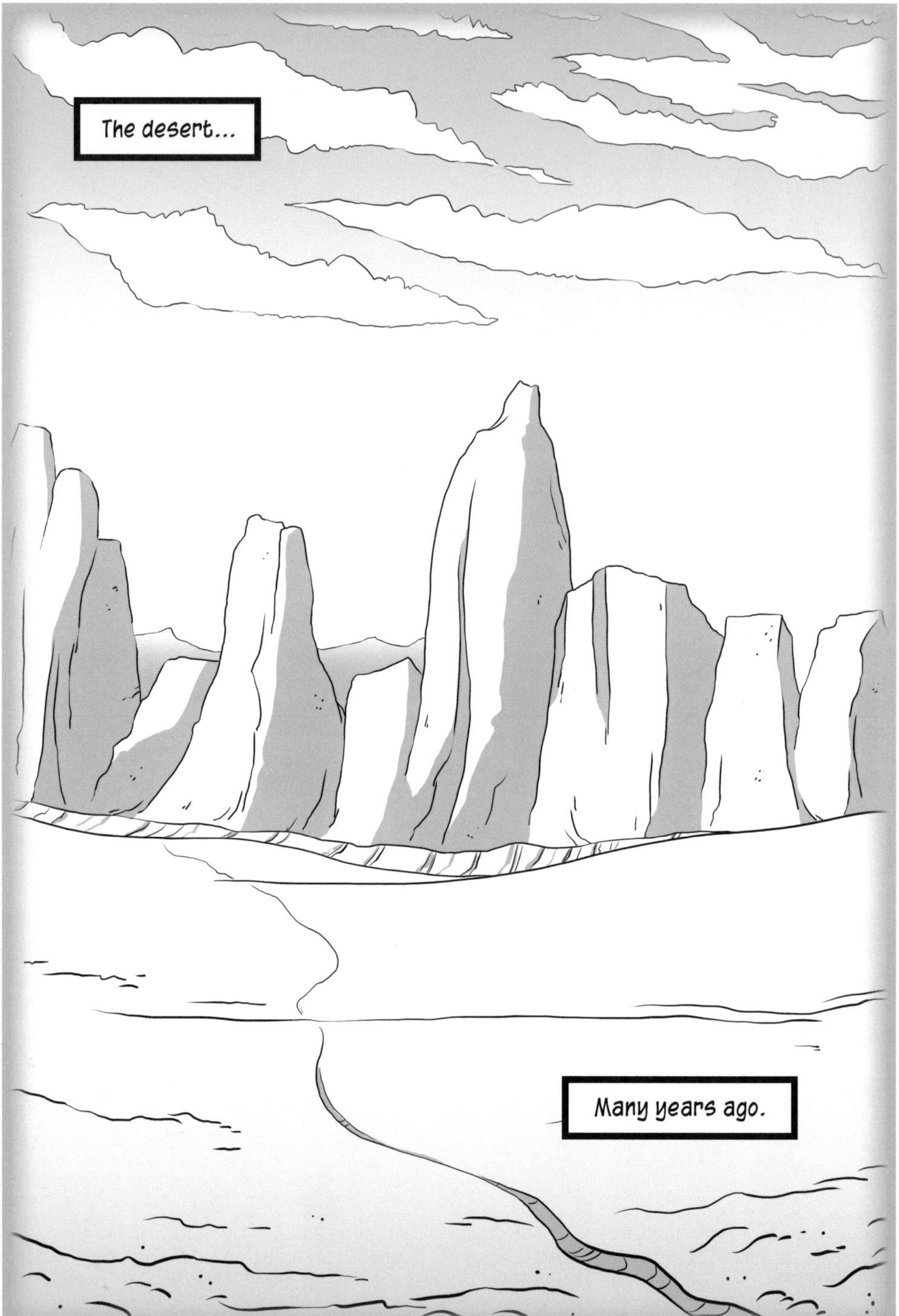
The desert...
Many years ago.

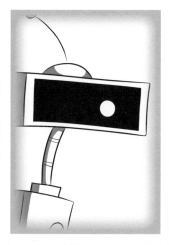
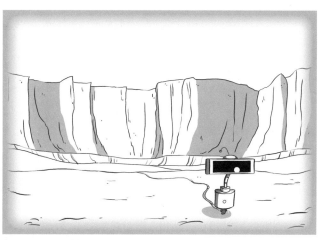

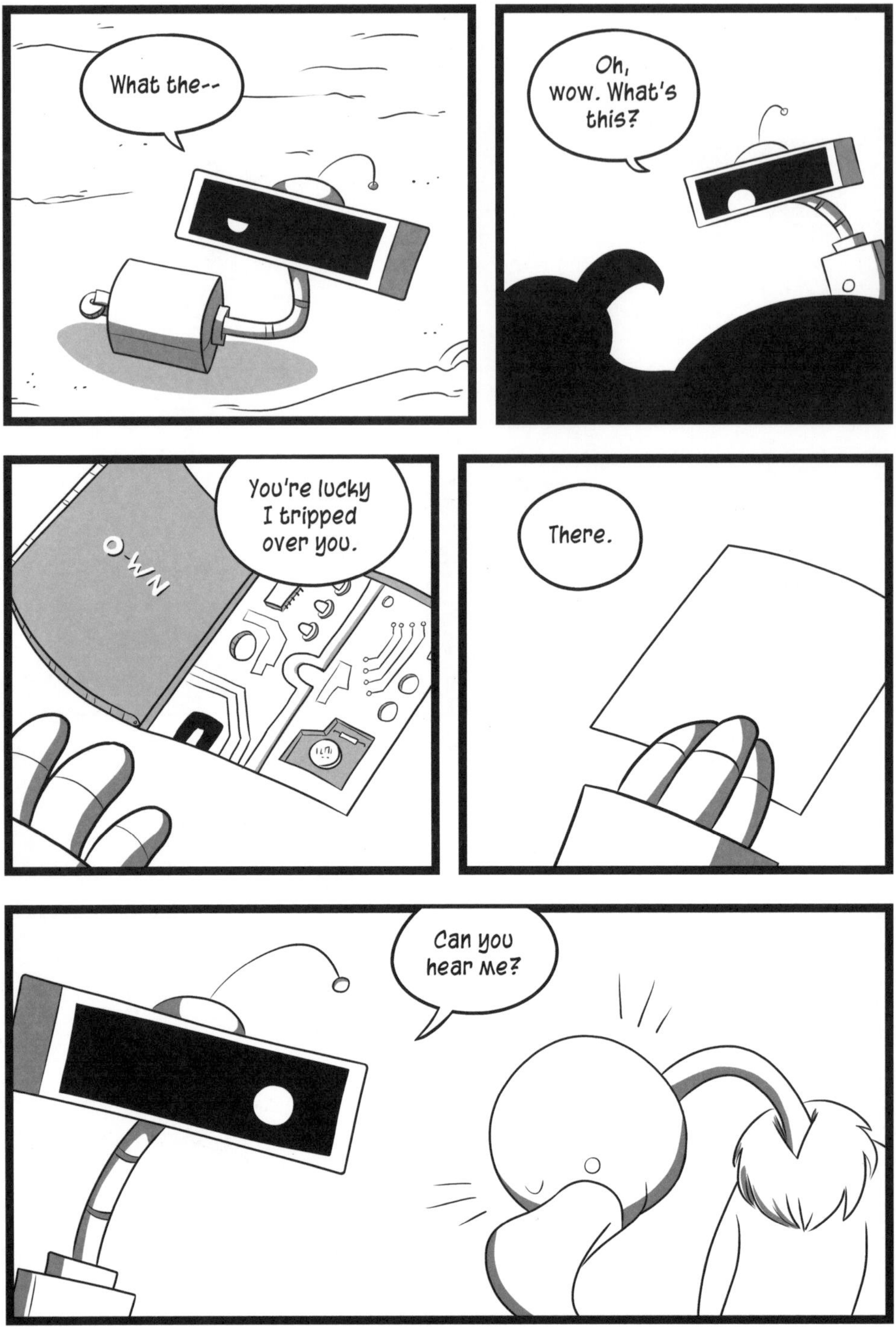
What the--
Oh, wow. What's this?
You're lucky I tripped over you.
O-WN
There.
Can you hear me?

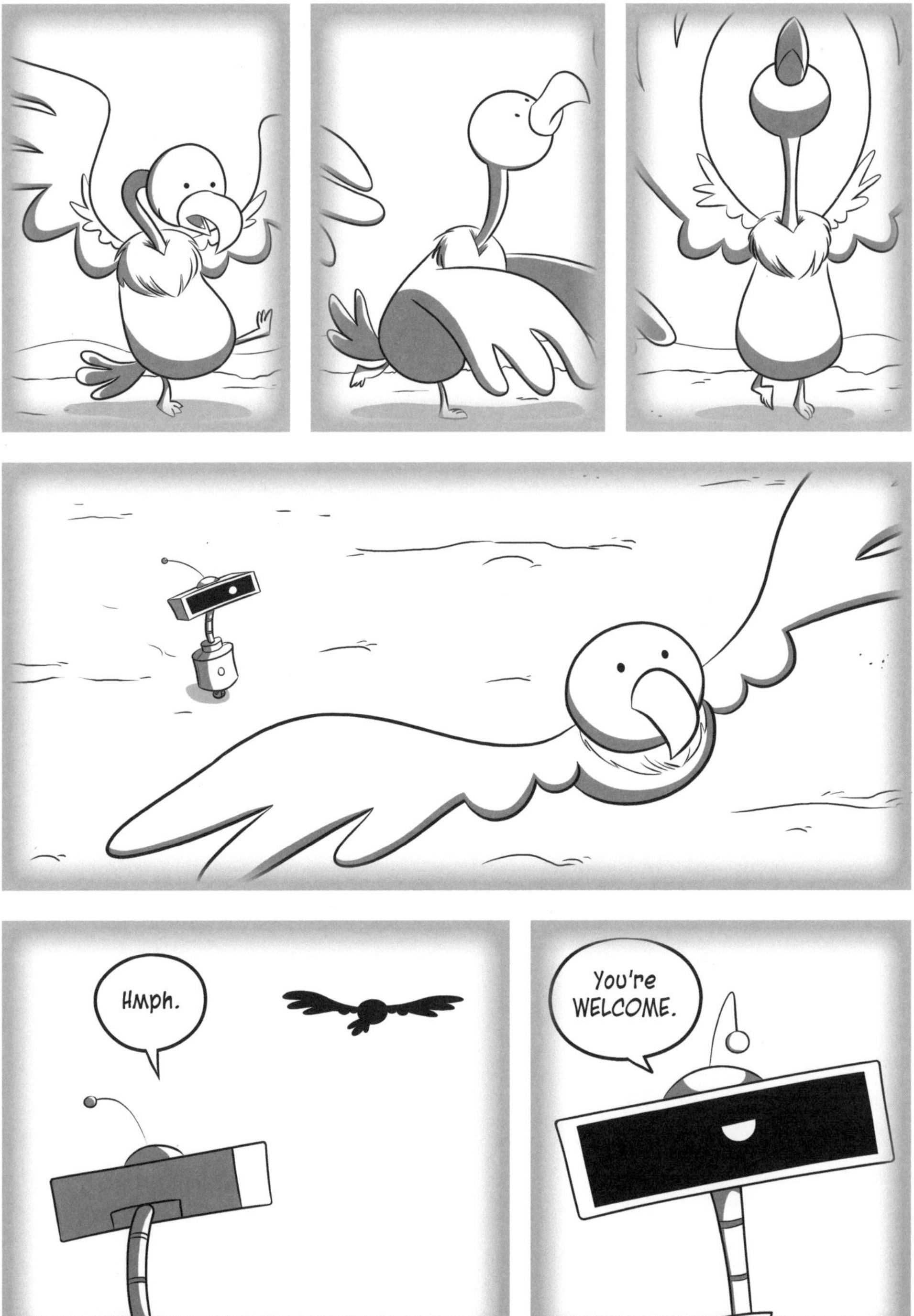
Hmph.
You're WELCOME.

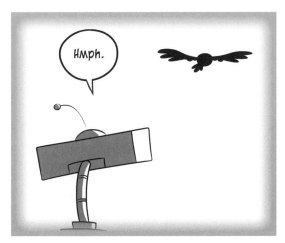

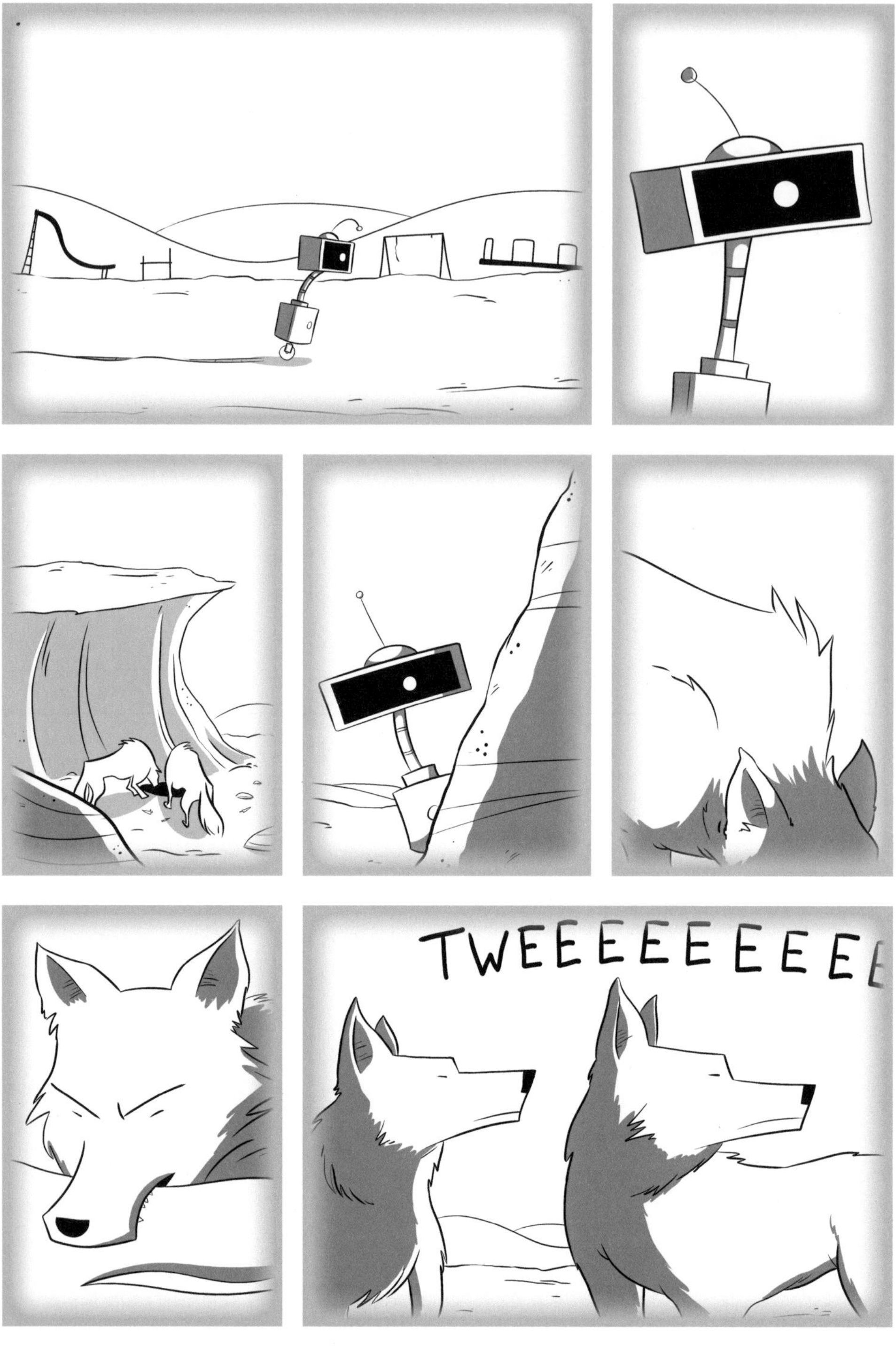
TWEEEEEEEE

TWEEEEE—

Are you okay?

Hey! Are you OKAY?

...okay.

Okay, good.

Good.

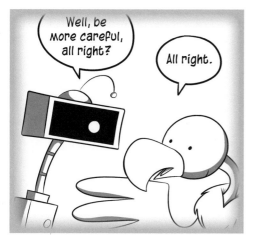

Well, be more careful, all right?

All right.

OH!
Uh, hello again. Can I help you? Again?
What's your name?
My serial number is R-TY.
Artie?
Sure.
What's my name?
O-WN.
But, uh...
...how about Owen?

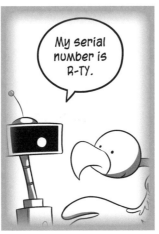

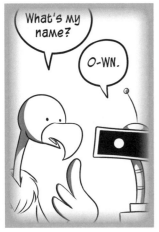

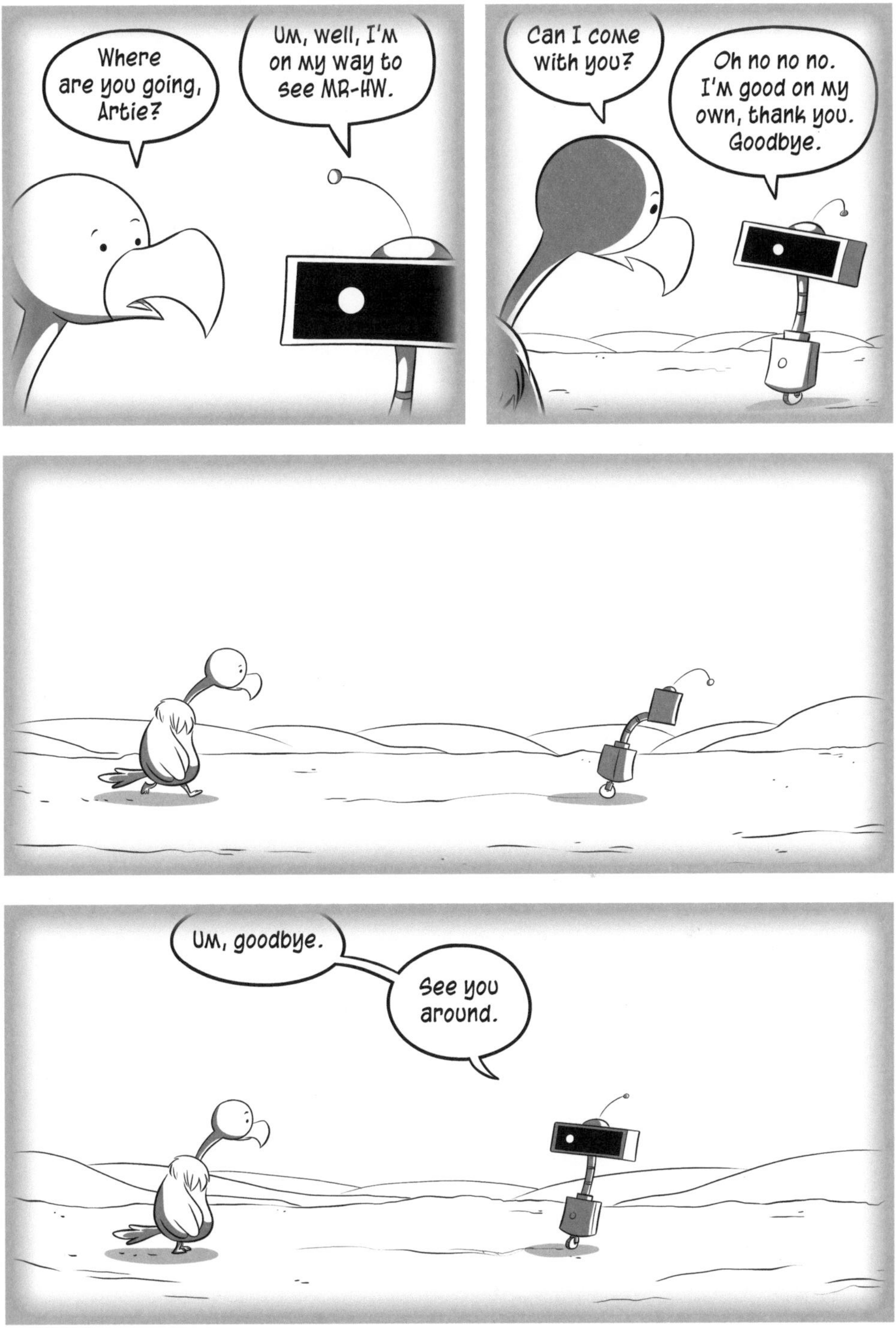
Where are you going, Artie?
Um, well, I'm on my way to see MR-HW.
Can I come with you?
Oh no no no. I'm good on my own, thank you. Goodbye.
Um, goodbye.
See you around.

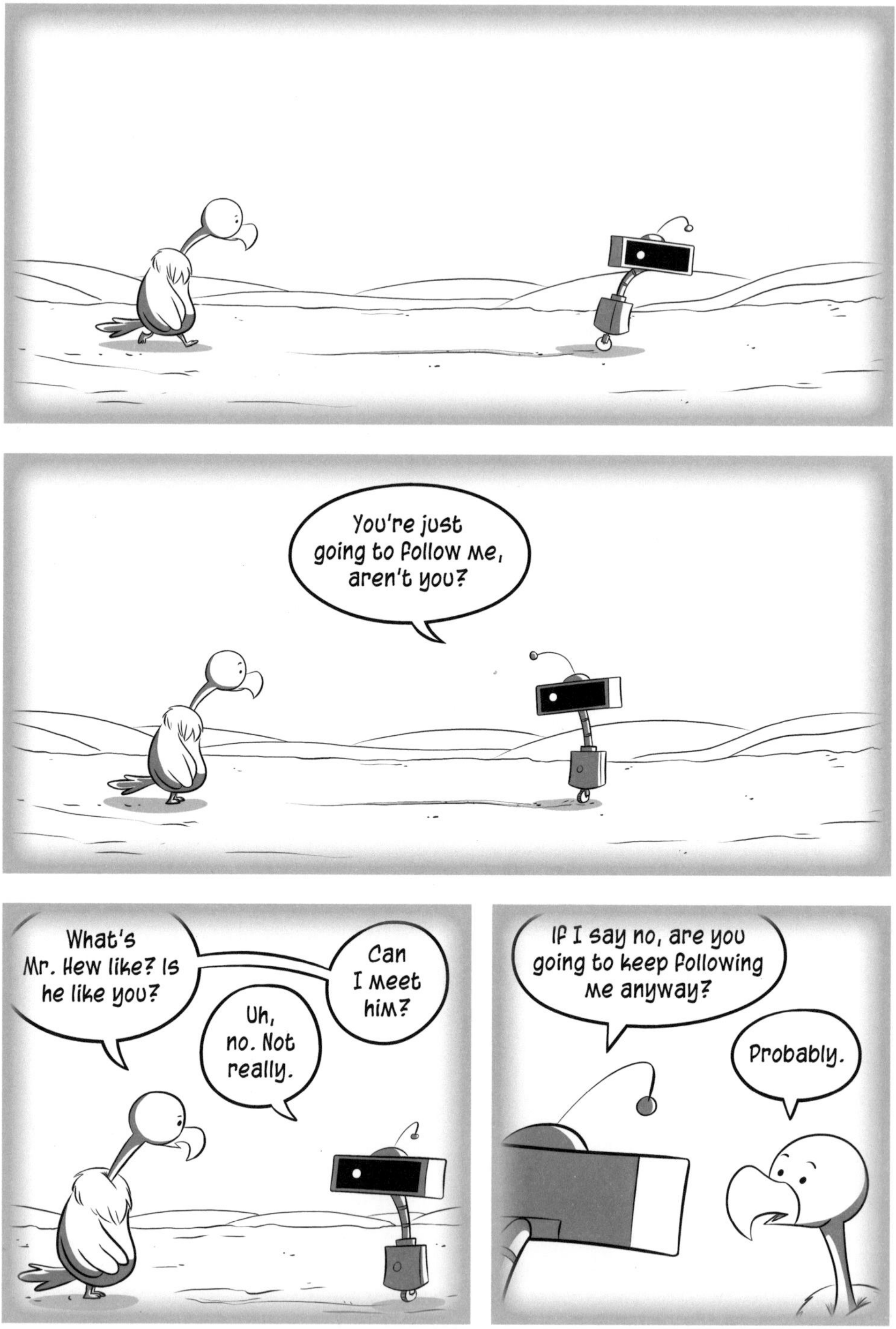
You're just going to follow me, aren't you?
What's Mr. Hew like? Is he like you?
Can I meet him?
Uh, no. Not really.
If I say no, are you going to keep following me anyway?
Probably.

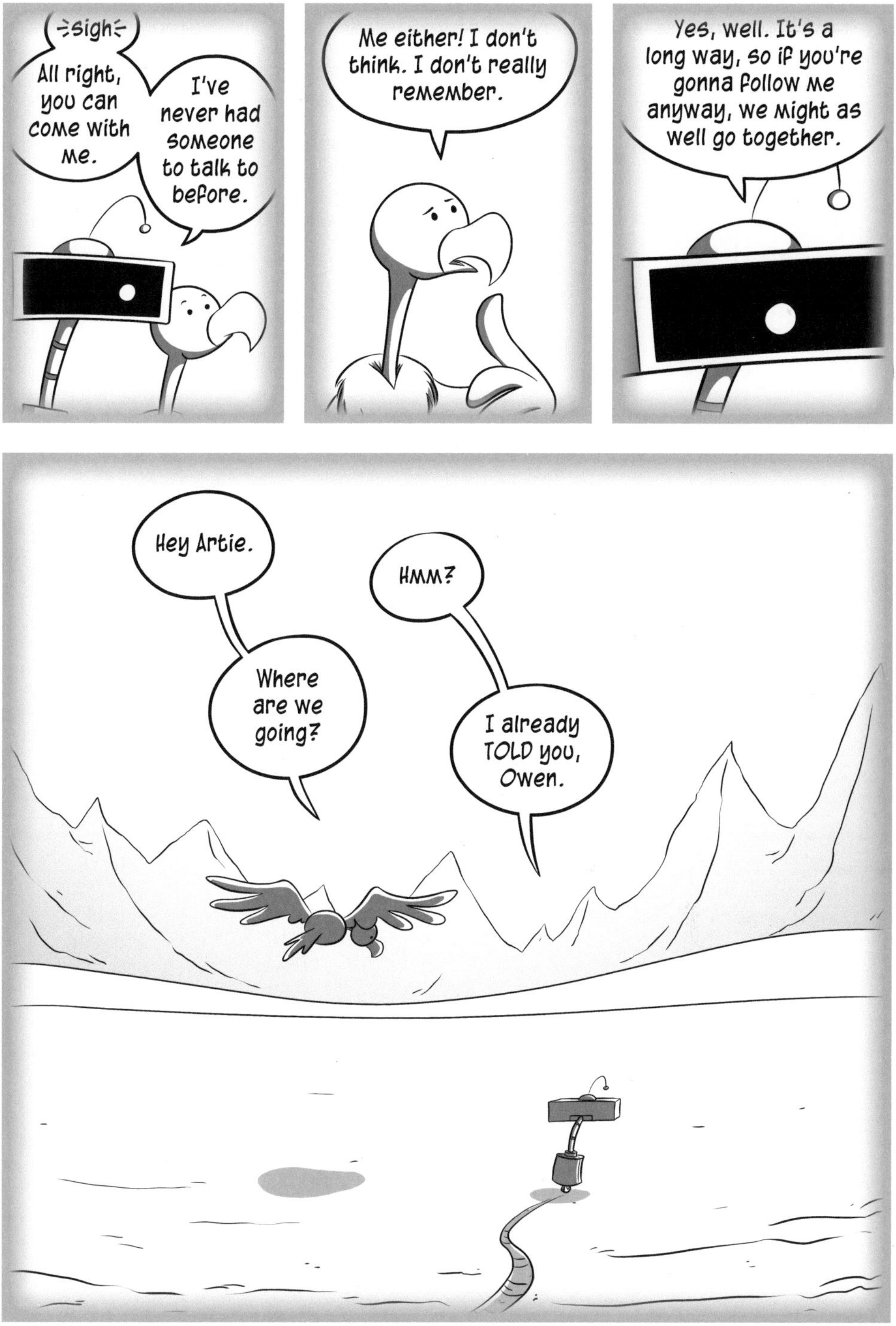
≈sigh≈
All right, you can come with me.
I've never had someone to talk to before.
Me either! I don't think. I don't really remember.
Yes, well. It's a long way, so if you're gonna follow me anyway, we might as well go together.
Hey Artie.
Where are we going?
HMM?
I already TOLD you, Owen.

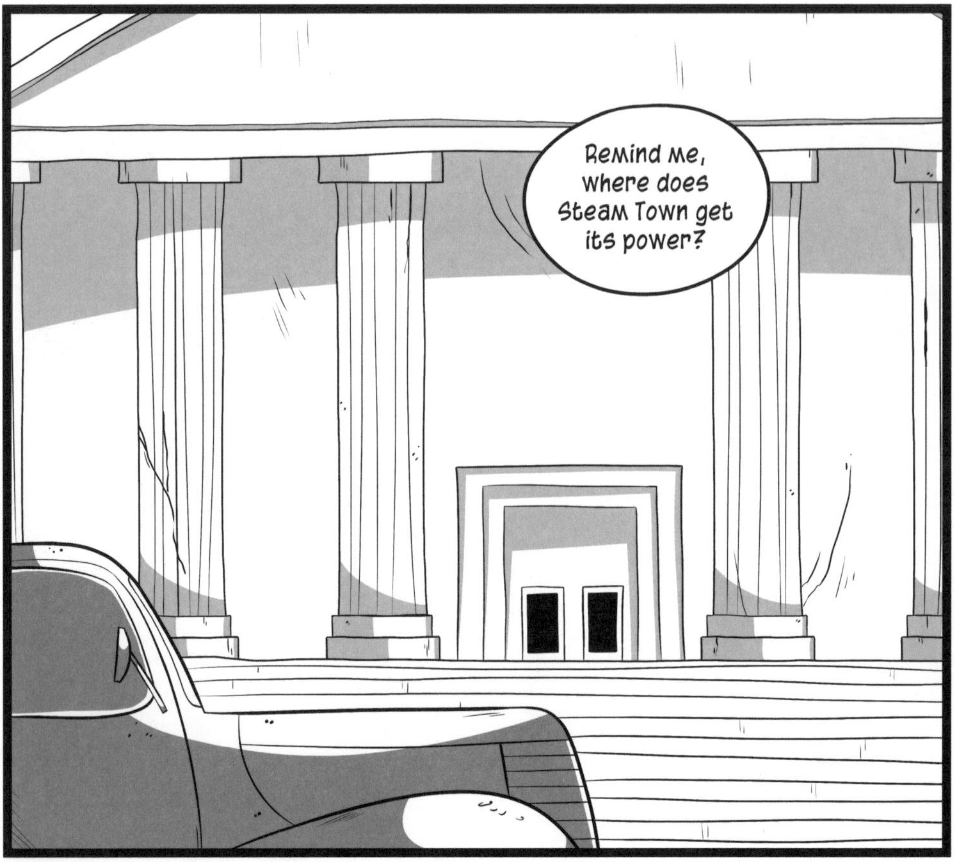
Remind me, where does Steam Town get its power?

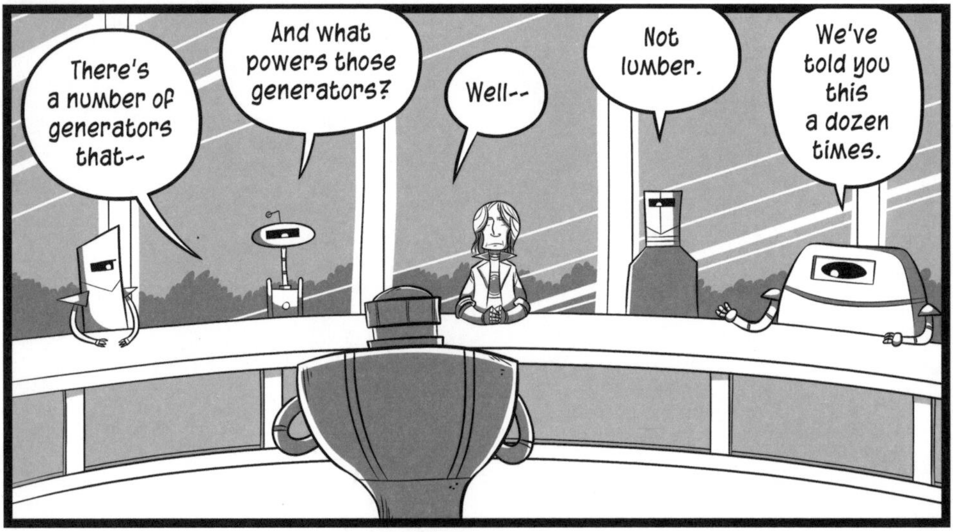
There's a number of generators that--
And what powers those generators?
Well--
Not lumber.
We've told you this a dozen times.

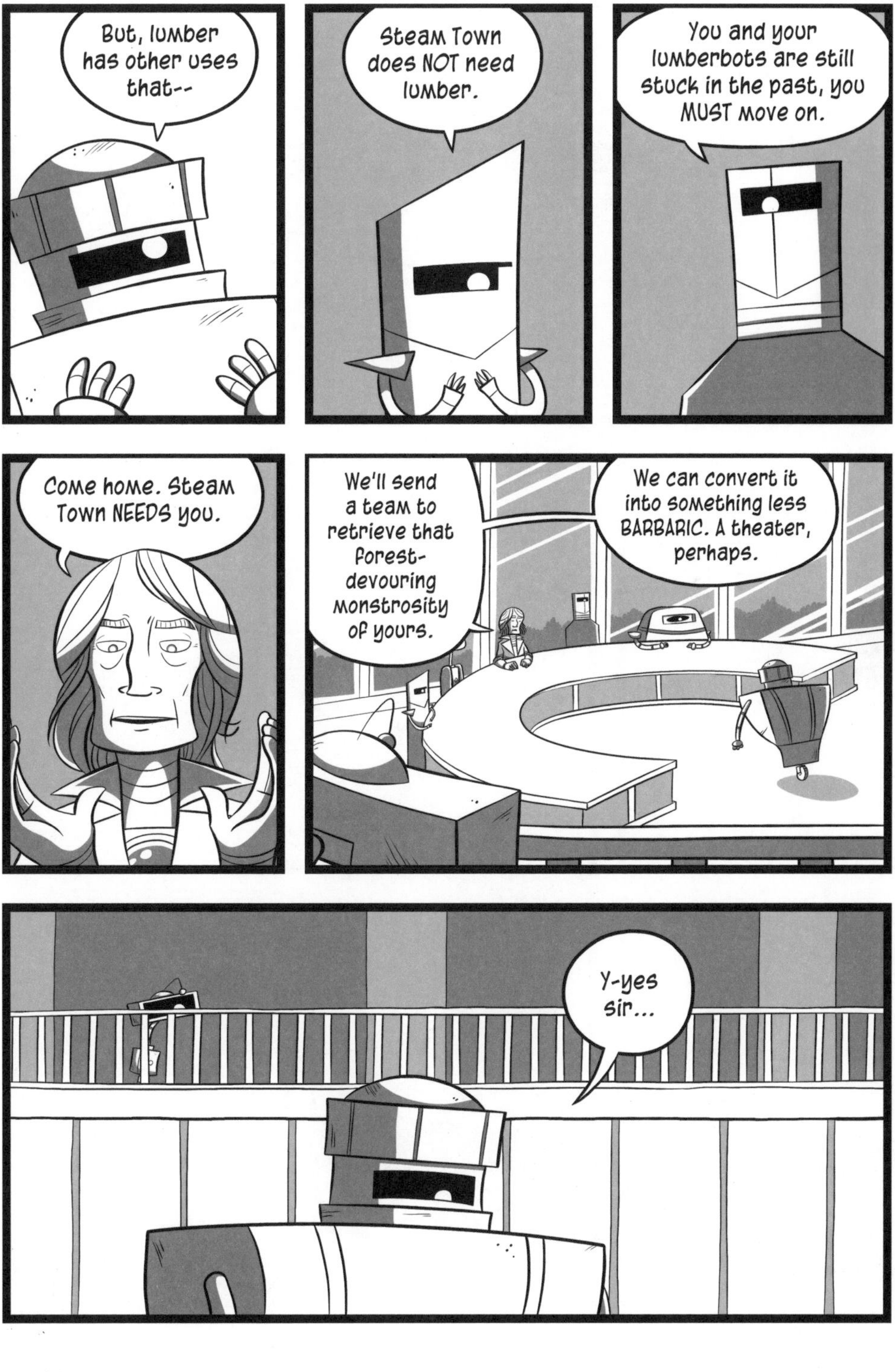
But, lumber has other uses that--
Steam Town does NOT need lumber.
You and your lumberbots are still stuck in the past, you MUST move on.
Come home. Steam Town NEEDS you.
We'll send a team to retrieve that forest-devouring monstrosity of yours.
We can convert it into something less BARBARIC. A theater, perhaps.
Y-yes sir...

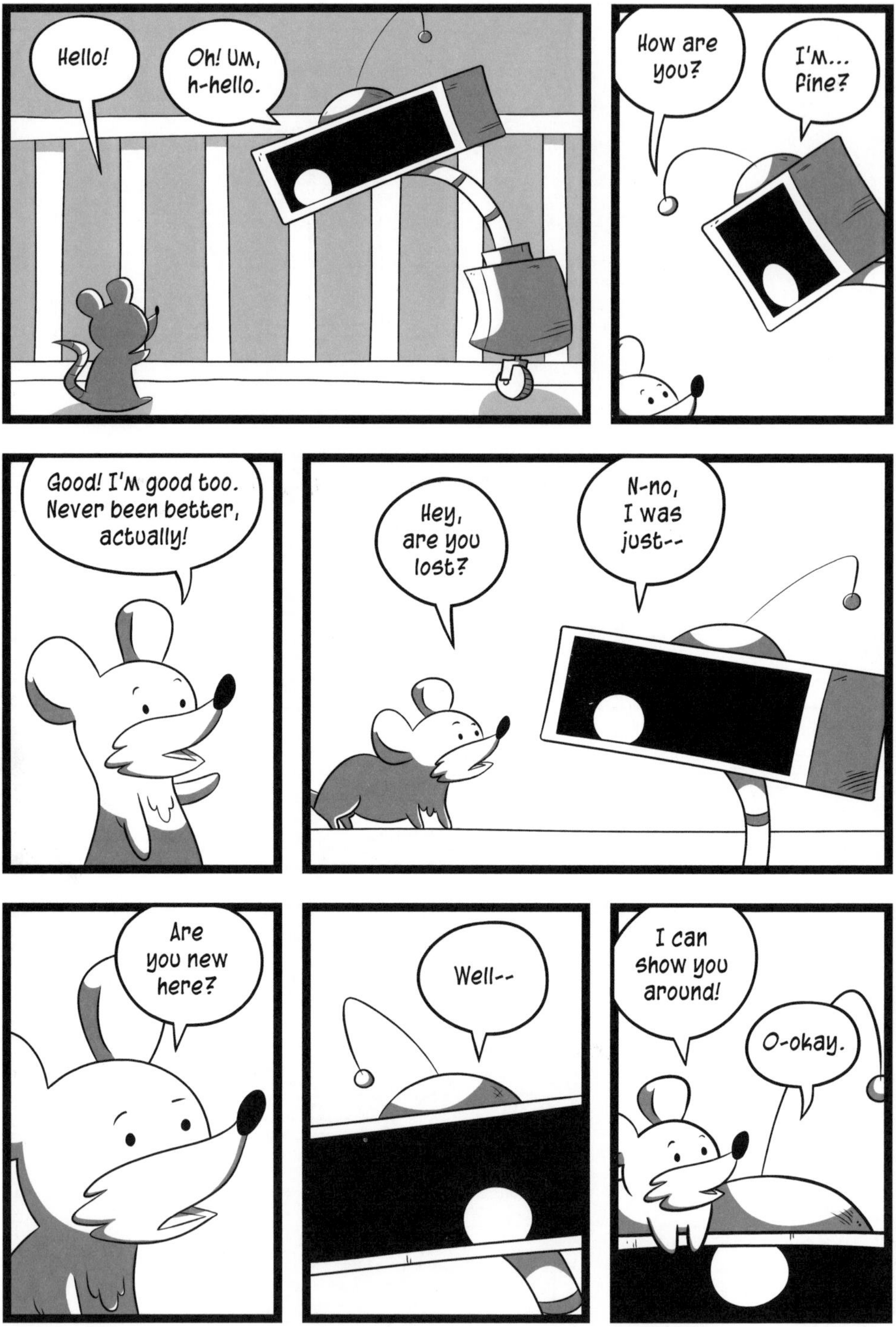
Hello!
Oh! Um, h-hello.
How are you?
I'm... fine?
Good! I'm good too. Never been better, actually!
Hey, are you lost?
N-no, I was just--
Are you new here?
Well--
I can show you around!
O-okay.

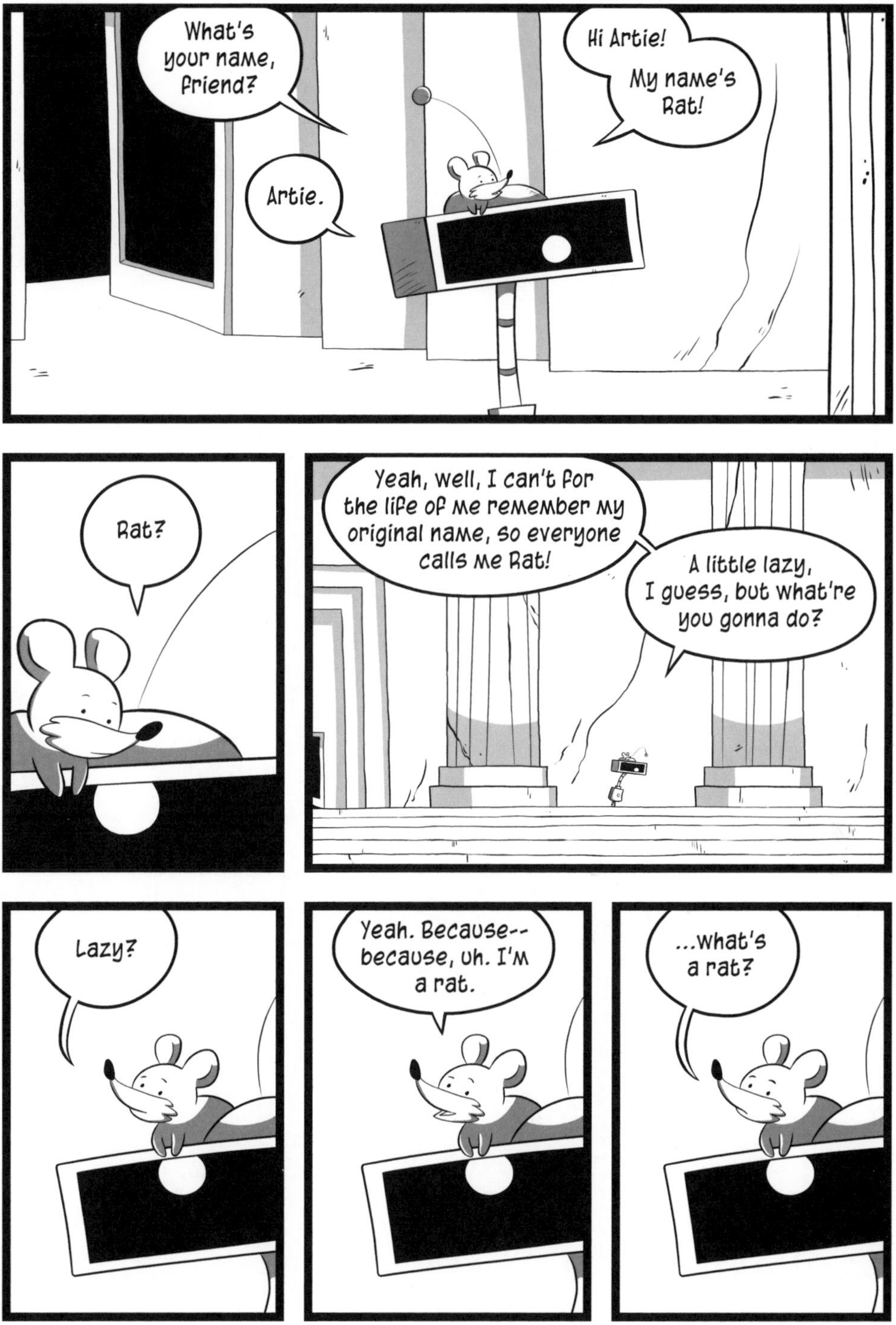
What's your name, friend?
Artie.
Hi Artie!
My name's Rat!
Rat?
Yeah, well, I can't for the life of me remember my original name, so everyone calls me Rat!
A little lazy, I guess, but what're you gonna do?
Lazy?
Yeah. Because-- because, uh. I'm a rat.
...what's a rat?

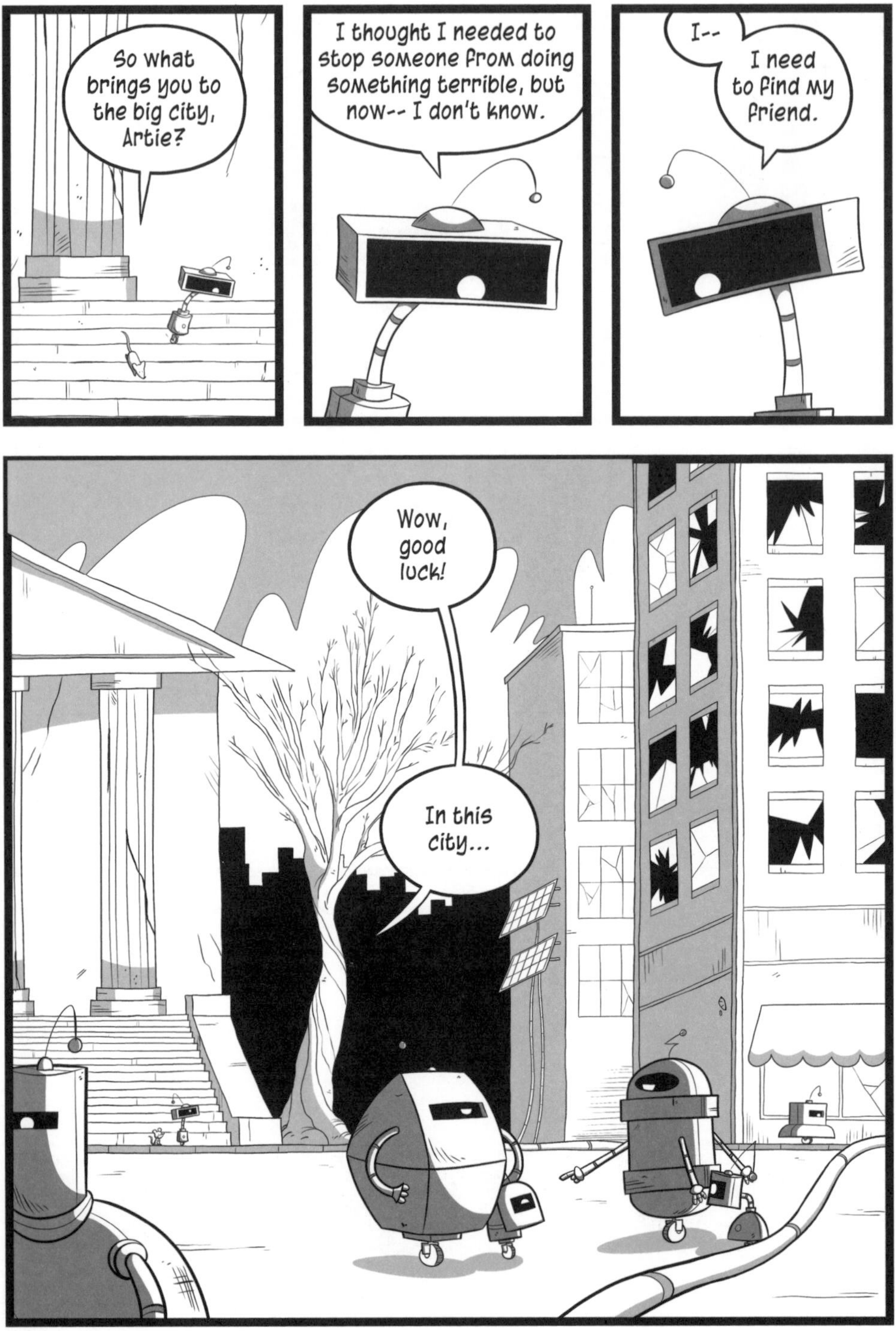
So what brings you to the big city, Artie?
I thought I needed to stop someone from doing something terrible, but now-- I don't know.
I--
I need to find my friend.
Wow, good luck!
In this city...

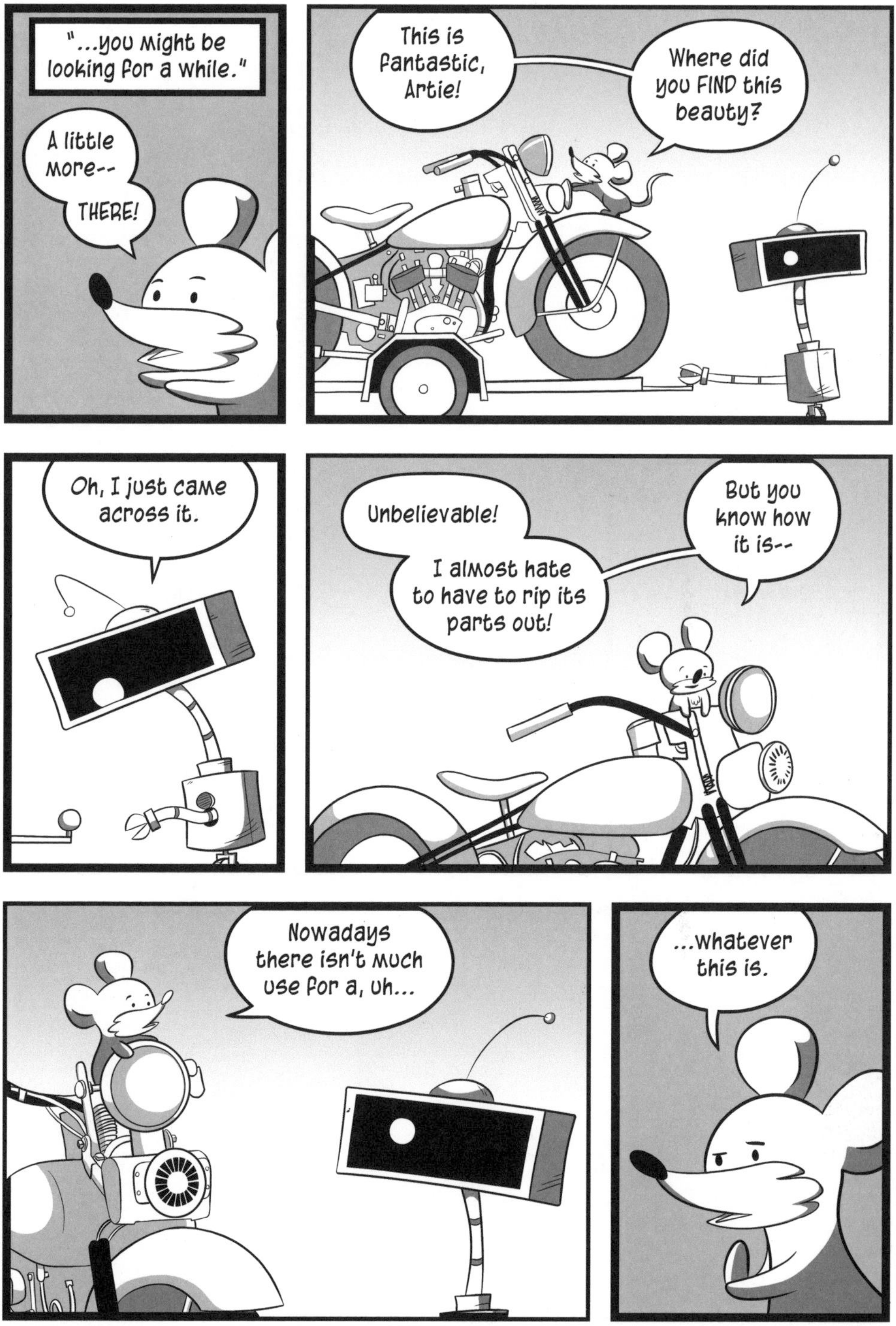
"...you might be looking for a while."
A little more--
THERE!
This is fantastic, Artie!
Where did you FIND this beauty?
Oh, I just came across it.
Unbelievable!
I almost hate to have to rip its parts out!
But you know how it is--
Nowadays there isn't much use for a, uh...
...whatever this is.

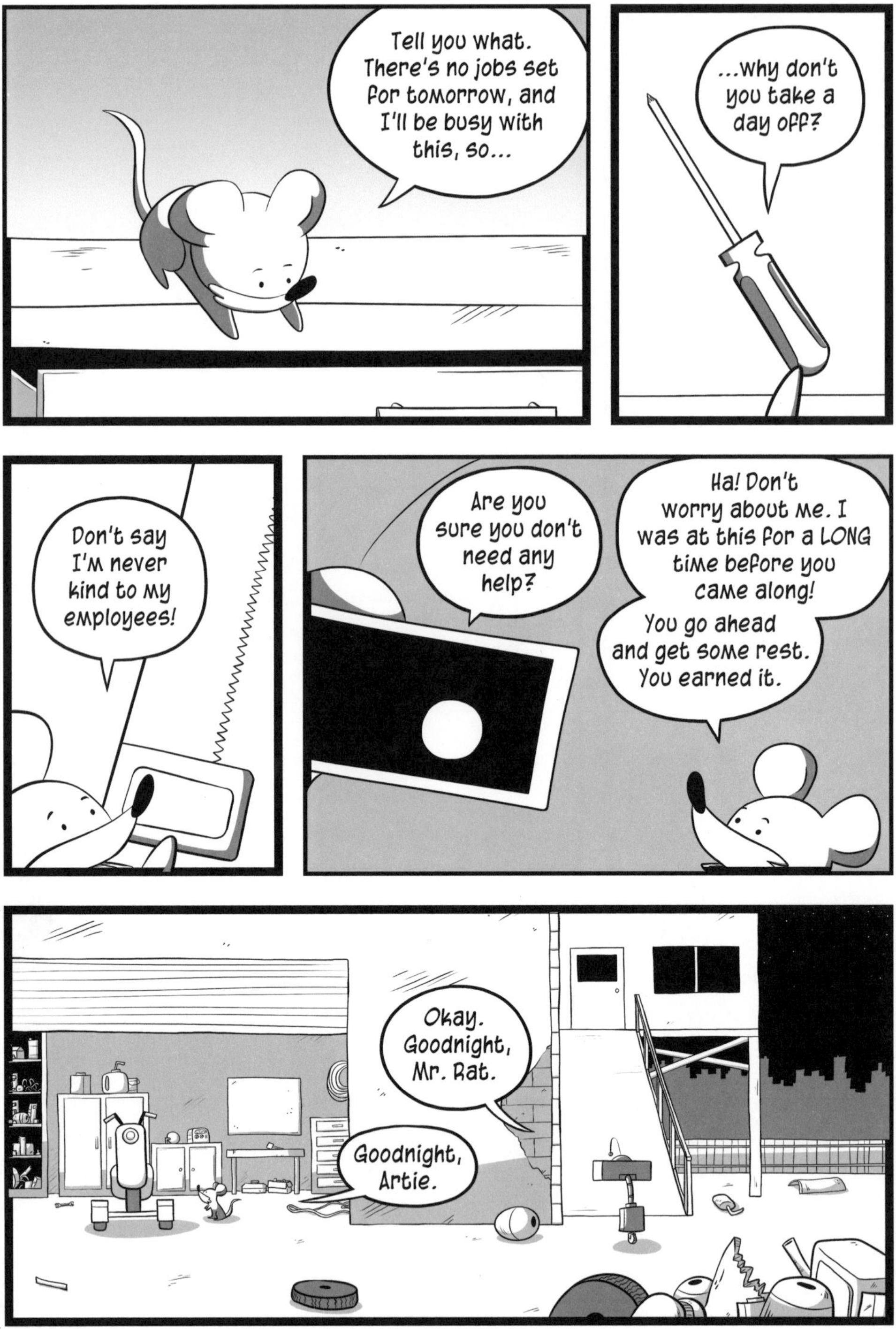
Tell you what. There's no jobs set for tomorrow, and I'll be busy with this, so...
...why don't you take a day off?
Don't say I'm never kind to my employees!
Are you sure you don't need any help?
Ha! Don't worry about me. I was at this for a LONG time before you came along!
You go ahead and get some rest. You earned it.
Okay. Goodnight, Mr. Rat.
Goodnight, Artie.

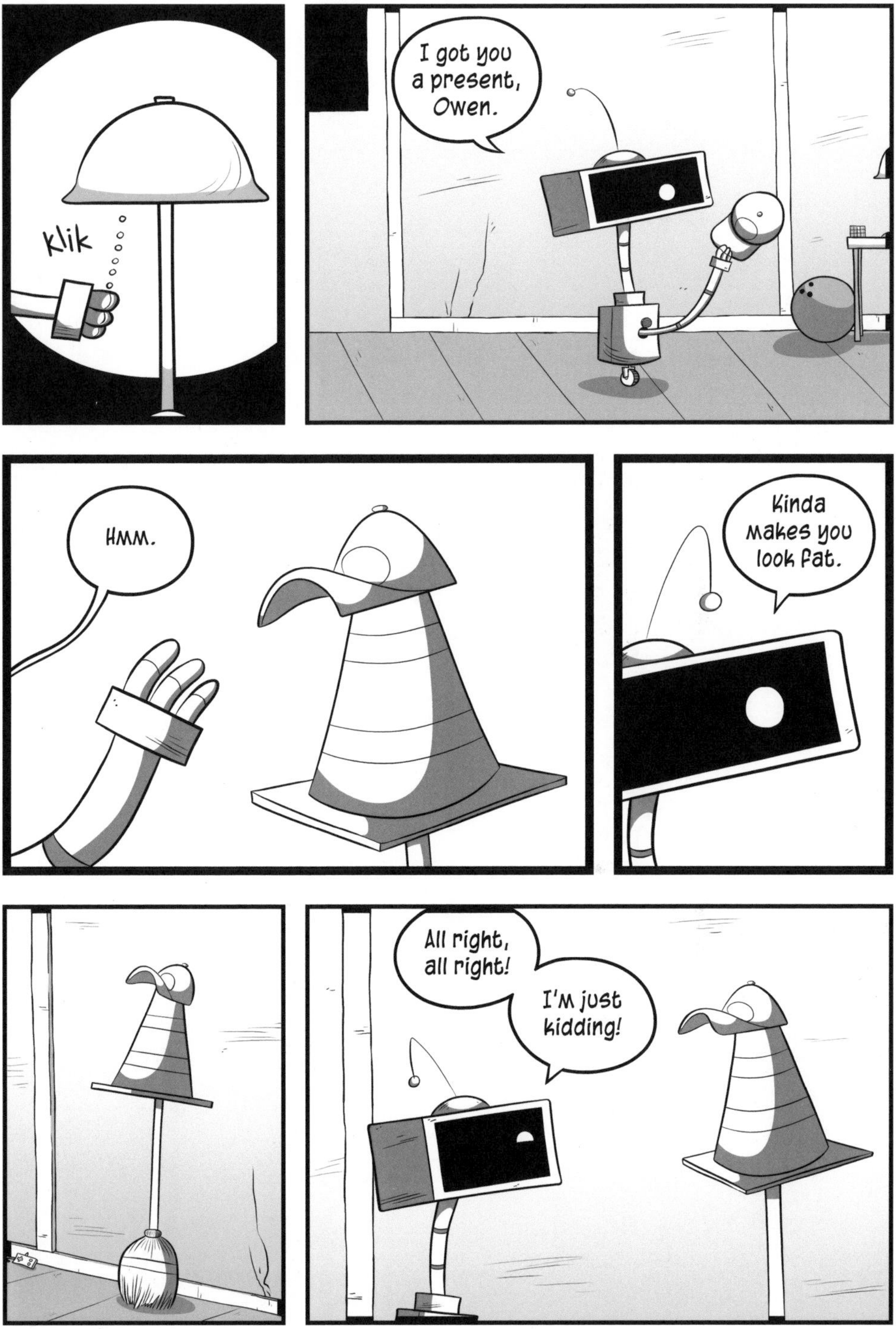
klik
I got you a present, Owen.
HMM.
Kinda makes you look fat.
All right, all right!
I'M just kidding!

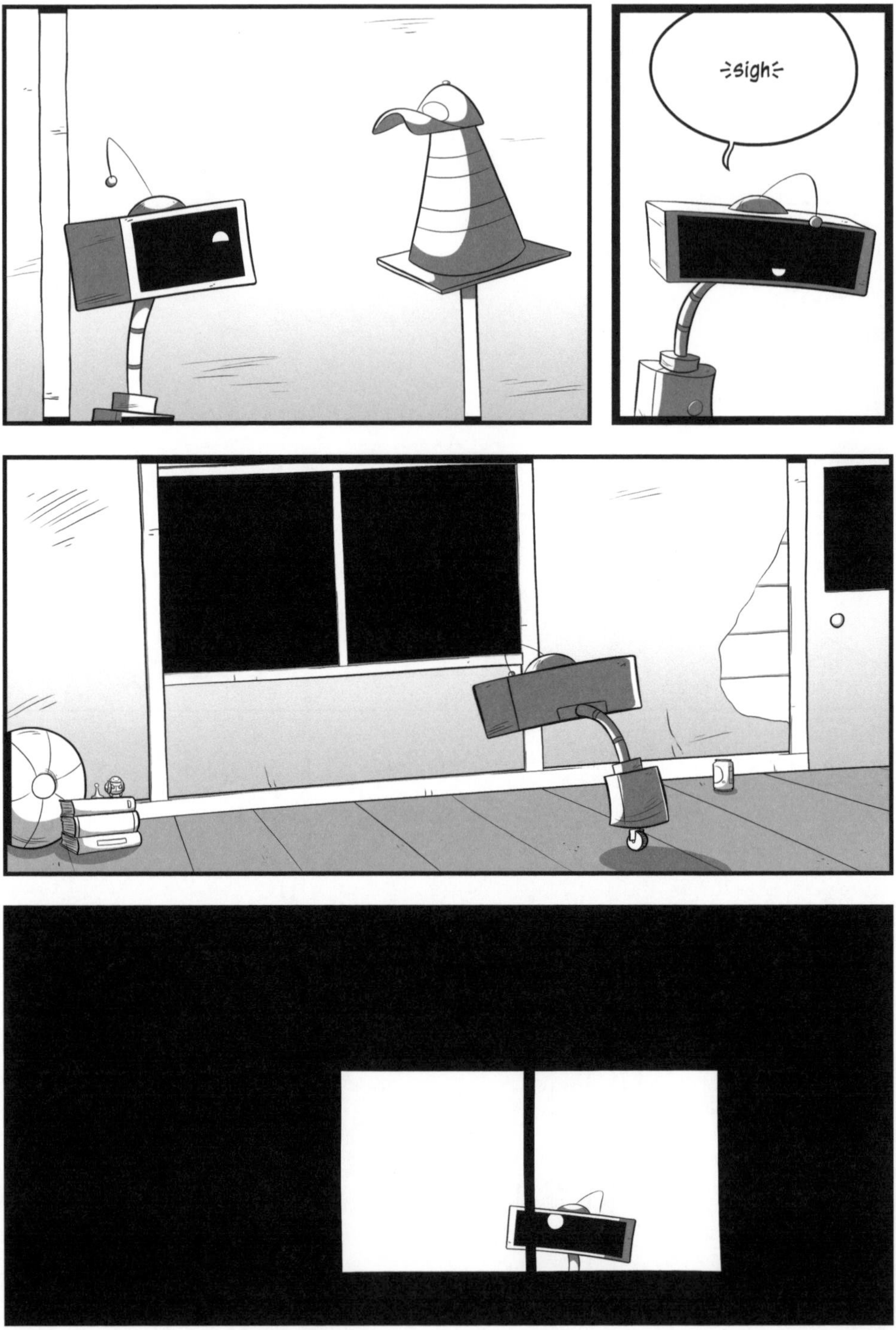
sigh

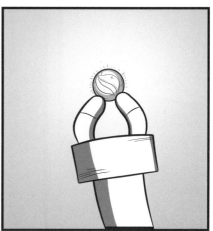

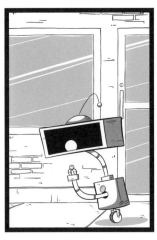

Owen?

Owen!

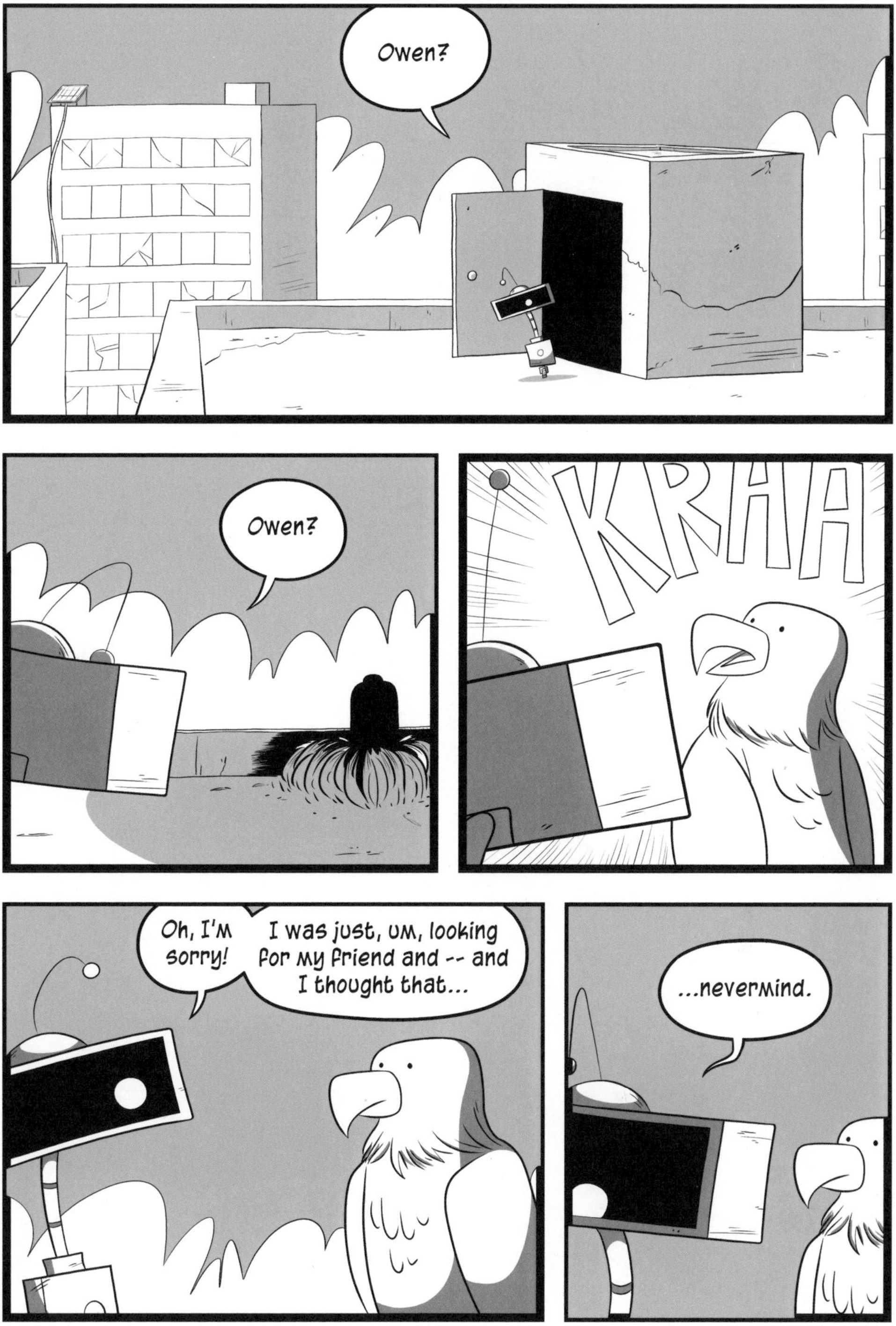
Owen?
Owen?
KRAA
Oh, I'm sorry!
I was just, um, looking for my friend and -- and I thought that...
...nevermind.

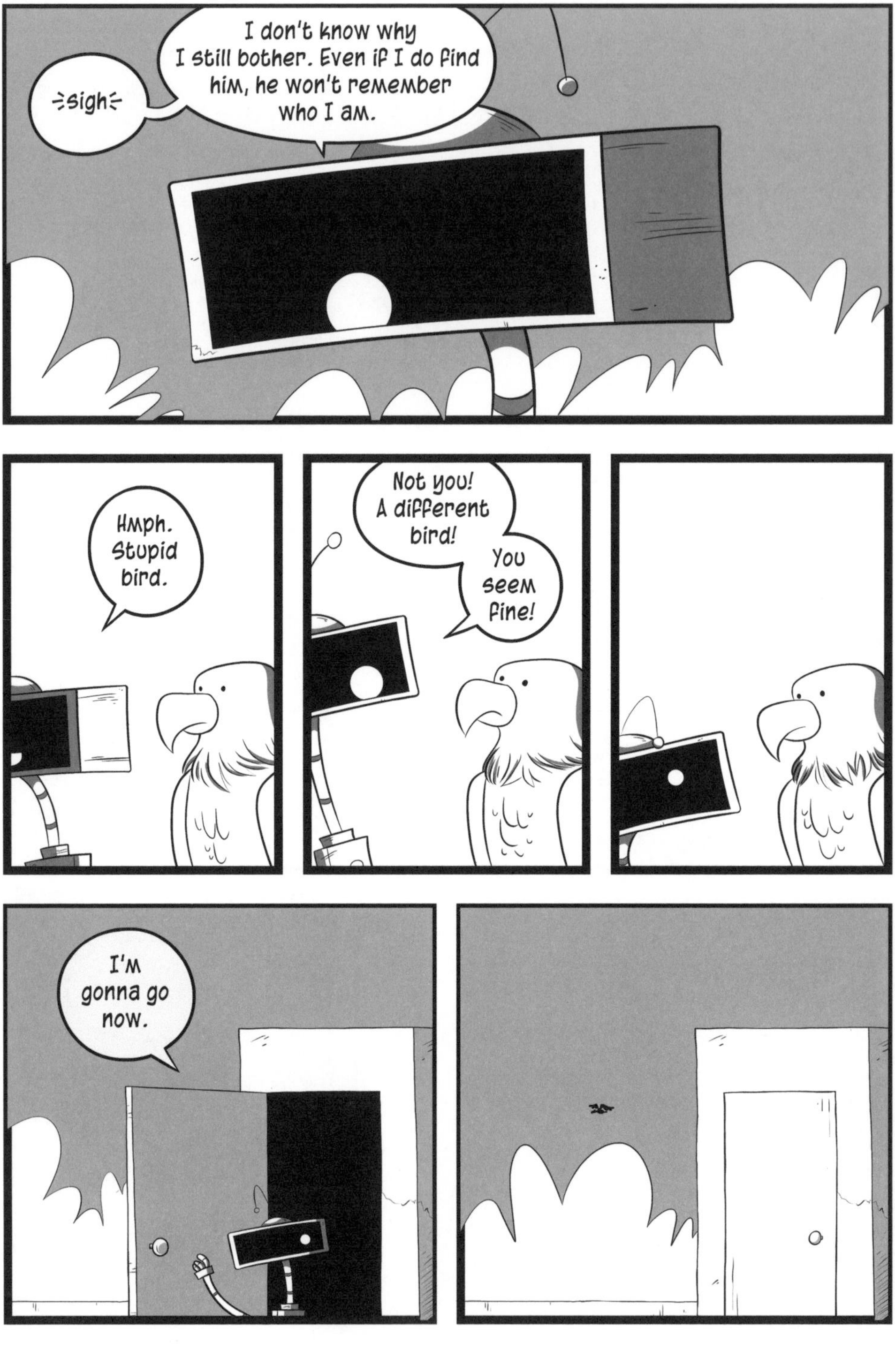

≈sigh≈
I don't know why I still bother. Even if I do find him, he won't remember who I am.
Hmph. Stupid bird.
Not you! A different bird!
You seem fine!
I'm gonna go now.

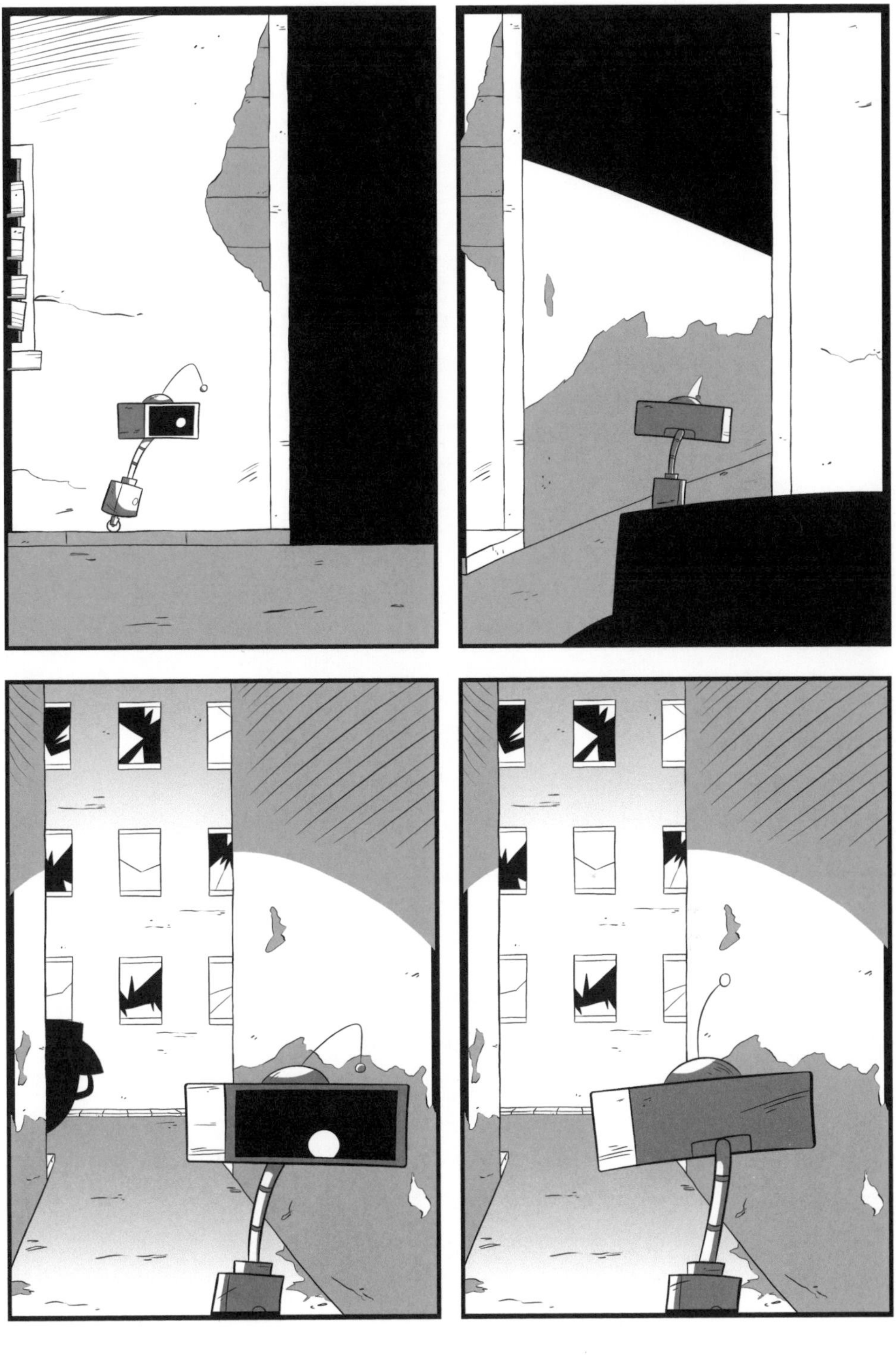

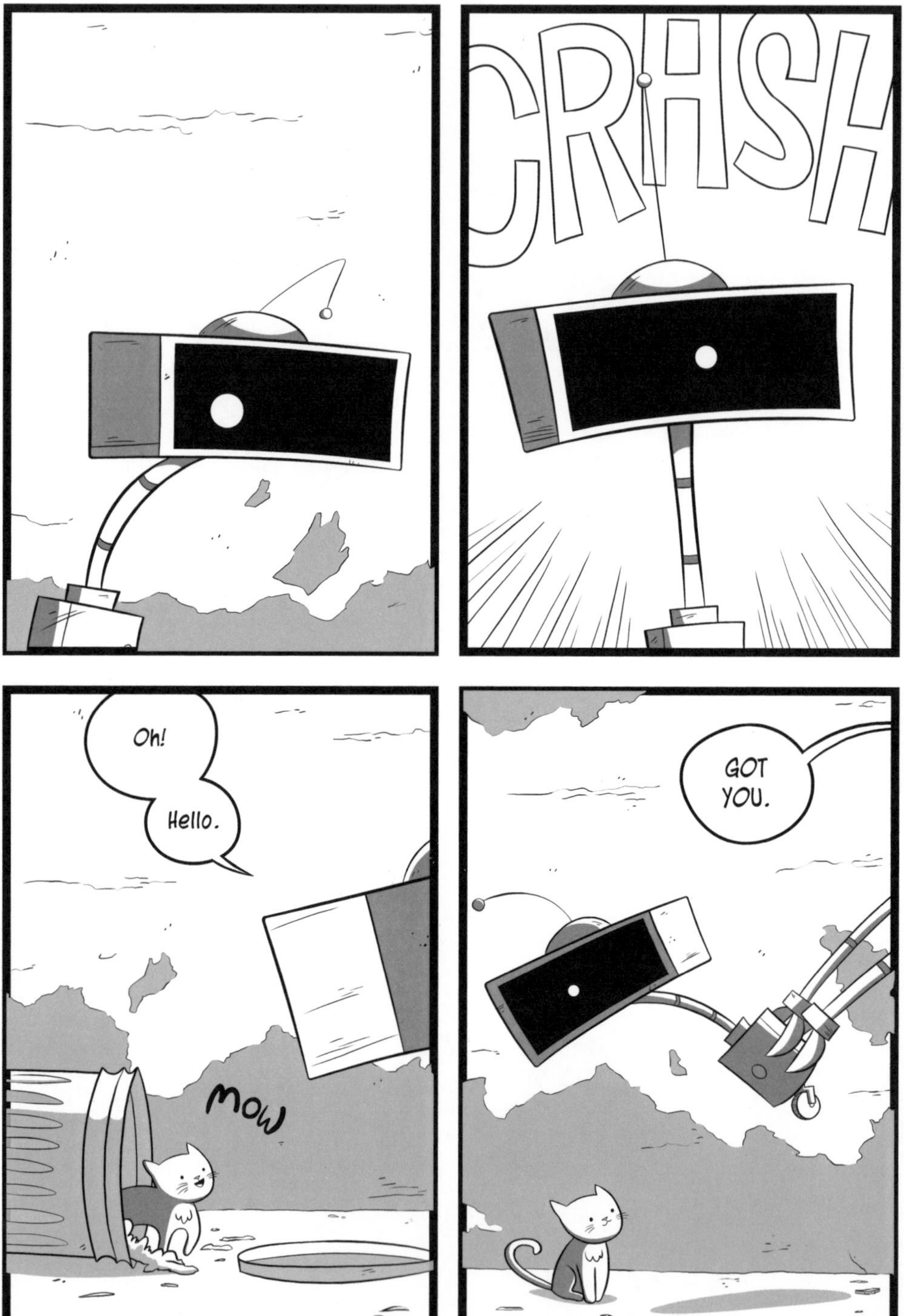
CRASH
Oh!
Hello.
MOW
GOT YOU.

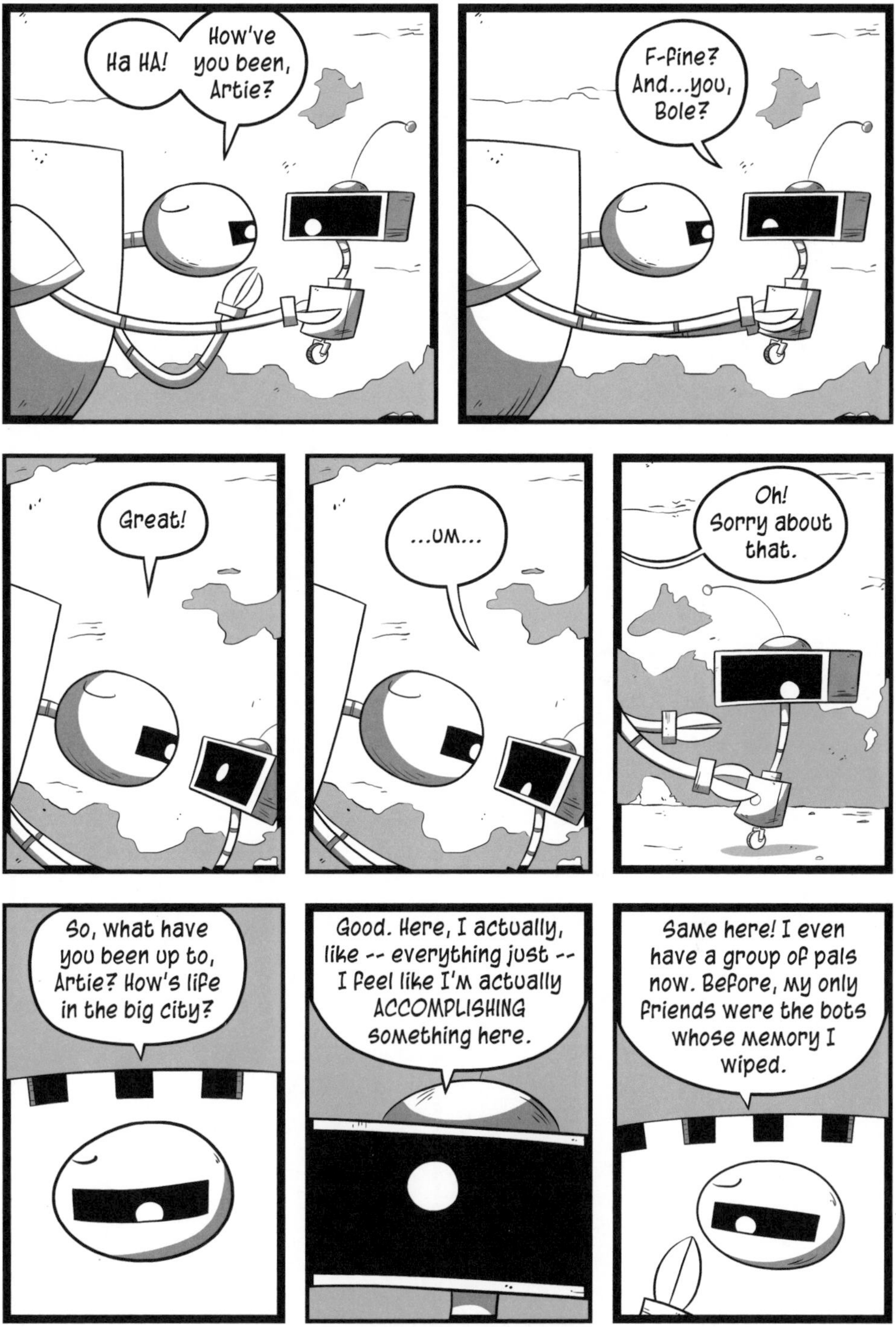
Ha HA!
How've you been, Artie?
F-fine? And...you, Bole?
Great!
...UM...
Oh! Sorry about that.
So, what have you been up to, Artie? How's life in the big city?
Good. Here, I actually, like -- everything just -- I feel like I'm actually ACCOMPLISHING something here.
Same here! I even have a group of pals now. Before, my only friends were the bots whose memory I wiped.

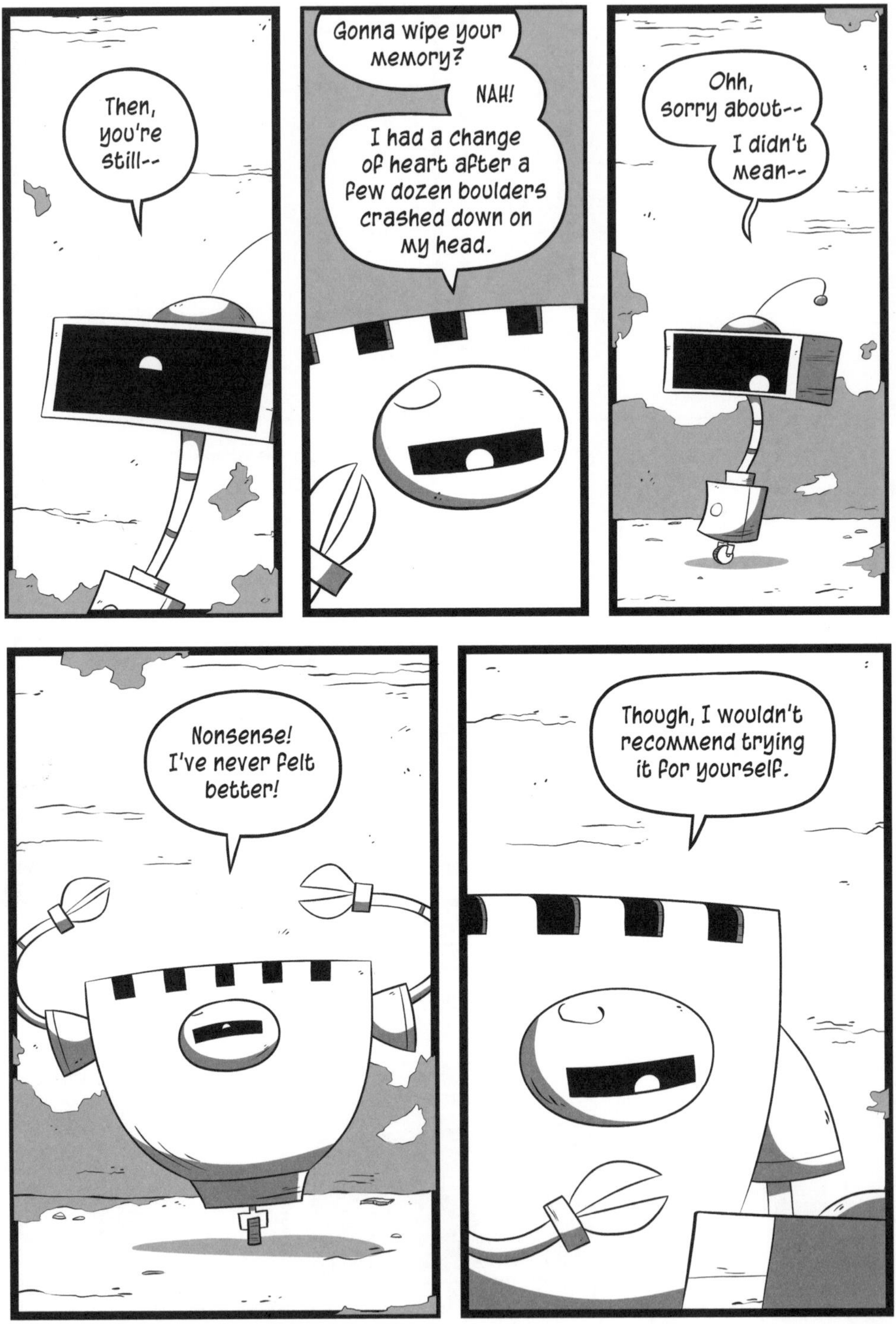
Then, you're still--
Gonna wipe your memory?
NAH!
I had a change of heart after a few dozen boulders crashed down on my head.
Ohh, sorry about--
I didn't mean--
Nonsense! I've never felt better!
Though, I wouldn't recommend trying it for yourself.

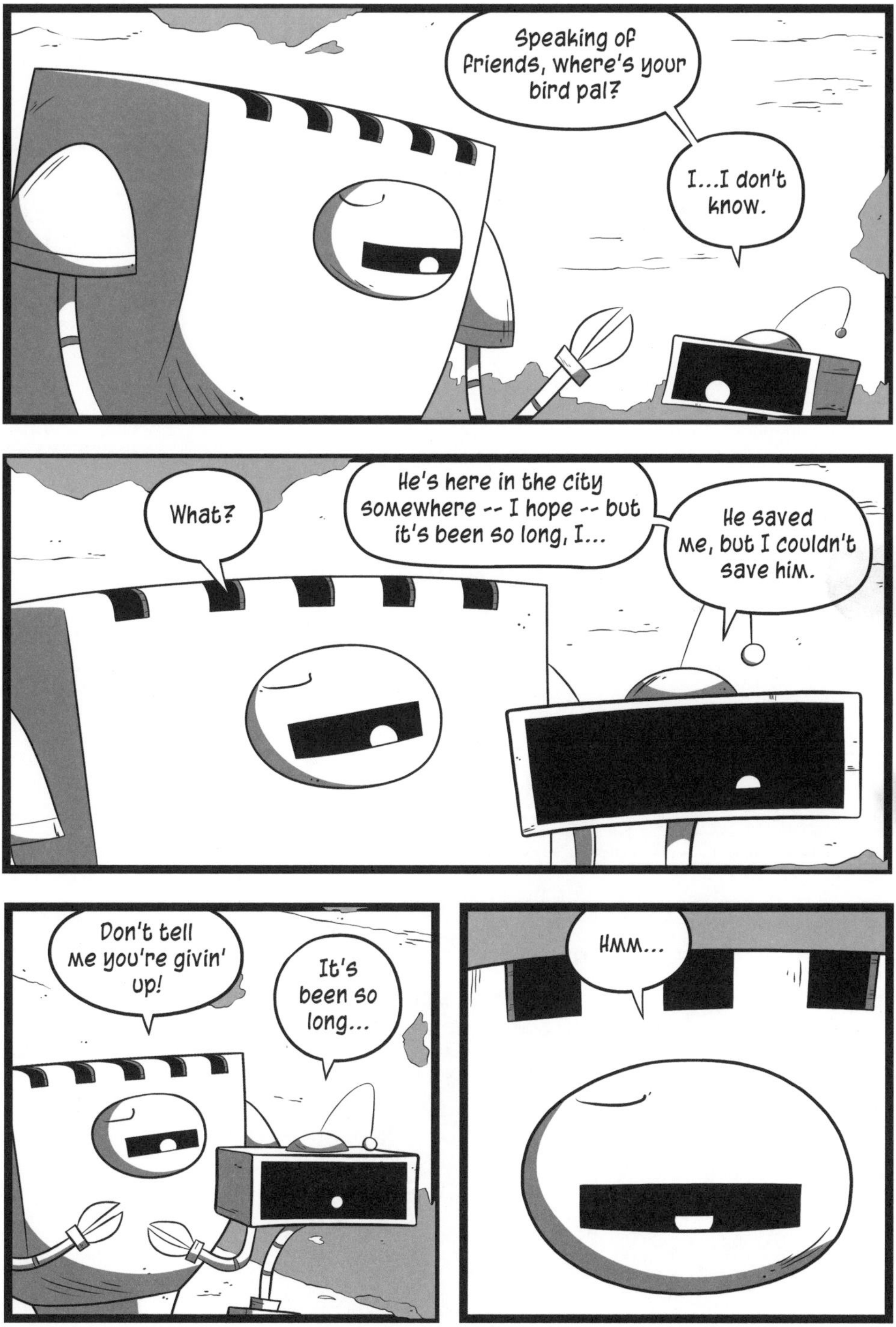
Speaking of friends, where's your bird pal?
I...I don't know.
What?
He's here in the city somewhere -- I hope -- but it's been so long, I...
He saved me, but I couldn't save him.
Don't tell me you're givin' up!
It's been so long...
HMM...

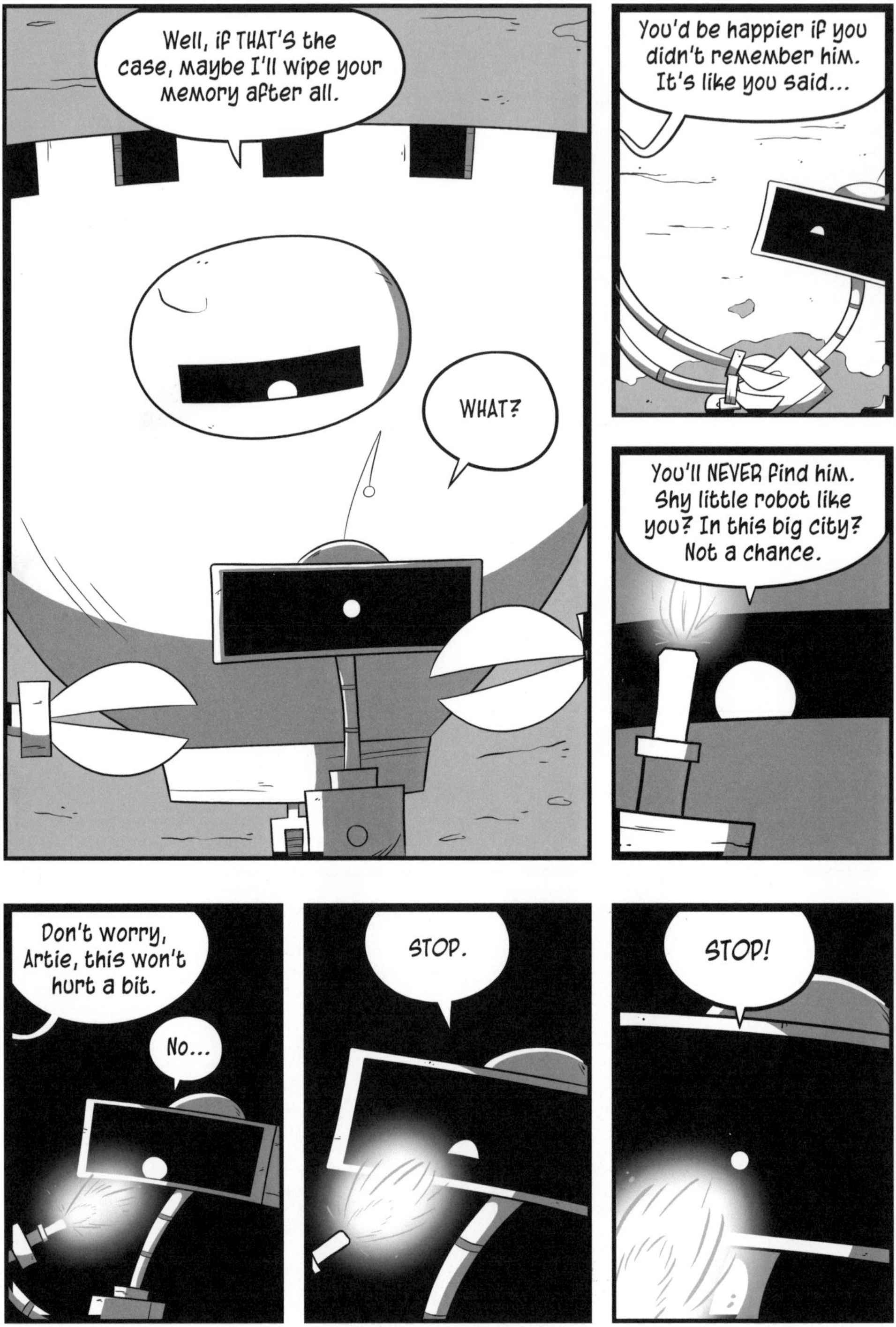
Well, if THAT'S the case, maybe I'll wipe your memory after all.
WHAT?
You'd be happier if you didn't remember him. It's like you said...
You'll NEVER find him. Shy little robot like you? In this big city? Not a chance.
Don't worry, Artie, this won't hurt a bit.
No...
STOP.
STOP!

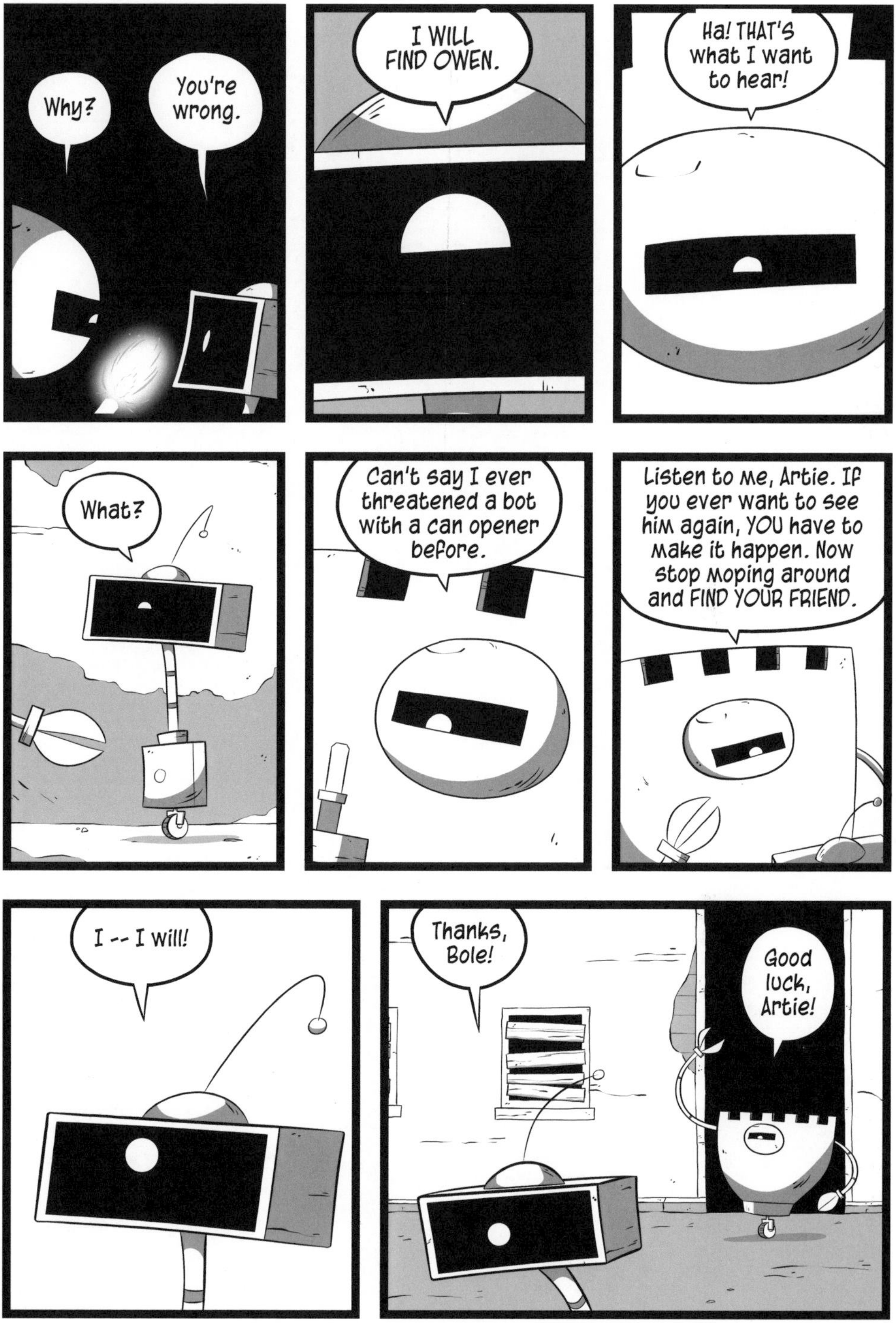
Why?
You're wrong.
I WILL FIND OWEN.
Ha! THAT'S what I want to hear!
What?
Can't say I ever threatened a bot with a can opener before.
Listen to me, Artie. If you ever want to see him again, YOU have to make it happen. Now stop moping around and FIND YOUR FRIEND.
I -- I will!
Thanks, Bole!
Good luck, Artie!

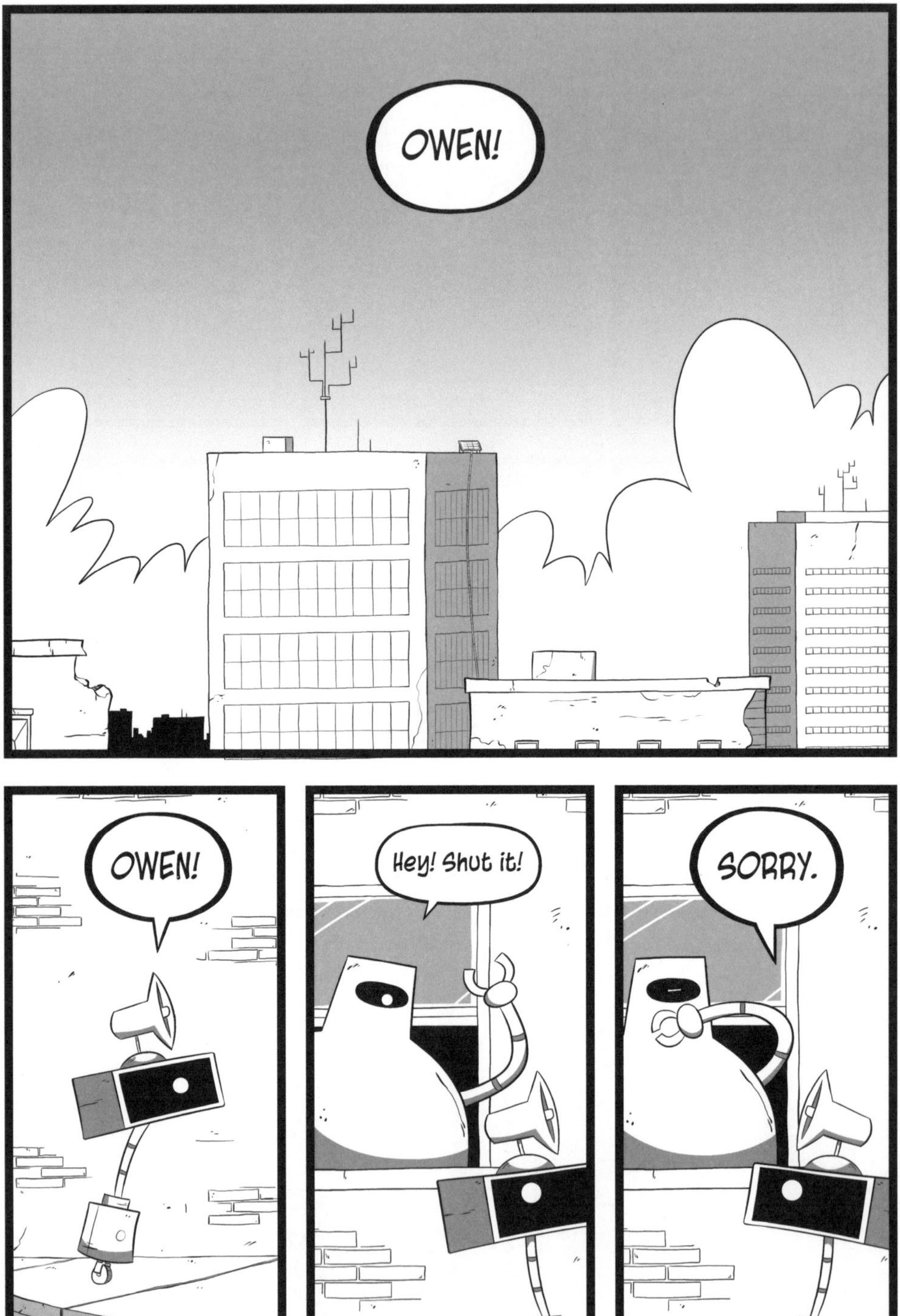
OWEN!
OWEN!
Hey! Shut it!
SORRY.

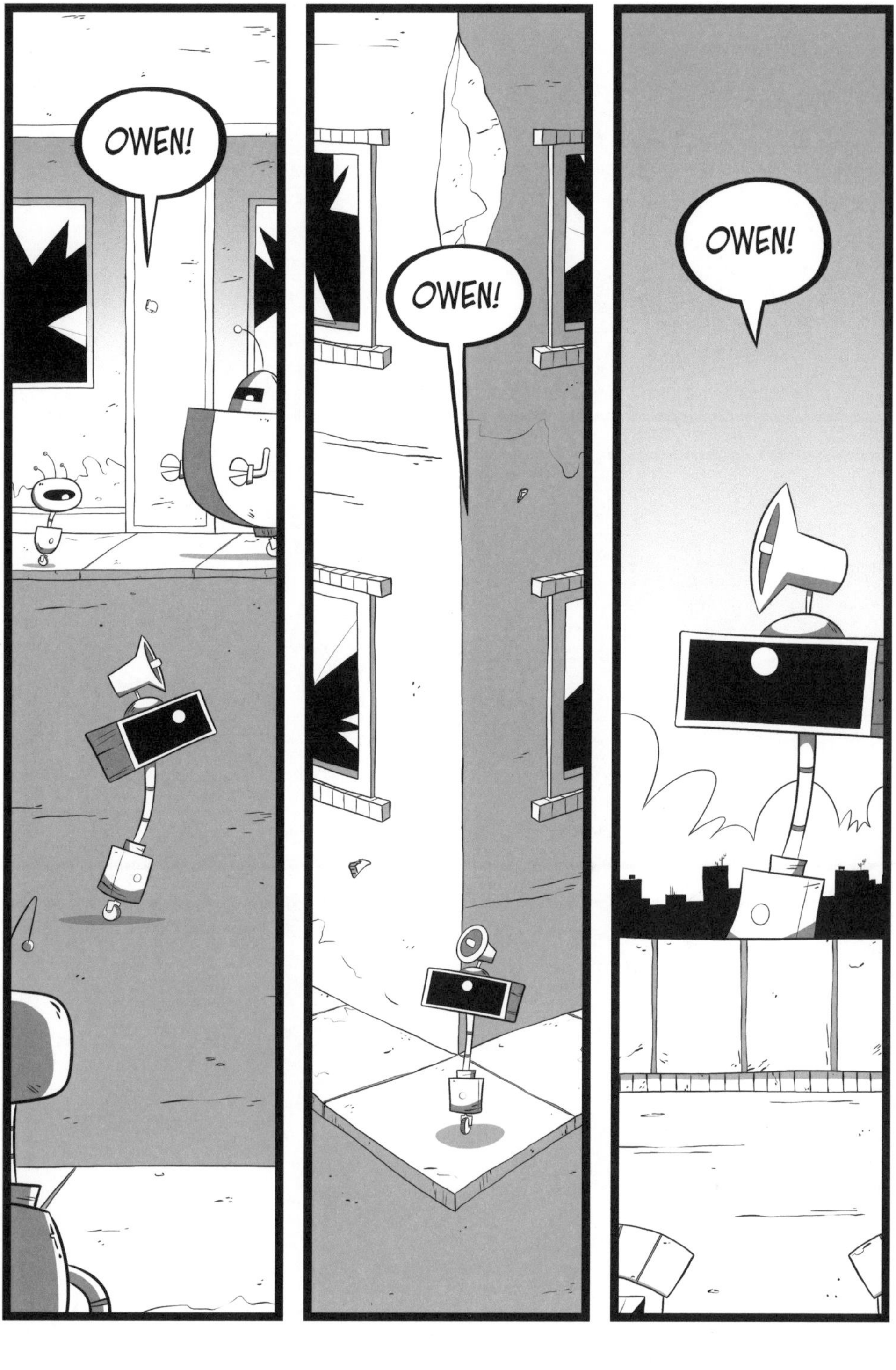
OWEN!
OWEN!
OWEN!

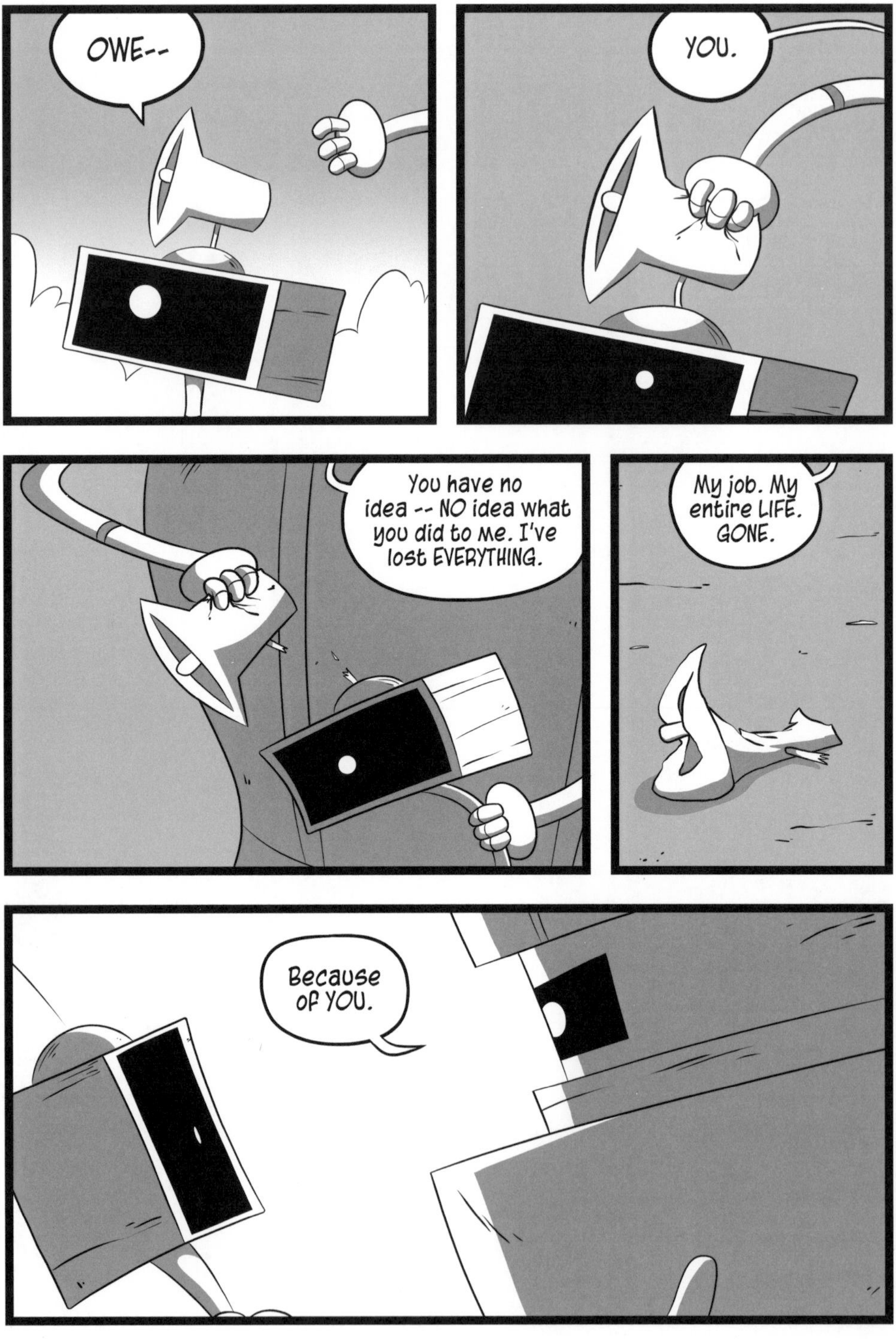
OWE--
YOU.
You have no idea -- NO idea what you did to me. I've lost EVERYTHING.
My job. My entire LIFE. GONE.
Because of YOU.

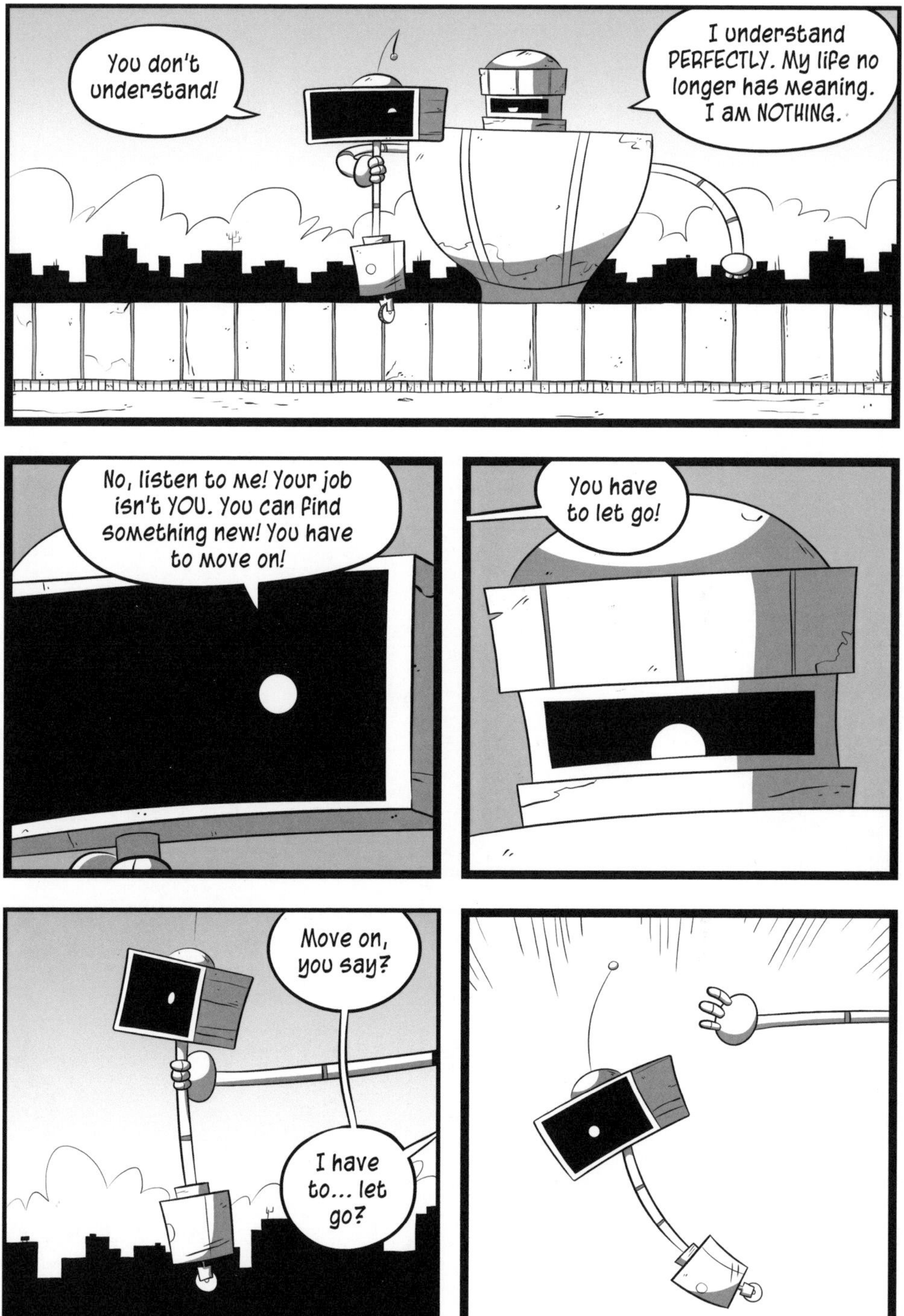
You don't understand!
I understand PERFECTLY. My life no longer has meaning. I AM NOTHING.
No, listen to me! Your job isn't YOU. You can find something new! You have to move on!
You have to let go!
Move on, you say?
I have to... let go?

What are you doing jumping off buildings?

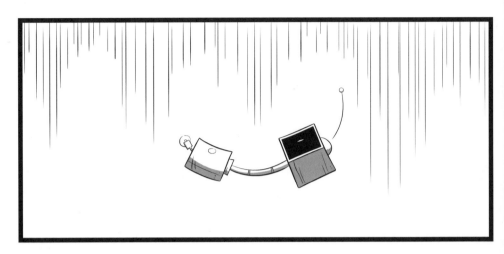

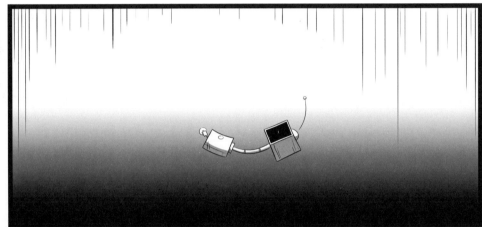

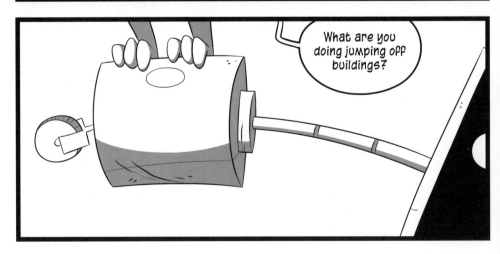

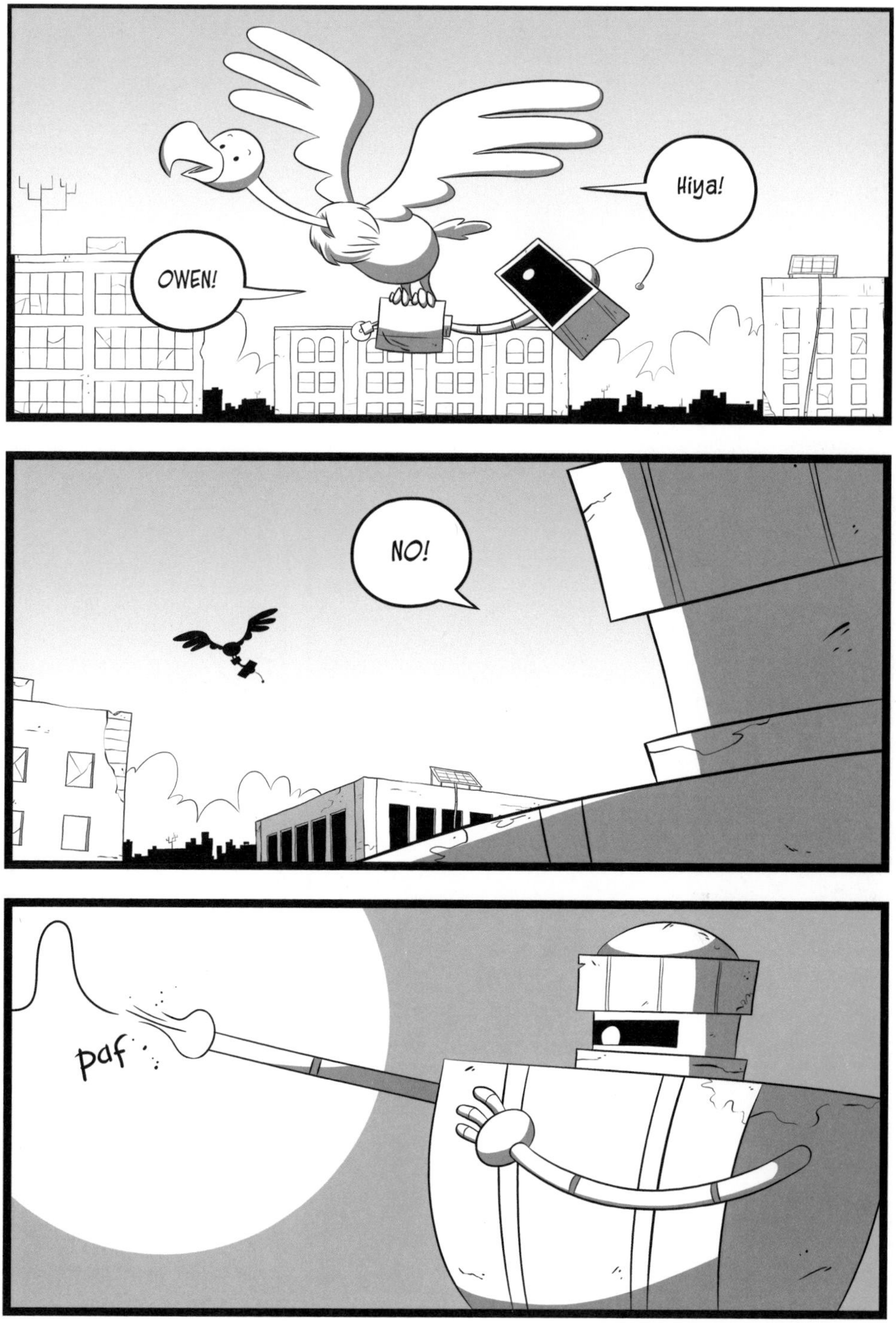
OWEN!
Hiya!
NO!
paf

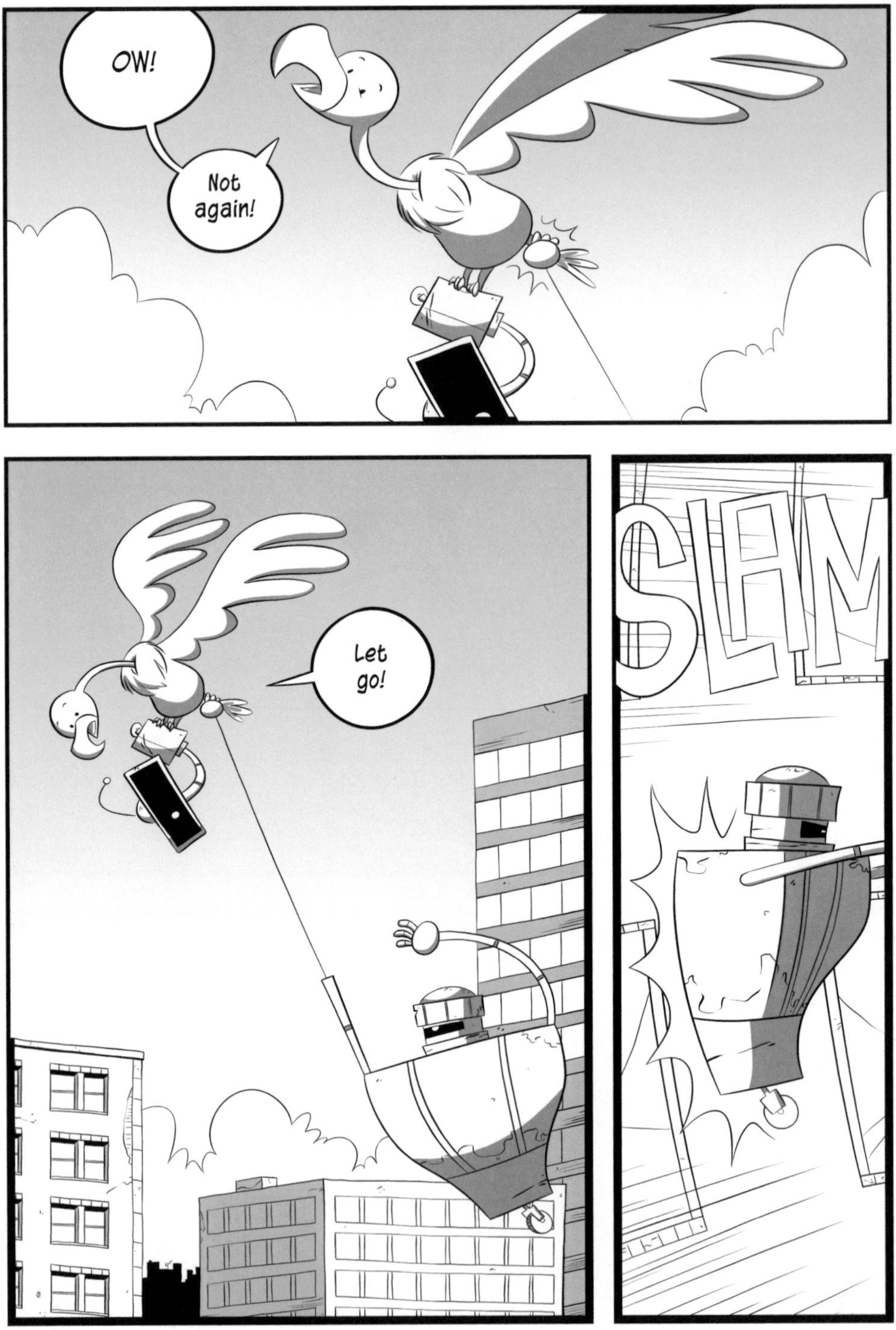
OW!
Not again!
Let go!
SLAM

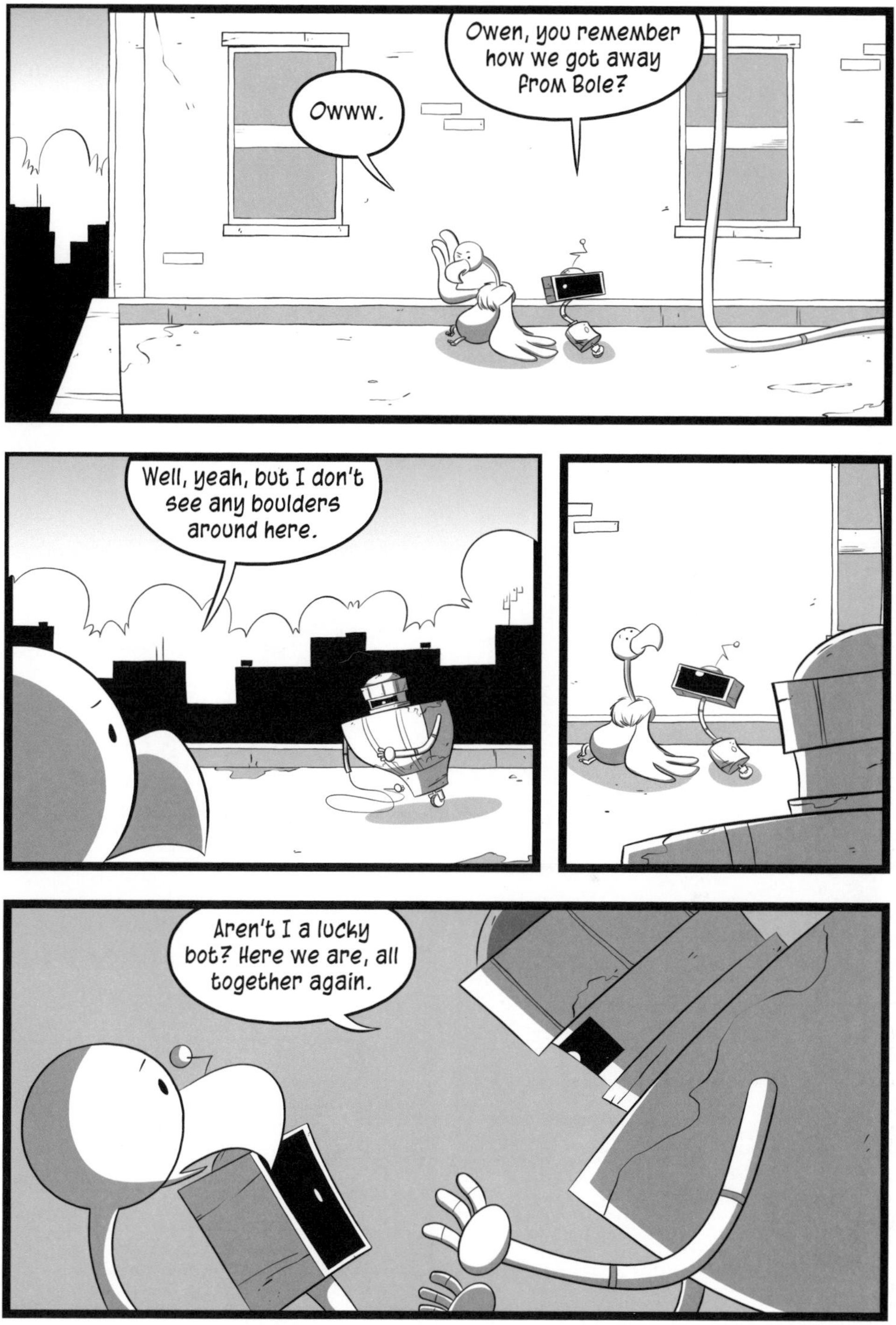
Owww.
Owen, you remember how we got away from Bole?
Well, yeah, but I don't see any boulders around here.
Aren't I a lucky bot? Here we are, all together again.

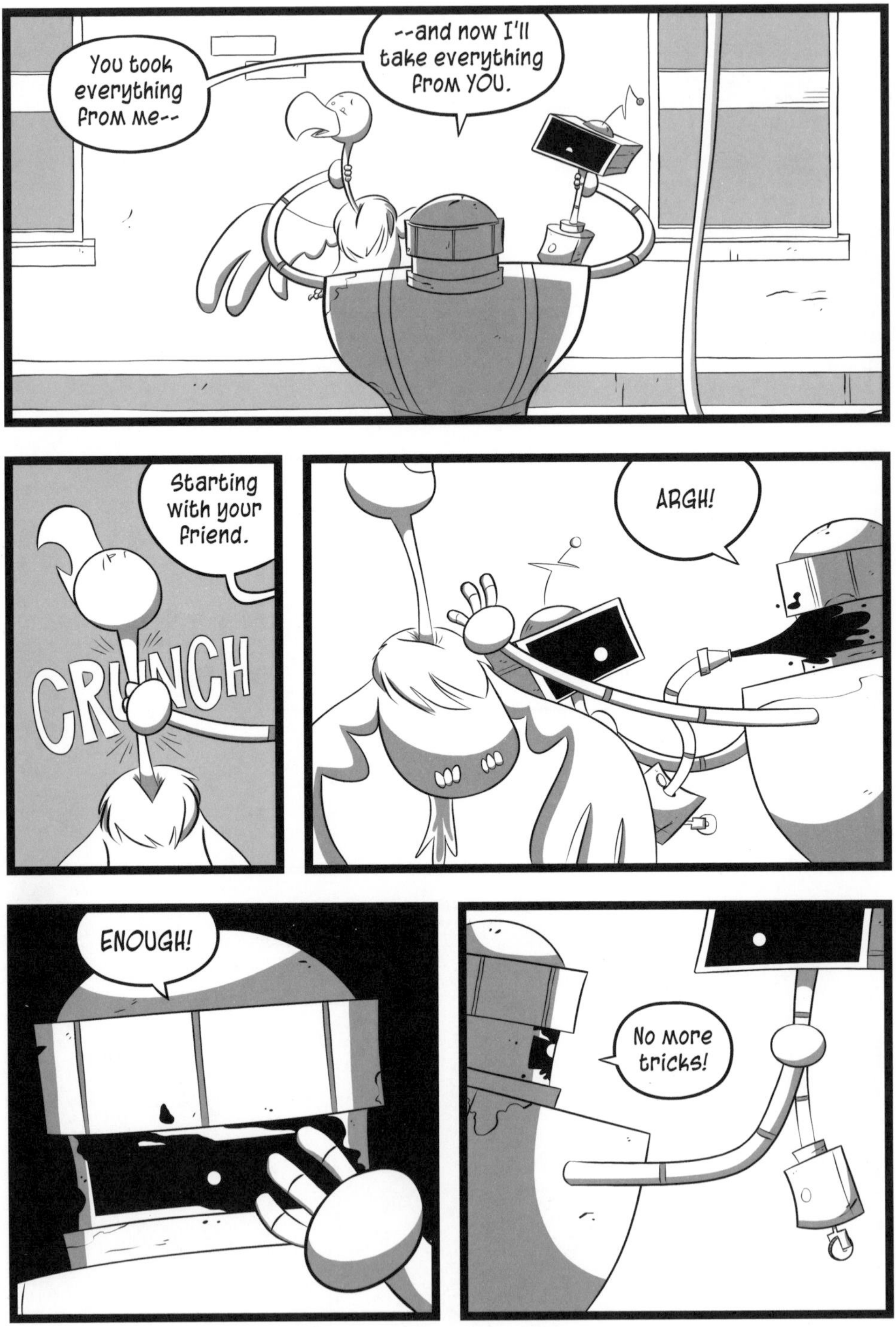
You took everything from me--
--and now I'll take everything from YOU.
Starting with your friend.
CRUNCH
ARGH!
ENOUGH!
No more tricks!

HOLD.
STILL.
NOW!

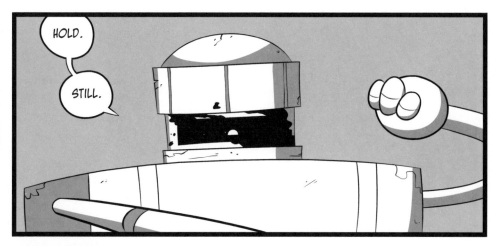

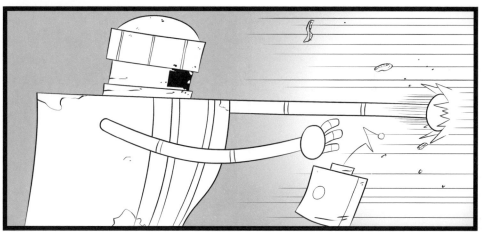

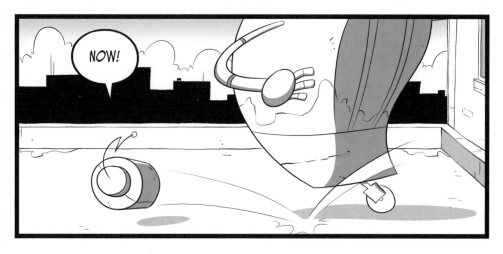

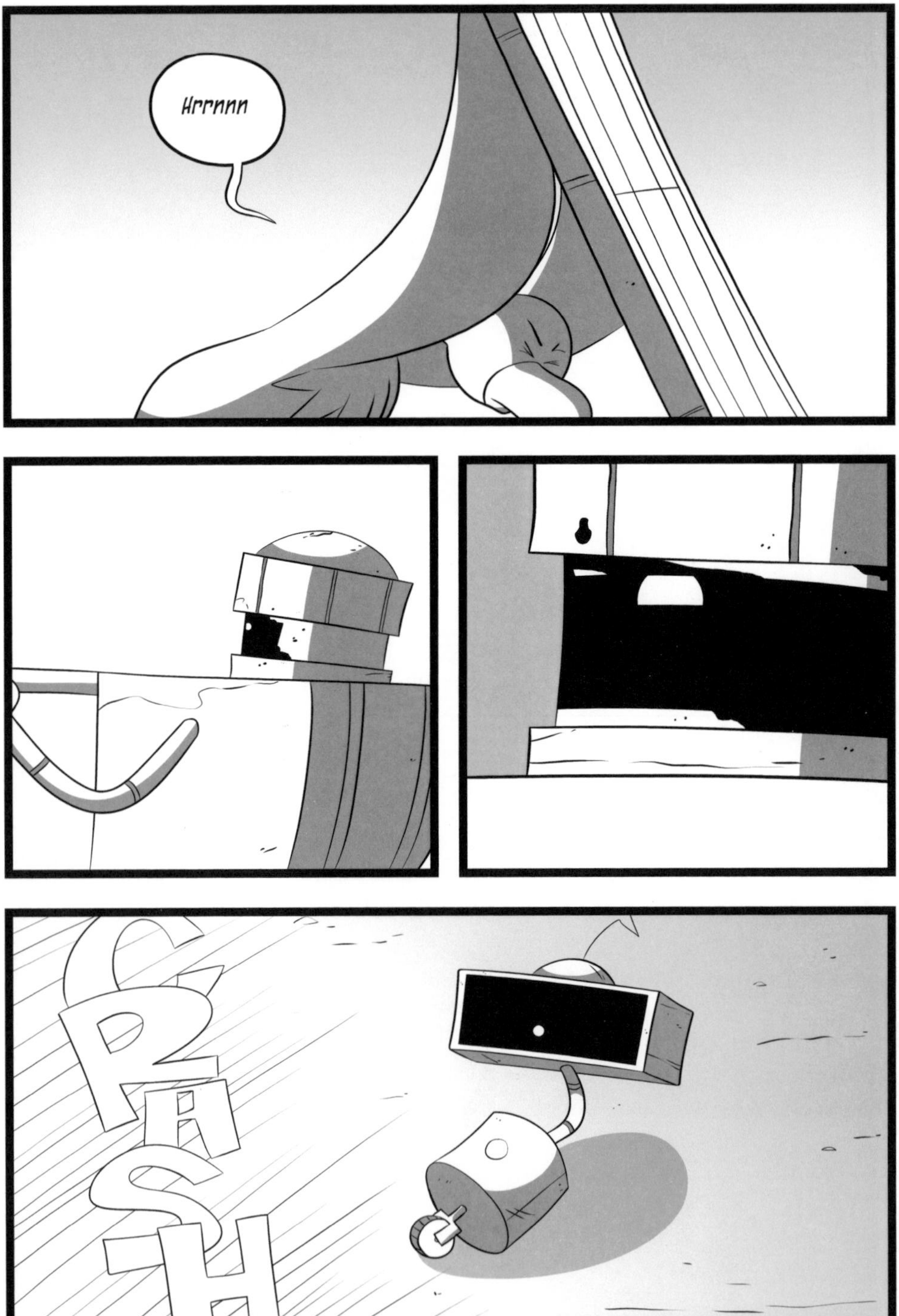
Hrrnnn
CRASH

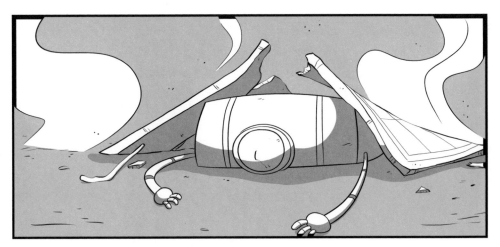

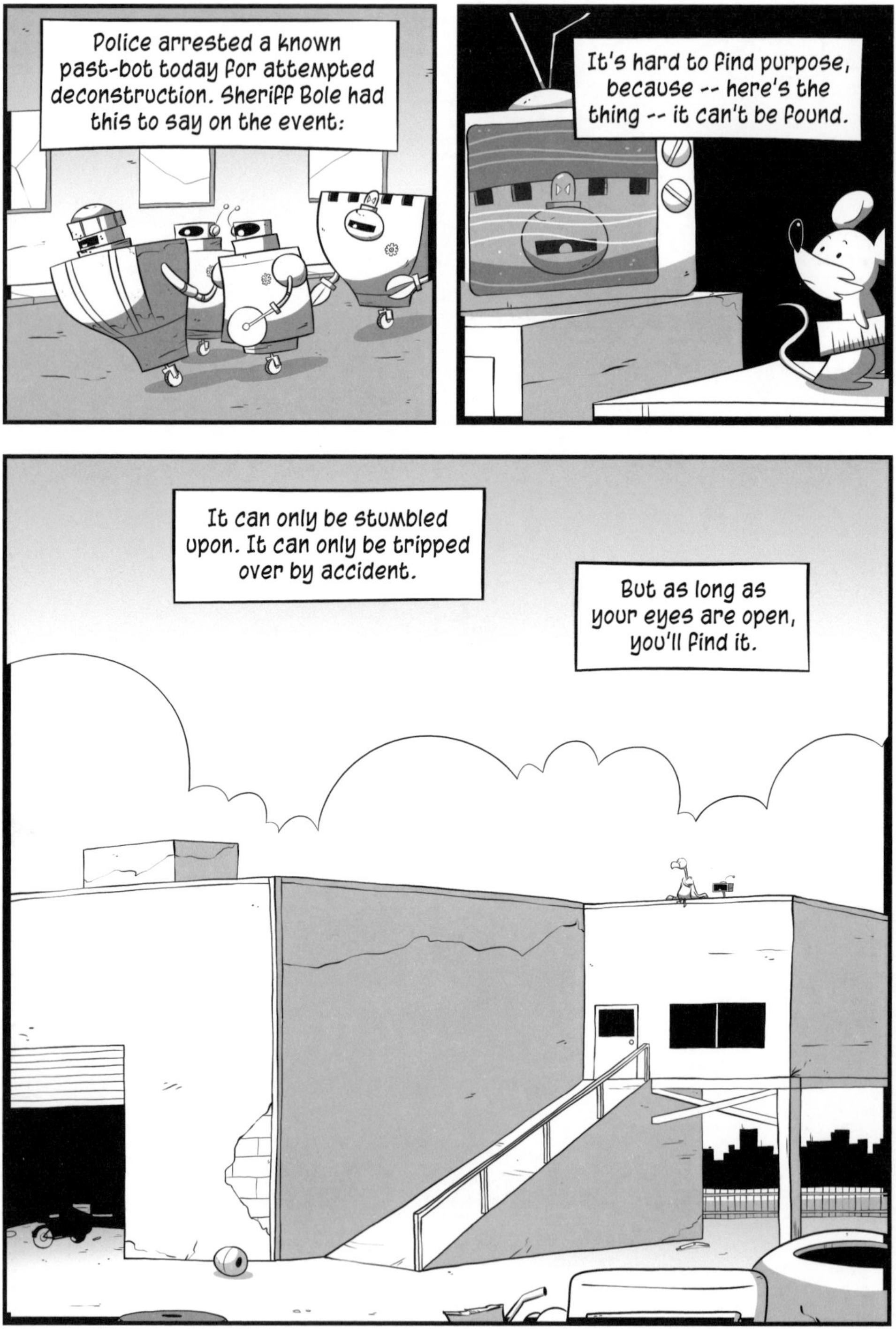
Police arrested a known past-bot today for attempted deconstruction. Sheriff Bole had this to say on the event:
It's hard to find purpose, because -- here's the thing -- it can't be found.
It can only be stumbled upon. It can only be tripped over by accident.
But as long as your eyes are open, you'll find it.

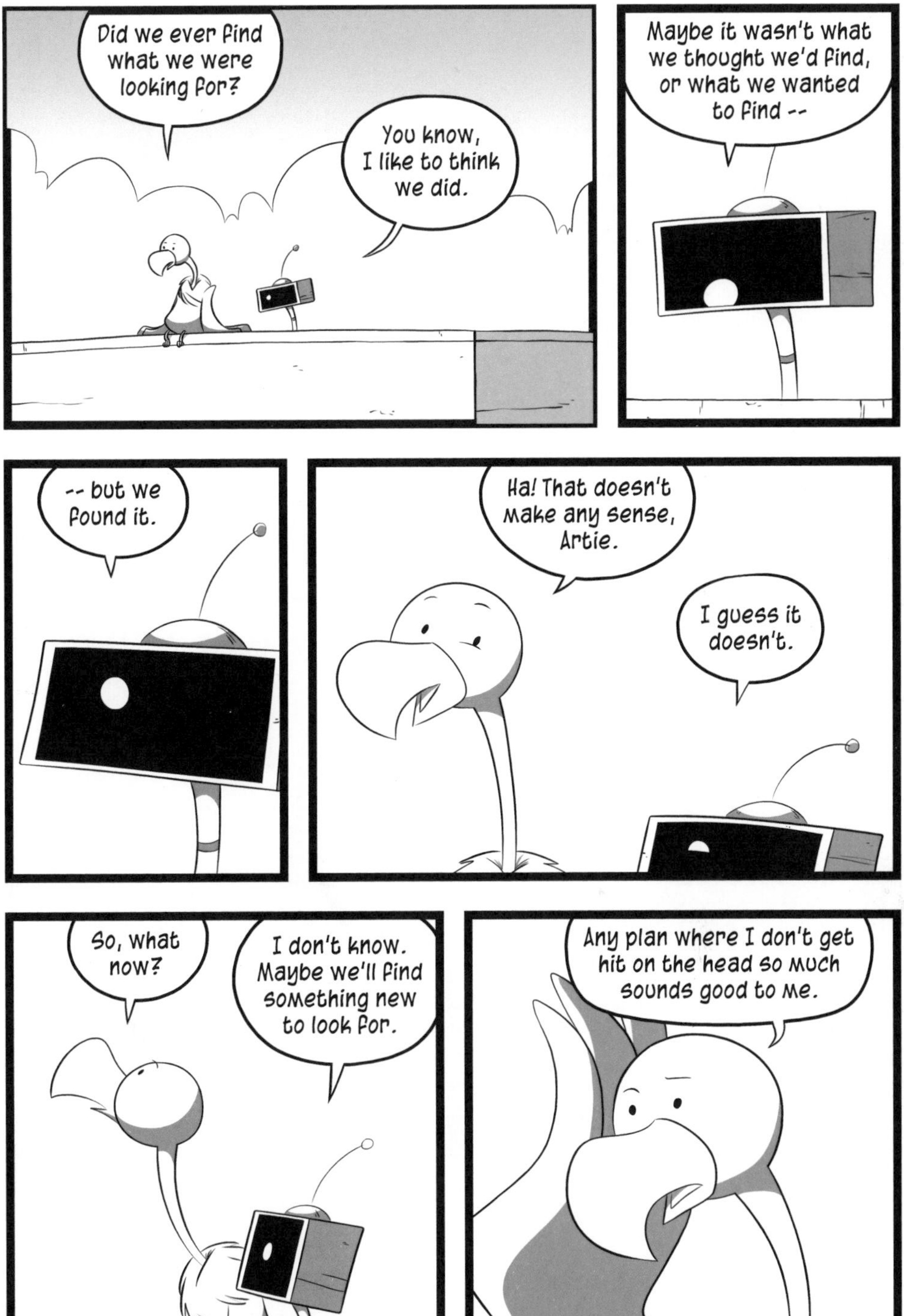
Did we ever find what we were looking for?
You know, I like to think we did.
Maybe it wasn't what we thought we'd find, or what we wanted to find --
-- but we found it.
Ha! That doesn't make any sense, Artie.
I guess it doesn't.
So, what now?
I don't know. Maybe we'll find something new to look for.
Any plan where I don't get hit on the head so much sounds good to me.

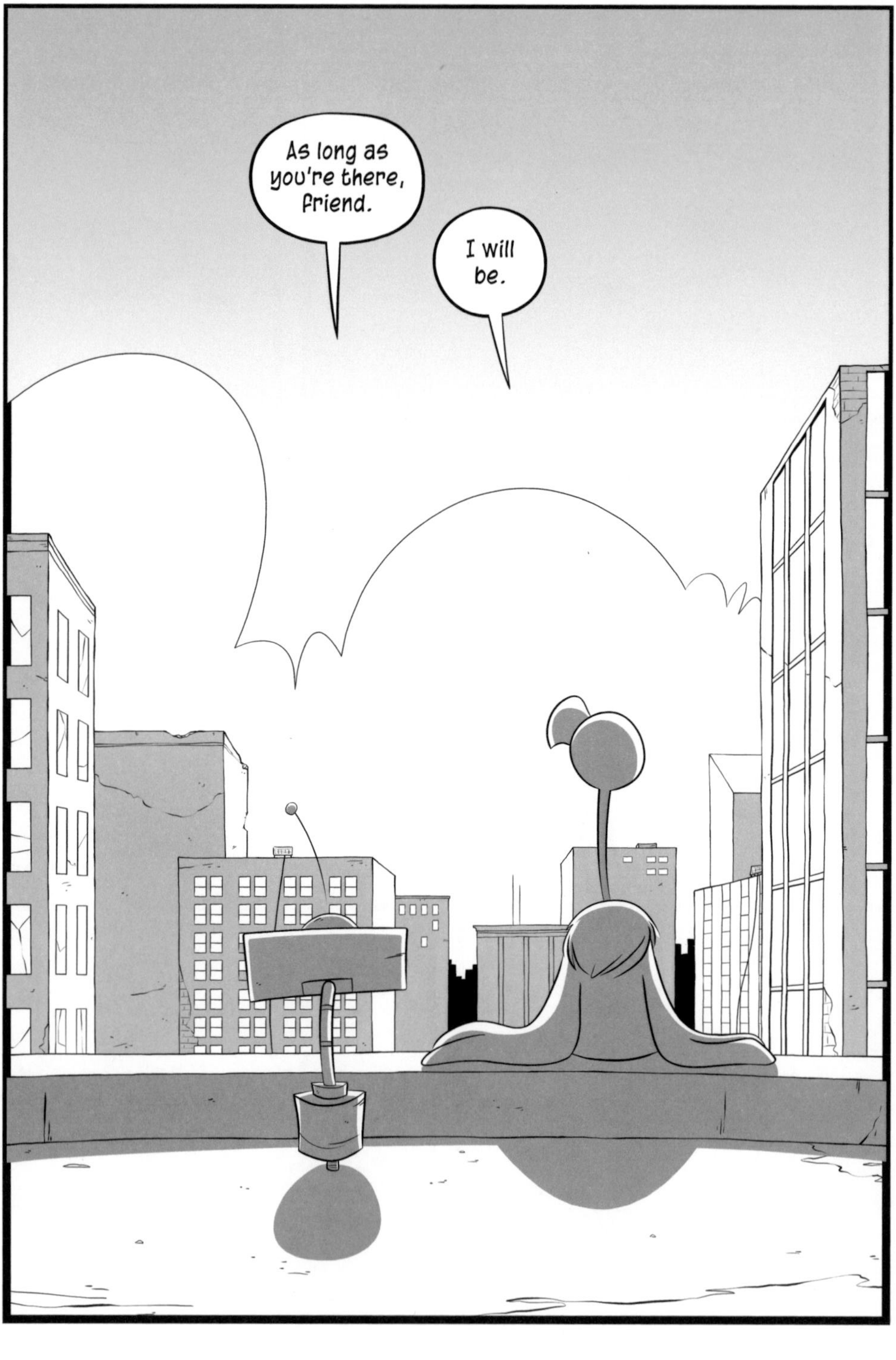
As long as you're there, friend.
I will be.

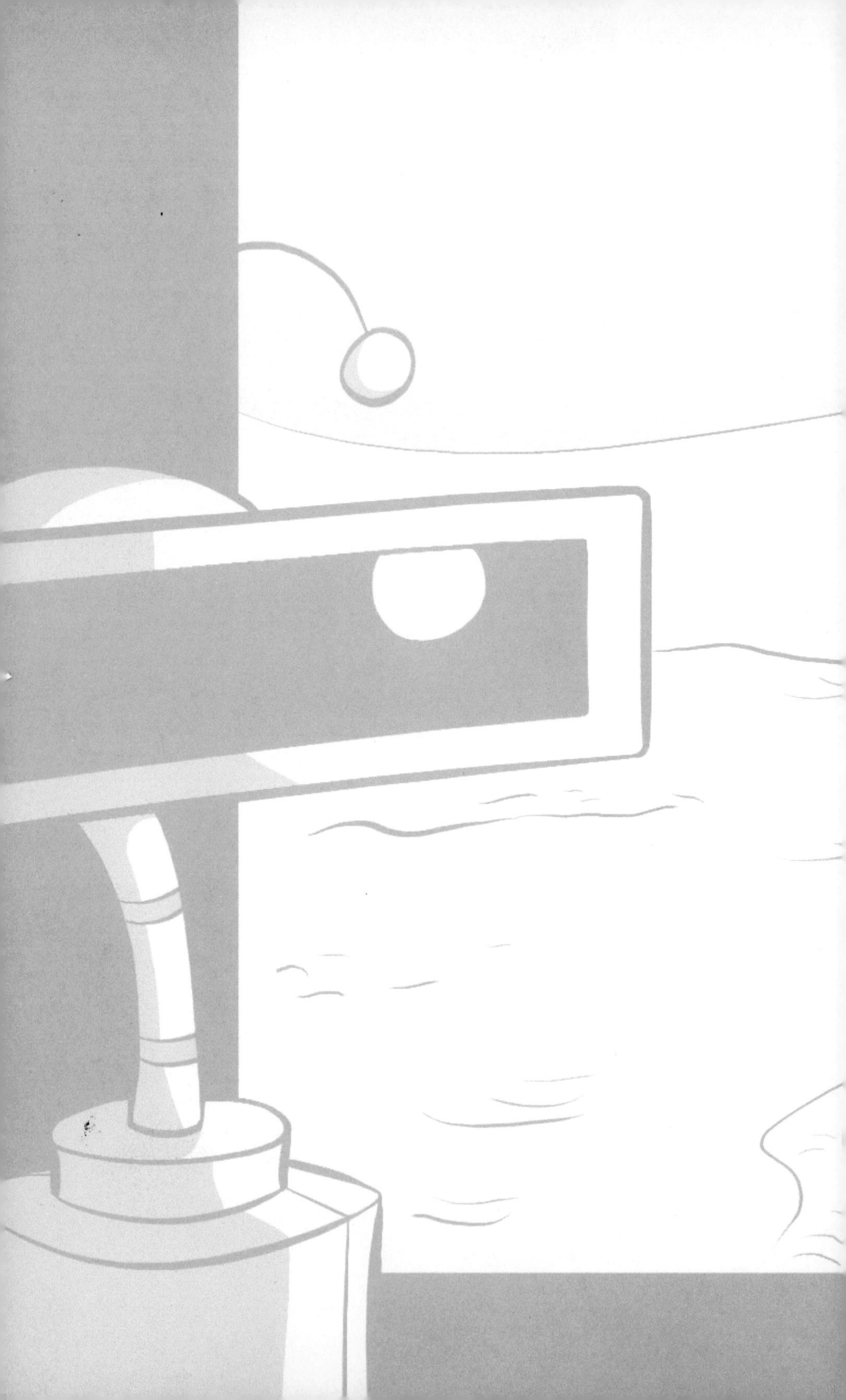

Jon Nielsen has been drawing silly pictures and putting them on the internet for at least a decade. He is known for his long running webcomic, Massive Pwnage, which ran for eight years. When he's not drawing comics or animating short cartoons for YouTube, he works at his local library, putting books away, and occasionally getting lost in the graphic novel section. He lives in Portland, OR with his small but formidable family. This is his first graphic novel. He currently works at the Multnomah County Gresham Library.

See more on Jon at www.darkmagicpress.com

SFAR • TRONDHEIM • BOULET
Dungeon
Zenith
Vol. 3: Back in Style

ARTHUR DE PINS
Zombillenium
3. Control Freaks

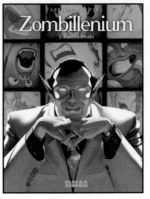

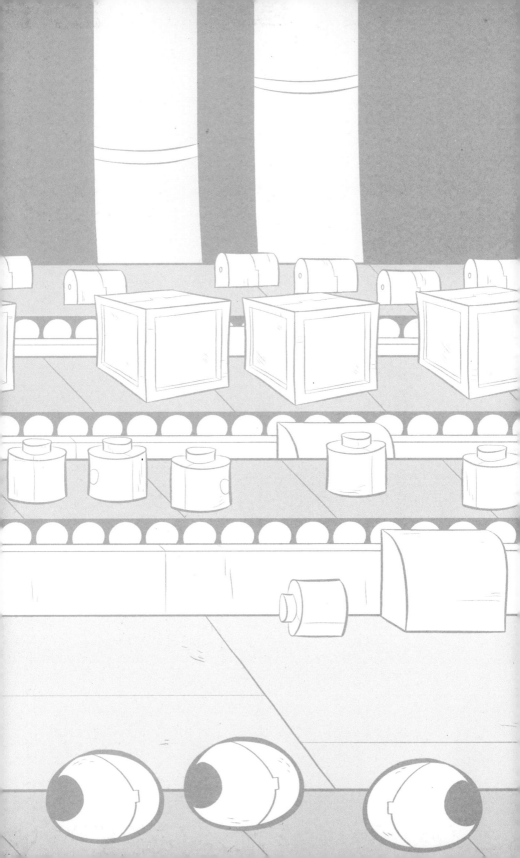